T0354704

PORTRAITS *of* PROVIDENCE

For People in Potholes

STEVE STEWART, TH.D.

WESTBOW
PRESS®
A DIVISION OF THOMAS NELSON
& ZONDERVAN

Copyright © 2022 Steve Stewart, Th.D.

All rights reserved. No part of this book may be used or reproduced by any means, graphic, electronic, or mechanical, including photocopying, recording, taping or by any information storage retrieval system without the written permission of the author except in the case of brief quotations embodied in critical articles and reviews.

This book is a work of non-fiction. Unless otherwise noted, the author and the publisher make no explicit guarantees as to the accuracy of the information contained in this book and in some cases, names of people and places have been altered to protect their privacy.

WestBow Press books may be ordered through booksellers or by contacting:

WestBow Press
A Division of Thomas Nelson & Zondervan
1663 Liberty Drive
Bloomington, IN 47403
www.westbowpress.com
844-714-3454

Because of the dynamic nature of the Internet, any web addresses or links contained in this book may have changed since publication and may no longer be valid. The views expressed in this work are solely those of the author and do not necessarily reflect the views of the publisher, and the publisher hereby disclaims any responsibility for them.

Any people depicted in stock imagery provided by Getty Images are models, and such images are being used for illustrative purposes only. Certain stock imagery © Getty Images.

All Scripture quotations are taken from the New King James Version®. Copyright © 1982 by Thomas Nelson. Used by permission. All rights reserved.

ISBN: 978-1-6642-6617-9 (sc)
ISBN: 978-1-6642-6618-6 (hc)
ISBN: 978-1-6642-6619-3 (e)

Library of Congress Control Number: 2022908569

Print information available on the last page.

WestBow Press rev. date: 05/11/2022

CONTENTS

This book is dedicated to the Lord Jesus Christ.
He has rescued me from many potholes!

INTRODUCTION

Potholes! A dangerous, distracting, menacing part of maneuvering the highways. Potholes are those unsightly blemishes in the highway that cause our driving from point A to point B to be nothing less than a test drive on an obstacle course. Sometimes I wonder if our highway departments don't purposely and strategically place potholes in just the right places to cause us motorists even more stress than we have in just driving from one place to another. Perhaps the highway departments have some kind of coalition with the area front end alignment shops, and they get part of the take for the front-end work that has to be continually sought after by us innocent motorists. Or perhaps they just like to see us motorists squirm uncomfortably in our driver's seats as we try to maneuver around those problematic potholes.

Of course, I am sure there is no such conspiracy at work here, but, none-the-less, regardless of the why's and the how's, potholes can make driving on some of our roads and highways a pretty demanding task.

However, potholes are not confined to the highways upon which we drive our vehicles. Potholes are a reality in all of life. Just when we begin to think that life is getting a little easier, a little more comfortable, a little more relaxed: WHAM! We all of a sudden turn another curve on the highway of life, and we find ourselves frantically trying to maneuver ourselves around another of those pesky potholes that has seemingly popped out of nowhere. And just as it is practically impossible to keep the front end of our automobiles aligned because of the potholes on the highways, we find it just as difficult to keep our lives in alignment because of the continual potholes of life. Just when we think we have our lives going in the right direction, another pothole throws us off course, and we find ourselves in a frenzied, frantic attempt to realign our lives while repairing the damage done by the pothole.

It would be great if someone could offer us an easy, step-by-step, four-point plan in how to properly handle the potholes of life. That, however, would be an impossible task. Potholes come in all different shapes and sizes, whether they be the potholes on the highways, or the more devastating potholes of life. Each pothole is different. Hitting some of the smaller potholes on the highway may only require having the tires rebalanced. Other potholes may require having the front end realigned. Still others may do so much damage that more extensive structural repairs may be required.

And so it is with the potholes of life. Some are more easily handled than others. Some seem to be of no consequence at all, while others tend to be more destructive in nature. But, regardless of the size of the pothole and the damage done, all require attention.

All through the Biblical record we are confronted with people in potholes of life. Some of the potholes are large, devastating potholes which cause great harm and require much time and attention in getting things back on the right track. As a matter of fact, some are so devastating and destructive that lives are ruined, and individuals left reeling in the aftermath of falling into one of those damaging potholes of life. Others are small and are dealt with relatively easily. But damage is still suffered, and reparations have to be made.

Paul teaches us that certain things happened to the people of Israel, and now serve as examples for us, warning us about certain potholes of life. If we will take note of those occurrences, and learn lessons from them, perhaps we will be able to steer around some of the potholes that caught them off-guard. Perhaps by carefully examining them, we will be able to glean some information which will enable us to better handle the potholes that we are sure to hit as we go through the highways of life more safely.

CHAPTER 1

ABRAHAM

The Pothole of Uncertainty

This *is* the genealogy of Terah: Terah begot Abram, Nahor, and Haran. Haran begot Lot. And Haran died before his father Terah in his native land, in Ur of the Chaldeans. Then Abram and Nahor took wives: the name of Abram's wife *was* Sarai, and the name of Nahor's wife, Milcah, the daughter of Haran the father of Milcah and the father of Iscah. But Sarai was barren; she had no child.

And Terah took his son Abram and his grandson Lot, the son of Haran, and his daughter-in-law Sarai, his son Abram's wife, and they went out with them from Ur of the Chaldeans to go to the land of Canaan; and they came to Haran and dwelt there.

–Genesis 11:27–31

An obstacle of enormous proportions in life is facing the unknowns of an uncertain future. So many seem to be stressed out almost constantly by the uncertainty of what might lie ahead of them as they face the future. Youth will begin to experience this as they approach their junior and senior years in high school, if not before. Some go in to their first year of college without announcing a major, having no idea what they want to do with their lives. Others go into college thinking they have their lives planned out, with every detail in place, only to find out after a short while that they do not feel they are moving in the right direction. A change of major will result in so much distress for the young student. An uncertain future can cause overwhelming stress and anxiety.

Serving churches as pastor for forty years brought me into contact with quite a number of individuals who were overwhelmed with anxiety due to the uncertainty of their future. I always tried to assure those who were anxious about the uncertainties of the future that God was in control, and that whatever came their way in life was part of His plan. However, having tried to instill this Biblical truth in their minds, many still experienced devastating blows that destroyed their relationships.

A fellow pastor called me on one occasion to share with me the story of a couple he had counseled with prior to their marriage. The couple, neither of which were members of his church, asked if he would provide pre-marital counseling. They shared with him that they had just moved into the community and did not yet have a church home. My friend agreed to provide the counseling with the promise that if they completed the four sessions he required he would perform their marriage.

The husband and wife to be were truly delightful, showing open displays of affection in the pastor's office during their discussions about their future together. During the four sessions of counseling, they discussed many possibilities as they looked ahead to a bright and promising married life.

One of the sessions focused on the potential of things not

turning out as they had planned. The pastor had given them the assignment to write down expectations and anxieties of where they would like their relationship to one year, five years, and ten years into their marriage. When they began discussing their thoughts and ideas, one of the major discussions focused on the possibility of one or the other becoming incapacitated due to illness which would result in a lengthy period of caregiving.

This subject was discussed at great length, with both stating adamantly that they would care for the other, giving their verbal assent to the part of the vows that state "in sickness and in health, till death do us part." They were very convincing in their commitment to each other, and the pastor believed that both were sincere and truly meant exactly what they said.

The wedding day came, the couple became husband and wife, and they began their marital journey with excitement and expectation. They had a beautiful relationship that many other young couples envied. They became actively involved in the church where the pastor served as they tried to live out their commitment to the Lord.

Not long after performing their marriage, the pastor moved to another pastorate and lost contact with this couple. He shared with me that he really expected this couple to make it for the long-haul. But then he became visibly distraught as he continued to share with me what he had just recently found out about this couple. He started by saying that he truly could not begin to explain the crushing blow he experienced when he heard of their divorce. Upon investigation into the matter he discovered that the wife had been diagnosed with a disease of the eyes that would ultimately cause her to go completely blind.

The husband then decided to divorce her. Why? He did not want to be married to a wife that he would have to care for and lead around because of her blindness. At this point the pastor literally broke down in my presence out of the deep pain he felt over the news of this marriage ending in this way.

As I have thought about this story since it was shared with

3

me, I have come to realize that it is a horrible story for several reasons. First, I remembered the pastor's testimony that both of them stated with assertiveness that they were committed to each other come what may. Yet, when things began to go south in the relationship one was ready to call it quits.

Second, I was appalled at the reason he gave. He refused to be put into the inconvenient situation where he would have to be her caregiver for the remainder of their lives. Had he forgotten those words he had spoken to the pastor during the pre-marital counseling and, more importantly, spoken at the altar? Perhaps he had conveniently forgotten, or maybe he just decided it was not worth it to be a man of his word.

The point of sharing this story is simply this: when we are speaking in the sterile setting of a counseling office, and then when we are faced with the unfolding uncertainties of life, we find that things are not at all like we had thought.

Life is not certain. We can make the best plans possible, giving attention to every possible scenario that we can think of. Yet when it comes down to it, those plans sometimes fall completely apart.

James has some very important words of instruction on this issue:

> Come now, you who say, "Today or tomorrow we will go to such and such a city, spend a year there, buy and sell, and make a profit"; whereas you do not know what will happen tomorrow. For what is your life? It is even a vapor that appears for a little time and then vanishes away. Instead you ought to say, "If the Lord wills, we shall do this or that." But now you boast your arrogance. All such boasting is evil.
>
> (James 4:13–16)

Those involved in this decision to make this business trip, expecting to get huge dividends from their investments were being extremely presumptuous. They were presuming so many things in this planned excursion. They were going to a certain place, with certain plans, for a certain length of time, to make certain profit. But they did not know what the future held for them. As a matter of fact, they did not even know if they would have a future. Even life itself is uncertain and fragile. Like a vapor it is here one moment and gone the next.

One of the major characters in the Bible was an individual who experienced firsthand the struggles of uncertainty. He probably thought his life was pretty much mapped out for him, as most probably did in his historical period. It was not like it is today, where people move from place to place, from job to job, from career to career. Usually, children would follow in the footsteps of their parents, not traveling very far in their entire lifetime.

Abraham was probably one of those who thought his life was pretty much mapped out for him. He was the son of Terah, a descendant of Noah's son Shem. His early life was spent in Ur of the Chaldees, a prominent Sumerian city. At birth, he was given the name Abram by his parents, a name which means "exalted father" or "'the father is exalted'." Later, God changed Abram's name to 'Abraham', which means "father of a multitude."

Abraham was reared in an idolatrous home. Terah is said to have been a worshipper of other gods (Joshua 24:2), and this would certainly have been passed down to his son. So, it was out of a pagan background that Abraham came. This makes his story even more remarkable. When thinking of Abraham, and the role he played in the Old Testament as well as the New Testament, we have the tendency to think that he was a worshipper of God from his childhood. We may even think that he somehow was such a committed follower of God that God would naturally choose him to be the father of the nation of Israel. Such was not the case. He was called out of a pagan background, and through the ensuing

5

years he would have to discard all that he had been taught in the home of his father as he learned to worship the true God.

This is certainly not a rare occurrence. Multitudes of individuals throughout history have come out of a pagan, even atheistic background only to become committed followers of the Lord. Josh McDowell and Lee Strobel are two prominent Christian apologists who were at one time professed atheists. They both set out to disprove the Bible, but in their attempt to do that they became convinced of the truth of scripture. God gloriously saved them, and they have been powerful witnesses for the Lord.

Back to Abraham. There are many potholes scattered throughout Abraham's life that oftentimes caught him off guard and to which he responded in a variety of ways. Some of his responses were based on his faith relationship with God. Anyone who is seriously striving to live a life of righteousness would do well to imitate these choices of Abraham. There were other times when he made poor choices, not responding in faith, but in fear. These should not be imitated but should be looked at as examples not to be followed. But again, we must remember that Abraham had to grow in his understanding of God just as we do. As a matter of fact, it could have been much more difficult for Abraham than it is for modern day believers. Remember, he came from a pagan background, having worshiped false deities his entire life up to the moment he was called by God. To follow God meant he had to discard all that he had been taught, and then learn to trust God and follow His directions. It was an ongoing journey toward spiritual maturity that Abraham traveled throughout the years of his life after receiving God's call to leave his homeland and travel to a place as yet undisclosed by God. This pothole of uncertainty was an extremely difficult pothole for Abraham.

The scene is set in Genesis 12:1–3, where we are told,

Now the Lord has said to Abram: "Get out of your country, from your family and from your father's house, to a land that I will show you. I will make you a great nation; I will bless you and make your name great; and you shall be a blessing. I will bless those who bless you, and I will curse him who curses you; and in you all the families of the earth shall be blessed.

That certainly doesn't sound much like a pothole, does it? God has just given Abraham one of the most unbelievable promises anyone could possibly imagine! Abraham is told that he is going to father a great nation – a nation through which all other nations of the world will be blessed. What an unbelievably astounding thing to consider.

There are very few of us who would deny that we would love to be the recipient of such a wonderful promise as this. It would be a blessing beyond description to receive this kind of news. Who would hesitate to jump at the chance to be the father of a great nation, and for all other nations of the world to be blessed through you? That isn't a pothole: that is a pedestal that pretty much anyone would like to be on!

But before we jump to hasty conclusions, let's consider the far-reaching ramifications of such a move as this. First, God commands Abraham to leave his country. This is not a move to a new neighborhood across town. This is not even a move to a new city, or a new state. It is not even a move across country. This is a move which entails leaving your country, your homeland, your place of birth, your place of upbringing. This is a move away from everything familiar and comfortable. This is a move away from the comforts of home. This is a move away from everything that you have ever known. Abraham is told to leave his country!

Missionaries who have felt God leading them to other countries must experience somewhat the same emotional upheaval as did Abraham. I have been privileged to go on seven mission trips to countries outside the United States. On most of these I have met long-term missionaries who have listened to the call of God to make these countries their home. They have completely left everything they had been accustomed to back home. I remember so clearly talking to one missionary in South Korea who shared with me that he and his wife had made that country their home. He explained that to do anything less would not have allowed them to have the impact on South Koreans as they had enjoyed.

He shared with me, with tears in his eyes, that he had witnessed so many missionaries who would come for one term, only to return home to the United States on furlough and never return to the mission field. He shared the damage that had been done to many who thought these were their long-term mentors and friends.

I was only there for a fifteen-day mission trip, and I missed home terribly. I can't imagine going to take up residence in a foreign country. I understand that it would have to be a divine calling of God on an individual's life to make such a long-term, or even a permanent commitment to the mission field. God is calling Abraham to make just such a permanent commitment.

Second, God commands him to leave his family. This would have been an extremely big thing for Abraham to even consider. We must remind ourselves that things were vastly different then than they are now. Family was all Abraham had ever known. Family ties were not to be broken. Generation after generation would reside in the same place. Father would pass down to son, and he to his son, and he to his. The old home place was the new home place for each succeeding generation. And now God commands Abraham to leave his father's house, his immediate family, his extended family, and all whom he knew and loved.

And third, God commands that he go to a land that God would show him. How utterly ridiculous! God did not even tell him where he was going. He was told to just go and allow God to direct the way. Maybe now we begin to see just how serious this move would be. There is no question about the fact that

8

the promise is great, but let's face it, the pothole is deep. God is asking too much! How could He ever expect Abraham to leave country, home, and family, and not even know where it is that he is supposed to end up himself?

So many get caught in this particular pothole and it can be one of the most devastating potholes imaginable. Uncounted lives have been ruined, multitudes of marriages have been wrecked, families have been shattered, because of this crippling pothole of life.

Our modern American society is filled with people who have been crippled by injuries sustained as they fell into this pothole. We live in a fragmented society. No longer do we see the old home places as we drive through the rural communities of our country. There was a time that you could drive through the rural areas of our country and see those beautiful old home places where families lived together – where children and parents and grandparents, and sometimes even great grandparents, all lived in the same place. It used to be that family was important, that family ties were solid, that family members relied on each other. It used to extend far beyond the nuclear family, consisting of parents and children. It used to be that "family" denoted parents, children, grandparents, uncles, aunts, cousins, nephews, and nieces.

As a young child growing up in South Carolina, some of my most cherished memories center around those times when we would meet, about every other Sunday afternoon, at Granny and Grandpa Gardner's house. This was something I looked forward to with great excitement and anticipation. Granny would usually have a delicious cake ready for all the grandchildren to devour upon our arrival. And all my mother's brothers and sisters, and all of their children, would all converge on Granny and Grandpa. What fond memories! What happy recollections!

But, alas, they are for the most part just that: memories and recollections. All the cousins, and now the nieces and nephews, are scattered here and there and everywhere. I have cousins now in so many different states that I can't keep up with them. And even sadder than that is the reality that I don't even try to keep up with them anymore. We have all grown up and gone our separate ways. The only time we might see each other is at a family reunion, and those are very rare events.

There was a closeness about those relationships back then. I actually knew all my cousins by name. I knew which uncle and aunt each cousin belonged to. Now, I can't remember either. It is a vague memory which fades more into oblivion with each passing year.

We can't begin to imagine how Abraham must have felt when God tells him to make such a drastic change. This would be a change that would alter everything for him and his wife. They are going to a new place, where they will make a new home, where they will start over. God gives them no indication that they would ever return to the homeland. They have no hope of ever seeing family again. Everything is going to change. Nothing will ever be the same again.

Abraham's new adventure is vastly different from the common experiences of our contemporary setting. In our fast paced, rat-race, dog-eat-dog world, the old traditional family values are becoming more and more a thing of the past. As children grow, they are prepared for the day when they will leave father and mother, and home, and possibly even homeland. They are taught that the important things in life are things which are attained in the work world, in the business world, in the daily grind of putting in those long, arduous hours so they might get to the top. So, they are prepared to leave it all behind in order to chase their dreams.

There is certainly nothing wrong with having dreams and setting goals. Once a young man or woman make decisions concerning education, career choice, place of residence in a city that will facilitate making their dreams come true, they then sell themselves out to make it a reality. Their choices could very likely demand that they move to a distant city, in a different state, or perhaps a different country. They make those moves, with huge dreams and aspirations motivating them to do whatever is necessary to make it all happen.

Oftentimes it is those diligent young men and women who are literally selling themselves for a mess of pottage. They are falling headlong into this devastating pothole because they are being torn from family and friend, from home and homeland, from all that is comfortable, familiar, and enjoyable. Many are able to dig themselves out, but far too numerous are those who live, and die, in this particular pothole. For the sake of career, or profession, or whatever dream they may be pursuing, many are leaving the nest, moving hundreds, or even thousands of miles away from home. In the search for happiness and fulfillment, too many are leaving the very thing behind that they are striving to find.

Back to the story of Abraham. How did he deal with this situation? How did he gain success even in the face of this formidable obstacle, this pothole of uncertainty? There are several things which stand out in the story of Abraham that shed some much-needed light on how he handled what could have been an extremely stressful and destructive situation.

First, it is obvious that Abraham sensed direction from God in making this move. It was by divine intervention in his life that he was led to leave family, friends, and the comforts of home and country. It was not that he just woke up one morning and decided to leave, but he was providentially directed by God to make this move.

It happens far too often that young men and women leave home to chase their rainbow. They have no idea where the end of the rainbow is, how far they will have to go to find it, or how many obstacles stand between them and it. They just know that they have to go. So they set out, without any clear direction, without really knowing where to start their journey, much less knowing where it might end. And because of that, for too many, it ends with them being stuck in a pothole. It ends in wasted efforts, and wasted years, and wasted lives.

One of the main reasons for this is the simple fact that they did not have divine guidance in making the decision to start their trek. They have decided on their own to move out, to find their way, to make it on their own. It may be that they decided at a relatively young age what they wanted to do with their lives. They had perhaps set some long-term goals, mapping out the journey they would have to make in order to make their dreams a reality. It may have been dreams of a career in a certain field that would require them to move to a distant city. It may have been that they would have to literally leave family behind, knowing that they would have very little chance to see them except on rare occasions.

Can you see yourself in this pothole? Have you ever been there? When I graduated from high school, I decided that I wanted to be out on my own. I gave no thought to seeking God's guidance in the matter, as at that time of my life I had no interest in anything godly. A friend invited me to share living expenses with him in an apartment in a city not far from my hometown. I thought it was the right thing to do because it was actually closer to my workplace than it was from my parent's home, where I was still living at the time. And, even more importantly than that, I would be free!

So, without giving it much thought, and to the disregard of my parent's warning that I would not be able to afford the cost of living in the apartment, I hastily moved out and moved in with my friend. Things went well for about three weeks, until the bills started coming due. I was asked by my roommate for my share of the expenses, but I had been so enamored with my newfound freedom that I had spent what should have been set aside for expenses. I still had enough to pay my share, but then I had nothing left over. Lesson learned, painfully.

Then, a very short time later, I was laid off unexpectedly at my job, and found myself out of work in a less than enviable job market. I searched in vain for the next several weeks to find work, only to have to return to my parent's home once again. Thankfully, my parents didn't hit me with "We told you so," but it was painful none-the-less to have to swallow my injured pride. Had I taken their advice to count the cost before making the move I would not have experienced this painful chapter of my life.

This is one of the major differences between Abraham and me. He left having received clear directions from God. Now this doesn't mean that God handed him a well-marked road map, showing him every step of the way, every obstacle he might face, every pothole he might encounter. He simply pointed him in a particular direction and told him to go.

God is still in the business of doing this. We hear of it often in the lives of those God calls to be pastors, evangelists, and missionaries. We love to hear those moving stories about how God has sent a missionary to the other side of the world. The vast majority of us love to hear how God calls His servants, and how He providentially places them in the exact location in which He wants them to serve.

But I am convinced that God wants to give this same kind of clear instruction and direction to all His children, not just those in 'full-time Christian service' (I really despise that phrase – all Christians are in full-time Christian service!). God has a particular plan for each of His children. We very seldom hear this taught, and this perhaps is one of the main reasons that very few of our young adults will spend any time seriously praying and seeking God's will for their lives. They don't feel called into any area of ministry, so they feel that they are left to figure out for themselves what they are supposed to do with their lives.

Not so. God will give direction and instruction if we will but take time to listen. That is the first step in the right direction of not getting trapped in this pothole. Wait for clear directions from God before making the first move. Doing this will protect us from suffering some form of pothole, as we will have the direction set for us.

However, even though Abraham received clear directions from God, it did not mean that he would never face any form of difficulties. He faced his share of the potholes of life. Following

God does not guarantee a life of ease and comfort. The Bible is replete with examples of individuals who were faithfully following God and yet they suffered some of the most horrifying potholes imaginable.

Abraham received the directives from God, and yet those directives were filled with uncertainty. He had no idea where he was going but was simply told to go. So what did Abraham do? After receiving His directions from God, Abraham obeyed. The record is clear: God told Abram to go, and he went. It might be tempting to think that since he did what God told him to do, that life was trouble-free from that point on. Wrong! Life was filled with pothole after pothole for Abraham. But his life of obedience made him the recipient of the vast blessings of God.

Let there be no mistake: the Christian life is not a trouble-free life. As a matter of fact, often it appears that those who are striving to follow God's direction with full obedience are the very ones who are picking themselves up from the potholes. But through it all, God is providentially guiding, working behind the scenes, bringing about His desired plans through the lives of His obedient children.

I remember well the occasion of God giving direction to my wife, Teresa, and me about making a move. It would be the biggest move we had ever made. It entailed leaving our home, our family, our friends, our rural setting in a small town where everybody knew everybody. As a matter of fact, it was the town we had already discussed as being the town in which we would one day retire. We loved it so much, in fact, that we didn't want to ever move away – we just wanted to stay there!

But then came the day. God had been preparing me for quite some time to pursue further education that would enable me to be able to teach in Bible colleges or universities. He had placed within me a tremendous desire to invest my life in the lives of those preparing for ministry. Therefore, we began to look at colleges, seminaries, and universities that I might possibly attend.

After a rather long process, Teresa and I felt strongly led to move to Dallas, Texas, so that I might be able to attend Criswell College. This would mean moving almost eleven hundred miles away from home! This would also mean taking our two sons eleven hundred miles away from their grandparents! This would further mean my wife, an only child, would be eleven hundred miles away from her parents. And finally, this would mean experiencing culture shock like I had never known, moving from small town Carolina to the Dallas/Fort Worth metroplex where millions reside!

We learned rather quickly that God had greater plans than we could have ever possibly imagined at the time. More of that story will be shared later in this chapter. Let it suffice to say at this time that God gave clear direction, without showing every pothole we might experience along the way. And once He had given the direction, the choice was simply to obey or disobey.

That is what it came down to with Abraham. Obey or disobey. God did not call Abraham to wander around aimlessly, even though it may have seemed that way to Abraham. God had a clear plan for him. However, the only way Abraham would ever see the fulfillment of God's plan, and enjoy the benefits of God's promises, was for him to obey. He had to commit himself to follow the Lord's guidance.

God issued the call. God gave directions for obeying the call. And God kept His word. Abraham received the call. He then followed the directions. And he received the blessings God had promised. What an amazing avowal to the providential guidance of God in the life of Abraham.

Granted, he did not receive all the details at once. Neither did he see the fulfillment of all of God's amazing promises in his lifetime. He was still looking by faith into an uncertain future at the end of his life. But he had seen God work in miraculous ways as he followed the directions of God. He witnessed God do things on his behalf that only God could have done. He lived by faith, and God blessed his faithfulness.

God is still in the business of issuing calls and giving direction.

What we must do is listen for those calls and be willing to follow the directions as He reveals them. He may not call us to leave family, home, and country. It may be to stay where we are and be faithful to God on our job, in our neighborhood, or in the classroom. It may call for us being involved in activities that would require getting out of our comfort zone into the realm of the uncertain and the unknown. Or it may call for us to remain right where we are, to be a faithful follower of the Lord in what might appear to be mundane and uneventful. This could very well be God's plan for us.

But the facts of the call are really not the important thing. What is important is that we be faithful and obedient to the call of God in our lives. If it is to go, then go. If it is to stay, then stay. Listen for God to speak and be quick to say yes to His direction.

Abraham listened and obeyed, and this was the beginning of a journey of adventure. This journey would take him through some rough terrain, with many potholes along the way. There were many twists and turns on the route God called him to travel. There were some potholes that may have caused Abraham to think, at least momentarily, that God's way may not be the best way after all.

One such instance in Abraham's life was that most awful occasion when God commanded him to sacrifice his son. Abraham must have thought that this could not be right, that God would never command such a thing. But again, we must remember Abraham's background. He was reared by an idolatrous father, who worshipped false deities. Being reared in this type of pagan environment meant that he would have participated in, or at least witnessed, the rituals and traditions of those religious systems.

Part of the religious ritual of many of the false religions was the sacrificing of sons and daughters as acts of worship to these false gods. These capricious gods would have to be appeased so that their anger would not be unleashed on the worshippers, and they had been taught that giving their sons and daughters as sacrifices to these gods would serve this purpose. Perhaps it had been part of the religion of his father. If so, then the practice would not have unfamiliar, nor would it have taken him by surprise.

Maybe this is one of the reasons the Bible shows no evidence that Abraham argued with God about this command. Perhaps he was so accustomed to this particular religious ritual that he accepted it without question. But he most assuredly would have been wondering how God was going to fulfill His promise to make of Abraham a great nation through which all nations would be blessed. How could the promise be fulfilled if the son of promise through whom Abraham's descendants would come is sacrificed? There must have been a sense of confusion and perplexity in the mind of Abraham as he tried to determine how God would fulfill His promises.

But again, Abraham obeyed. His faith in God and his faithfulness to God took him through this most arduous of potholes. God graciously stopped the sacrifice of Isaac by providing a ram for the sacrifice, but the pothole was real, the pain of going through it was agonizing, the faith of Abraham stood the test of giving his son, and the faithfulness of God to fulfill His promises was kept intact.

Abraham learned through this experience that no matter what the pothole may be, God will see us through. His way is always best, even when it might cause us to question what He is up to in our lives.

We will all face the pothole of uncertainty at times in our lives. There are seasons of life in which we will face an uncertain future, which has been caused by circumstances beyond our control. Of course, in one sense the future is totally uncertain simply due to the fact that no one knows what the future holds. The best plans will sometimes crash because an unforeseen event takes place – an event we had not thought about nor planned for. It is in those potholes that we have to trust God, remain faithful to God, and pray that He would graciously show us the path we are to follow from that moment on.

Abraham teaches us that God can be fully trusted. Even in

those moments when we can't see clearly where He is leading, He will give direction according to His will and His timetable. And when God calls us to change directions, then we should be willing to follow His call.

Abraham also teaches us that the life of the believer will be a life of adventure. Some would probably prefer to forego the adventurous aspect of the life of a follower of God, but there is nothing more exciting than seeing His plans unfold. I shared earlier in this chapter about moving our family to Dallas, Texas, so I could further my education. After much prayer my wife and I were convinced that this was the move we were to make. At the time I thought the reason of the move was for my education. However, it wasn't long before we realized that there was a much bigger picture to be considered.

Both of our sons eventually married Texas girls. They would never have met if we had not made the move. This taught us that God had much more in store for us as we made the move for me to attend Criswell. I share this to simply say that God has much bigger things in store as we follow Him. We may go in a certain direction with the knowledge we have at the time, but as we faithfully follow His guidance we see a plan unfold that we never would have dreamed.

Abraham is a great example of how to maneuver around the potholes that come our way as we face the uncertainties of life. His faith in God and his faithfulness to God resulted in him experiencing the manifold blessings of God.

QUESTIONS FOR THOUGHT AND DISCUSSION

1. Have you ever felt that you were in a pothole of uncertainty?
2. If so how did you find your way out?
3. Was the uncertainty in your personal life, professional life, married life, or some other area? Explain in detail.
4. Did you try to find your way out on your own, or did you seek God's guidance?
5. What lessons did you learn by your experience in this pothole.
6. How will your experience in this pothole help you assist others who may find themselves in one of this same type?

CHAPTER 2

JOSEPH

The Pothole of Temptation

Now Jacob dwelt in the land where his father was a stranger, in the land of Canaan. This is the history of Jacob. Joseph, being seventeen years old, was feeding the flock with his brothers. And the lad was with the sons of Bilhah and the sons of Zilpah, his father's wives; and Joseph brought a bad report of them to his father. Now Israel loved Joseph more than all his children, because he was the son of his old age. And he made him a tunic of many colors.

(Genesis 37:1–3)

Have you ever felt as if your life was just one continuous series of troubles and difficulties? Have you ever felt as if you were the subject being sung about in the old song from the "Hee Haw" television program?

"Gloom, despair, and agony on me,
Deep dark depression, constant misery,
If it weren't for bad luck, I'd have not luck at all!
Gloom, despair, and agony on me!"

The sad reality is, there are multitudes who feel this way about life. It seems that each year we hear of more and more who are succumbing to the effects of depression. Like the words of the song, they feel as if all they have in life is bad luck. Everything is a matter of gloom and despair. Each year we hear of those hard luck stories in which another poor soul has 'bit the dust' out of sheer desperation of life. Life has put so many potholes in their path that they have now reached the conclusion that it is not worth the hassle to carry on.

Let's face it: life is really tough at times. It can throw things at us that are unpredictable and that we are completely unprepared for. Oftentimes those things catch us totally off-guard, and we find ourselves trying to figure a way out of the mess.

From the biblical record we learn that Joseph certainly had his share of potholes. As a matter of fact, it seems that he actually had more than his share. His whole life seemed to be a continuous cycle of jumping out of one pothole, only to end in another. And for many years of his life, each pothole seemed to be a little deeper, a little more dangerous, and a bit more difficult to escape from, than those which had gone before. Each succeeding pothole was more ominous than those he had been in previously.

In order to get the full impact of the story, let's begin with a review of Joseph's life. Joseph was the eleventh of twelve sons born to Jacob. He had the distinction of being Jacob's favorite son, having been born to his favorite wife, Rachel, and having been born in Jacob's old age. It was obvious from the start that Joseph was his father's favorite, a fact which caused serious problems with his ten older brothers.

Jacob showed his favoritism toward Joseph by giving him a coat of many colors. This may have been an indicator that Jacob had plans to make Joseph the head of the family tribes, even though that distinction belonged to the first born son. Whatever the intent, it was obvious to his brothers that their father was playing favorites, and this created an intense jealousy between them. It is difficult enough to be in a family with eleven brothers. There would have been plenty of competition between the boys as they grew together. The brothers were born from four different mothers. The sons of Jacob's wives may have felt that they were more privileged than the sons of Jacob's concubines. Tensions were probably pretty high at times as the twelve brothers grew up. And then, added to the tension of being reared in a family with so many brothers, was the fact that Jacob visibly showed his favoritism toward Joseph.

However, the evident display of favoritism by Jacob was not all that contributed to their ill feelings toward Joseph. Joseph himself did much to earn their displeasure. He revealed to his brothers that he had dreamed dreams which depicted him in dominion over them.

Now Joseph had a dream, and he told *it* to his brothers; and they hated him even more. So he said to them, "Please hear this dream which I have dreamed: There we were, binding sheaves in the field. Then behold, my sheaf arose and also stood upright; and indeed your sheaves stood all around and bowed down to my sheaf."

And his brothers said to him, "Shall you indeed reign over us? Or shall you indeed have dominion over us?" So they hated him even more for his dreams and for his words.

Then he dreamed still another dream and told it to his brothers, and said, "Look, I have dreamed another dream. And this time, the sun, the moon, and the eleven stars bowed down to me."

So he told *it* to his father and his brothers; and his father rebuked him and said to him, "What *is* this dream that you have dreamed? Shall your mother and I and your brothers indeed come to bow down to the earth before you?"

(Genesis 37:5–10)

These dreams must have undoubtedly seemed like the epitome of arrogance to Joseph's older brothers. The text doesn't reveal the reason Joseph decided to share his dreams with his brothers, so the best that can be done is to speculate about his reasoning. Did he do it with the intent to anger his brothers? Or was it possible he did it to make his brothers jealous? Maybe he thought that to reveal the dream to his brothers would mean that they would give him more respect than they had in the past. He was, after all, the baby of the family. Perhaps he had been on the receiving end of some of the older brothers' practical jokes.

And then there is the possibility that his reason for sharing his dream was from a totally pure heart and with the purest of motives. Maybe he sees something in these dreams that caused him to think that he would in some way serve an important role in the family's future. Maybe, after sharing both dreams to his brothers and his parents, he felt that there was going to come a time in which he would be able to provide in some way for his family.

There is really no way that we can know his reasoning for sharing, nor his motive in sharing, but we do know that later on there would come the time in which his dreams would come true. But at the time in which he shared these dreams with his siblings, whatever the motive for his sharing, his brothers did not react with fondness toward their younger brother. Rather, they became infuriated at him for his lofty dreams.

As he shared his dreams it proved to be more than his brothers could bear, and when the opportunity presented itself, they made plans to get rid of their haughty brother. The initial plan was to murder Joseph! How awful jealousy and bitterness are when left unchecked. Joseph's brothers have witnessed the favoritism of their father through the years of Joseph's life. They have obviously seen their father lavish his love on Joseph while at the same time ignoring them. Their animosity toward Joseph has built to a point of exploding. And now, hearing Joseph speak of his prideful dreams, they are so incensed that they are moved to act. So, they plot and scheme, and finally decide that they will kill their brother.

It was only through the intervention of Reuben, one of the brothers, that the plot was not carried out. It seems that he could not bear the thought of having his brother's blood on his hands and could not put his father in grief by sharing the news of Joseph's death. Instead, they put Joseph into a pit (the first of many potholes!), and later sold him to a band of Midianite traders. These traders then took Joseph to Egypt, where they sold him to Potiphar, an officer of Pharaoh.

All these events were providentially guided by the invisible hand of God, even though there was no way for Joseph or his brothers to know this at the time. Joseph must have viewed these events as being a series of life's cruel jokes. He is taken from his family by the treachery of his brothers, and his life is about to be put through a series of events that would cause the strongest among us to cringe. He must have surely been thinking that those dreams were nothing more than that, just dreams.

Joseph is sold to the Midianites, who in turn sell him to Potiphar, who serves in the court of Pharaoh. This is another of the many potholes which will ensnare him while in Egypt. Volumes have been written about the experiences of Joseph. At the conclusion of his story as recorded in Genesis, it is revealed that everything which had happened to him was through the providential leadership of God. Joseph even testifies to his brothers:

> But as for you, you meant evil against me; but God meant it for good, in order to bring it about as it is this day, to save many people alive.
>
> (Genesis 50:20)

Joseph recognized all the awful events which had transpired in his life had actually been providentially orchestrated by the invisible hand of God so that Jacob's family might be saved through the disastrous famine that had ravaged the land. However, that is getting a little ahead of the story. Let's back up and consider one of those devastating potholes with which Joseph had to contend as part of the outworking of God's providential plan.

After having been sold to Potiphar by the Midianite traders, Joseph displayed a life of maturity and integrity. The Genesis record says,

> The Lord was with Joseph, and he was a successful man; and he was in the house of his master the Egyptian. And his master saw that the Lord was with him and that the Lord made all he did to prosper in his hand.
>
> (Genesis 39:2–3)

Undoubtedly, Joseph's life was a consistent display of integrity, honesty, and ability. His life bore testimony to the hand of God being at work in him, and it caused Potiphar to take note of the success which seemed to be part of everything Joseph did. This motivated Potiphar to quickly promote Joseph to a position of authority over his entire personal household. Everything Potiphar owned was placed under the authority of Joseph. Potiphar trusted him implicitly, which resulted in him placing Joseph as overseer of everything that Potiphar possessed. God's hand was obviously on this young man from Israel.

Scripture bears testimony to the gracious hand of God being upon Joseph. As he proved himself over and over to be a man who was totally committed to God and committed to serve God even in the midst of a nation that served and worshipped false deities, God proved faithful to Joseph. His hand of favor continued to set Joseph apart, and Joseph's faithfulness to God set him apart as one whose life was blessed by that invisible hand of providence. Read the following passage slowly, allowing the testimony of his life to encourage us in our walk with the Lord:

> So it was, from the time *that* he had made him overseer of his house and all that he had, that the Lord blessed the Egyptian's house for Joseph's sake; and the blessing of the Lord was on all that he had in the house and in the field. Thus he left all that he had in Joseph's hand, and he did not know what he had except for the bread which he ate.
>
> (Genesis 39:5–6a)

Who would ever have thought that this boy from the backwoods of Canaan could become so successful in such a short period of time? Joseph had come a long way indeed! From being hated and despised by his brothers, to being sold to the Midianite traders, to being sold as a mere slave to Potiphar, to now become the figure of authority in Potiphar's house. What a powerful illustration of an individual going from rags to riches! Potiphar had so much confidence in this young man that he put everything he possessed under his care.

These actions of Potiphar clearly showed his total trust in Joseph. This young man of utmost honesty, personal integrity, and personal ability could be trusted with everything. Potiphar had no worries at all knowing that everything he owned was in good hands with Joseph. What could possibly go wrong with everything under his care? Potiphar could rest easy knowing that his entire estate was in Joseph's capable hands.

Everything that had now happened to Joseph since being sold by his brothers must have been a source of consolation to this young man. Even though he has been sold as a mere slave, he had now been elevated to overseer of Potiphar's possessions. The only thing that was not under his control was Potiphar and Potiphar's wife. Everything else was under his direct supervision. His life of being a slave was somewhat comforted by being promoted to a life of relative ease, even though he was still a slave. Perhaps some of the pain had now eased, at least to some degree, after being so mistreated by his brothers.

But the calm is about to be disrupted. Now comes the pothole. Joseph's honesty and integrity are about to be put to the ultimate test. He is about to find himself in a pothole of enormous proportions. The Genesis account records it as follows:

> Now Joseph was handsome in form and appearance. And it came to pass after these things that his master's wife cast longing eyes on Joseph, and she said, "Lie with me."
>
> (Genesis 39:6b–7)

What an astonishing turn of events! This must have undoubtedly caught Joseph totally by surprise. How could he have ever possibly imagined in his wildest dreams that his master's wife would make such a request of him? How could she ever expect him to betray the trust of his master by being swayed by her sultry seductions?

And what's more, Joseph must have been wondering how he could ever have gotten into such a situation as this. Here is this young man, who could still vividly remember those wonderful dreams of old: those dreams which had revealed to him that he would in some way not yet known to him be in a position of authority over his older brothers. Up to this point he had probably been trying to put it all together. Perhaps he had tried to figure out all the details of how his present situation would fit into the overall plan of God as revealed in those dreams. But how could this present dilemma possibly be part of the providential plan of God? How could he escape this disastrous pothole?

Joseph's decision is recorded in his response to her seductions:

> But he refused and said to his master's wife, "Look, my master does not know what *is* with me in the house, and he has committed all that he has to my hand. There is no one greater in this house than I, nor has he kept back anything from me but you, because you *are* his wife. How then can I do this great wickedness, and sin against God?"
>
> (Genesis 39:8–9)

Joseph's response to her temptations revealed that he was a man of integrity in his personal life as he was in his professional life. How could he even consider such a thing since his master had placed so much confidence in him? Potiphar had trusted him with everything! Clearly, he had every confidence in this young Hebrew. And what is more than that, Potiphar had obviously benefited tremendously from having Joseph in the position of authority over all his possessions. So, Joseph's response to Potiphar's wife showed that he was not going to do anything to chance losing Potiphar's trust.

However, as lofty as those commitments were, his role of responsibility to Potiphar is not Joseph's main concern. Note again the final words in the above quote: *"And sin against God."* Yes, Joseph was concerned about the physical ramifications of becoming involved with his master's wife, but he was more concerned about the spiritual ramifications. How could he ever commit such an act of disobedience against God? His answer is a definitive "NO!"

So, his master's wife never propositioned him again, right? WRONG! The record says,

> So it was, as she spoke to Joseph day by day, that
> he did not heed her, to lie with her or to be with her.
> (Genesis 39:10)

The seductive enticements continued daily. Every day as Joseph would come and go in his master's house, she would tempt him to lie with her. Over and over, she propositioned, and over and over Joseph refused.

This is the usual mode of operation Satan will use in his attempts to lure someone into his deceitful traps of seduction. He uses just the thing that will appeal to the senses. In Joseph's case, he appealed to his natural, God-given attraction to the opposite sex. There is nothing sinful with enjoying this beautiful gift God has given to mankind, as long as it is within the parameters of God's prescribed manner of human sexuality. It is only when it is taken outside of those Biblical guidelines that trouble ensues.

Temptation comes in all shapes and sizes, and Satan is relentless in keeping it before us. He appeals to our natural human urges, placing before us sights, sounds and images that attract us. He strives to ensnare us in that trap of temptation, to keep it before us so much that we eventually find ourselves thinking about it constantly. Just as we see in this episode in Joseph's life, the seductions of Potiphar's wife were relentless – day after day after day the same thing.

Joseph could have allowed these daily seductions to wear him down. He could have gone back to his living quarters each day, allowing his imagination to picture how it would be to give in to her sexual suggestions. He could have easily allowed it to become a consuming desire within him, until finally giving in to her invitation to join her in her bedchamber.

Joseph could have given in to her enticements and could have justified himself for doing it. He could have reasoned that he now lived in a different country, in a different culture. He could have consoled himself by reaching the conclusion that just because this action would be wrong back over in Canaan does not necessarily dictate that it would be wrong now that he is in Egypt. He could have convinced himself that adultery was not viewed with such scorn in Egypt as it had been back home, so, now that he was in Egypt, why not do as the Egyptians?

Still another way he could have justified taking advantage of her sexual enticements would have been to do what the situation dictated. He was there: she was there. Her desire was to have relations with him, so why not just go ahead and give in to her seduction? They could possibly, perhaps even probably, have had a sexual relationship with each other that never would have been discovered. He was a young man with emotions and feelings and desires just like anyone else. He could have taken advantage of the situation that had been placed before him, while maintaining his relationship with Potiphar.

There were so many ways Joseph could have mentally and emotionally justified himself in becoming involved with his master's wife. But he refused. Time and time again he refused. He refused on the grounds that to do anything else would be to involve himself in activity which was nothing less than sin against God.

Countless is the number of those who have been swallowed by this pothole. In our ever-changing world, in which ethical standards have for the most part been thrown to the wind, it is so easy to give in to the seductive temptations of everyday life. It would stagger the imagination if the statistics were known as to how many lives have been destroyed because of this pothole.

Think for a moment about the sexual permissiveness of our modern society. Marital fidelity is a matter of scorn and ridicule in most circles today. Our society has placed its stamp of approval on premarital sex, extra-marital affairs, living together out of wedlock, and homosexual and lesbian partnerships. The sanctity of the marital relationship is no longer taken seriously. Far too many live by the soap opera philosophy of life, believing that the road to fulfillment takes the individual through many different sexual relationships with many different people. We look up to those who embrace this type of lifestyle and applaud those who are willing to "come out of the closet" so that their sexual exploits are openly displayed.

Having served in pastoral ministry for forty years I have counseled with dozens of individuals whose marriages have been destroyed because of marital infidelity. I have spoken with others who have offered their excuses for engaging in pre-marital sex. I have witnessed the crushing pain caused by an adulterous spouse, and the ensuing difficulties it caused. I have seen children's lives shattered due to the infidelities of their parents. When the biblical parameters for sexual relationships are neglected, we open ourselves up for heartache and heartbreak as lives and families are destroyed by this devastating pothole.

But these things should come as no surprise. Why? The answer is so simple, yet so profoundly sad. No longer does our society look with scorn on those who involve themselves in deviant sexual behaviors and lifestyles, but rather it looks with scorn on those who live by the old fashioned, outdated ethical standards which are based on the ethical absolutes of God's word. It really wasn't that long ago when those who were caught in premarital sexual relationships or extra-marital relationships would have been the talk of the town. But now, they are the toast of the town. Our society has become so twisted and perverted that we are doing as Israel of old: calling right wrong, and wrong right. We live by the dictates of our fallen, sinful nature. And we have embraced what might be called the 'beer commercial mentality' which exhorts us to get all the gusto out of life. We have even been encouraged by one country and western singer that if we are not with the one we love, then we should just love the one we are with. So many in our sexually permissive society would give

31

hearty assent to that statement, and then turn to kiss the nearest person of the opposite sex, or, for that matter, for those who have now "come out of the closet," the nearest person of the same sex.

Joseph could have so easily been swayed by his master's wife's persistent temptations, just as so many in our day and time are doing. But instead, Joseph refused to allow himself to become entangled in this web of sin. Just as she persisted in her seductions, he persisted in his resistance.

But where is the portrait of providence in this strange set of circumstances? We have already made note of Joseph's response to his brothers at the end of the story, but that is looking back on all the events which have transpired from beginning to end. It is at that point of his life that Joseph can look back and see the providential hand of God that had brought about the physical deliverance of Jacob's family. But what about all these pesky potholes along the way? What about all the heartache and trauma that were part of the out-working of this providential plan of God? Surely, we are not to understand that these potholes were part of God's plan, are we?

Undoubtedly that is the way Joseph interpreted all these events. He recognized it as God's plan to save His people. This included all the potholes which he encountered along the way. Joseph saw everything that happened to him along this long journey as part of a grand plan that could not be seen or understood until he had gotten to the end and looked back. Then, it became crystal clear that there was an invisible hand of providence leading the way through it all.

What a truly phenomenal thing this is to consider. At the end of the story, when Joseph has had opportunity to look back over the events of these many years and evaluate them in light of his understanding, he reaches the conclusion that God was in control all along. There must have been times when he had to have felt that everything was out of control. The pothole we have considered was only one in a long series of potholes. Joseph had problem after problem, just as we do through all of life. But the lesson he learned through these experiences was that all of it was part of God's providential plan.

There may have been times when Joseph questioned everything that he had ever been taught about God. He could have questioned God's involvement in daily life. He could have questioned God's goodness, His tender, compassionate care, His wonderful provision for His people. Joseph could have even questioned if God was really there for him at all. But instead, we hear Joseph giving testimony to the fact that God had been in control all along, and that His plan had been worked out through all these situations that had come his way in life.

As we look at the story, we see that for a long period of Joseph's life he may not have been able to see or understand what God was doing, but we also see that God was guiding in all these events. In order for Joseph to be the deliverer who could physically save his family from the ravages of famine, he had to be in the right place at just the right time. This called for him to be in a position of authority in Egypt, not just in Potiphar's house. In order to get Joseph where he needed to be when he needed to be there, God providentially guided in all of these events so that His plans for Jacob's family could be fulfilled.

Does that mean it was part of God's plan for Joseph to be put to this sexual test? Could we honestly say that God tempted Joseph to sin? Absolutely not! God did not tempt Joseph, just as He tempts no one to commit sin. But we need to take note of the fact that it was through the providential leadership of God that Joseph was in the place where he was tempted.

If this should be of concern to anyone, let us remind ourselves of the temptations of Jesus in the desert. The testimony of scripture is that the Holy Spirit led Jesus into the wilderness to be tempted by the devil. The Spirit did not do the tempting, but He led Jesus to the place of temptation. Why? Because this was part of the providential plan of God the Father for God the Son, Jesus Christ.

And so it was with Joseph. He was placed in a position in

which he could be tempted, because it was through the temptation and the following series of events that Joseph was ultimately led to be in a position of authority from which he could deliver his family from sure destruction. It is relatively easy for us to see the hand of God at work in these events because we have the whole story. But for Joseph, it must have been a difficult thing trying to see God's hand at work in all of the troubles and tribulations he faced.

There are times when we may question what God is doing, or why God is allowing certain things to happen to us, or if God really cares about us or is the least bit concerned about those daily struggles we all face. If there is anything we should learn from Joseph's experiences in the potholes of life, it is that God is still in control, providentially working in and through all the different situations that arise throughout our lives, and that He will guide us through that maze of experiences just as He did with Joseph.

Joseph's handling of this particular pothole also teaches us a much-needed lesson as we face (fall into) our own personal potholes. As he was confronted time and again with the sexual advances of Potiphar's wife, the one all-controlling factor which enabled him to continue to be a man of integrity was his level of commitment and obedience to God. His one desire was to live his life in such a way as to glorify God, and he would do whatever it took to accomplish that desire.

God providentially guides us into a continually deeper understanding of His word, and how that word relates to our daily experiences of life. One thing that Joseph had learned was that God demands sexual purity, and he gave himself in obedience to live according to that knowledge. God has not changed His mind concerning this matter. He still demands sexual purity, and He then providentially provides His children with the ability to say "No" when temptation comes. Potholes may come which cause us to question where God is, or if He cares, and it is in those moments of darkness that we are given opportunity to display our God-given integrity by living lives of obedience to what He has revealed to us in the light.

Joseph's obedience to the word of God is then coupled with his willingness to do whatever it took to remain pure. The narrative in Genesis goes on to reveal that Potiphar's wife became so obsessed with the thought of a sexual liaison with Joseph that she literally grabbed him and tried to force him to have sexual relations with her. So what did Joseph do? Did he stand toe to toe with this woman and strive to give explanation as to why this would be wrong? Did he witness to her about God's demand for sexual purity? Did he give her a lecture on the dangers of adulterous relationships? No! He did none of these. Instead, he turned around and ran. He fled from the temptress, and the temptation.

There are times when this is the only course of action. There are times when the most Christian, godly thing we could possibly do is to turn around and run. Paul's admonition to young Timothy reverberates with this same thought:

> Flee youthful lusts; but pursue righteousness, faith,
> love, peace with those who call on the Lord out of
> a pure heart.
>
> (2 Timothy 2:22)

Spiritual courage is oftentimes best displayed in a well-timed retreat. Joseph learned this lesson as he struggled in the pothole. Perhaps we can learn the lesson from him so that we don't have to fall in the hole at all.

There are times of temptation when we may be caught completely off-guard. We need to be prepared spiritually, mentally, and emotionally to respond to the temptation with actions based on the word of God. Something may seem to be right at the moment, but if we are committed to the teachings of the Bible, and obedient to those instructions from the Lord, then we will be able to do as Joseph: flee the temptation.

The life of Joseph is a display of Godly integrity, courage, and commitment. Every believer in Jesus Christ could, and should, learn lessons from the life of this young man as he faced his potholes, so that we can be guided by the same principles that gave such clear direction to his life.

QUESTIONS FOR THOUGHT AND DISCUSSION

1. Can you identify with Joseph in the pothole of temptation?
2. If you answered yes to #1, were you able to withstand the temptation, or did you succumb to it? If you withstood, to what would you attribute your ability to say no.
3. How do we prepare for the constant battering of temptation? How can we, as Joseph, develop the courage and stamina to withstand?
4. Paul instructed Timothy to flee youthful lusts. When is it right to run away from temptation?
5. It was mentioned in this chapter that countless numbers of individuals have been destroyed by this particular pothole. Do you agree with this assessment? If so, explain your answer.
6. Do you personally know of someone in this pothole? If so, what can you do to help them escape before permanent damage is done?

CHAPTER 3

MOSES

The Pothole of the Impossible Task

Now Moses was tending the flock of Jethro his father-in-law, the priest of Midian. And he led the flock to the back of the desert, and came to Horeb, the mountain of God. And the Angel of the Lord appeared to him in a flame of fire from the midst of a bush. So he looked, and behold, the bush was burning with fire, but the bush *was* not consumed. Then Moses said, "I will now turn aside and see this great sight, why the bush does not burn."

So when the Lord saw that he turned aside to look, God called to him from the midst of the bush and said, "Moses, Moses!"

And he said, "Here I am."

Then He said, "Do not draw near this place. Take your sandals off your feet, for the place where you stand *is* holy ground." Moreover He said, "I *am* the God of your father—the God of Abraham, the God of Isaac, and the God of Jacob." And Moses hid his face, for he was afraid to look upon God.

And the Lord said: "I have surely seen the oppression of My people who *are* in Egypt, and have heard their cry because of their taskmasters, for I know their sorrows. So I have come down to deliver them out of the hand of the Egyptians, and to bring them up from that land to a good and large land, to a land flowing with milk and honey, to the place of the Canaanites and the Hittites and the Amorites and the Perizzites and the Hivites and the Jebusites. Now therefore, behold, the cry of the children of Israel has come to Me, and I have also seen the oppression with which the Egyptians oppress them. Come now, therefore, and I will send you to Pharaoh that you may bring My people, the children of Israel, out of Egypt."

(Exodus 3:1–10)

I sn't it amazing how God always has just the right person in just the right place at just the right time? Whenever there is a need, God supplies the resources and the personnel to meet that need. The book of Exodus tells us of a time when the need was overwhelming. The people of Israel had now been in Egypt for almost four hundred years. What started out as a friendly and cordial relationship had deteriorated over the years to the point that the descendants of Jacob were nothing more than slaves. They were performing forced labor, being used to build Pharaoh's cities. God comes to the rescue by raising up a man whom God will use to bring about deliverance for Israel.

Moses is that man. He is born to Amram and Jochebed at the worst time imaginable. Pharaoh had commanded the Israelite midwives to kill all the male infants born to Israelite women. The names of these midwives would lead us to believe that they were very likely Egyptian rather than Israelite. This adds so much insight into the miraculous element of God's providence revealed in this text. The Israelites were multiplying exponentially, and this command to kill all the male infants was Pharaoh's plan to thwart this massive population explosion. The midwives, however, refused to follow through on this wicked edict from Pharaoh, and continued to allow the Israelite children to live.

This is just one of the many powerful displays of God's providence at work in this historical record of God's personal participation with the people of Israel. It is amazing to see how He constantly works to bring about His plans. Sometimes His work is open and obvious while at other times it is hidden from view. The people of Israel were probably wondering where God was and what He was up to as they languish in servitude to the Egyptians.

It may be that many of them, perhaps most of them, had long ago forgotten the promises God had made to Abraham. And many of them, even if they could remember, had probably developed a spirit of bitterness toward God as He had seemingly forgotten all about them. Or, maybe they thought that He had simply forsaken them, having changed His mind about the promises He had made.

But God is about to do something that they would never have believed. After all, four hundred years is an extremely long time. Why should they have any confidence in these promises after all that time? Why would any of them hold out hope for God to deliver them, much less give them the land He had promised so long ago?

Can you imagine the despair and hopelessness many, if not most, or perhaps even all of them must have felt? Perhaps a spirit of sheer hopelessness had now become the common way of thinking among the masses. They are laboring day after day, week after week, month after month, and yes, year after year. They are languishing under the cruel hand of the taskmasters who are only interested in meeting their daily quota assignments. They probably could not have cared any less about their health, their welfare, their suffering. Those cruel taskmasters must have just demanded of the Israelites to give what is expected today, and then do it all over again tomorrow.

It was during this time of extreme anguish and suffering that Moses was born. He was providentially protected by God's gracious hand of providence even from birth. The story is nothing short of amazing, even miraculous. The events recorded here are an unbelievable display of how God protects and provides for His own.

The text reveals first that the midwives allowed the child to live. They were putting their own lives at risk by going against the direct order of Pharaoh, and yet they took no thought of the personal consequences they might have to endure. They simply were not willing to take the lives of every male child born to Hebrew mothers.

Then, again orchestrated by the hand of providence, the child's mother is able to protect him for the first three months of his life. Somehow this wise mother protects him from the regular searches conducted by Pharaoh's assigned guards. She is able to hide him from those who would do him harm. But it finally becomes obvious that it would be impossible to keep him concealed any longer.

This is such a shocking story! The events that are transpiring here are unbelievable. How could anyone be so barbaric? How could anyone give orders to wantonly and recklessly take the lives of these innocent male babies? How could Pharaoh be so cold and cruel? How could anyone be this heartless? Pharaoh has become accustomed to having the Israelites do all their menial labor, but now he is concerned that the Israelites are going to become more numerous than the Egyptians. He is so stricken with fear that he issues the command to have all the male children killed so that they will not be able to continue this massive population explosion.

So, even though the mother has been able to successfully hide the infant for three full months, she is now convinced that he could no longer be hidden. She then, out of what must have been sheer desperation, came up with a plan that she hoped would save her son's life. This plan once again proves to be an amazing display of God's providential protection.

> And a man of the house of Levi went and took *as wife* a daughter of Levi. So the woman conceived and bore a son. And when she saw that he *was* a beautiful *child,* she hid him three months. But when she could no longer hide him, she took an ark of bulrushes for him, daubed it with asphalt and pitch, put the child in it, and laid *it* in the reeds by the river's bank. And his sister stood afar off, to know what would be done to him.
>
> (Exodus 2:1–4)

Can you imagine the anxiety, the stress, the distress this would have caused to develop in the heart of the child's mother? She has protected him as long as she thought it was safe to do so, but now has determined she can no longer provide that protection. She has probably been thinking about what she could do to protect her son from a sure and sudden death if he was found. How could she protect him? How could she save his life? How could she possibly protect him from this evil plan of Pharaoh? I imagine she and her husband, Amram, have spent many hours trying to come up with a plan that could possibly save his life.

The pressure to come up with a plan was growing more intense with each passing day. They had probably thought of every possible scenario in which his life could be spared from the death sentence decreed by Pharaoh. Desperate circumstances call for desperate measures. And they were beyond a state of desperation. They had reached the point of no return. Something had to be done, and it had to be done immediately.

Finally, they come up with a plan that could perhaps save the child. It was a risky plan, but under the circumstances it was probably the best thing they could come up with. The pressure kept mounting every day to figure out some way to protect the young boy. From Amram and Jochebed's perspective it may have been a matter of sheer desperation, but from God's perspective it was the plan of providence: God had His hand in the plan.

The plan seems to be utterly insane. They decide to place the child in a basket and set it afloat in the Nile River. Jochebed's heart must have been crushed as that small, fragile basket begins to float downstream with the current. Everything was now out of her hands. She stood there, helplessly watching as the basket bobbed up and down on the waves, weaving back and forth with the changing current. It must have felt like an eternity as she stood there, not knowing what would happen to the precious human cargo inside that basket.

At this point anything could have happened to the baby. The basket could have easily flipped over by the waves of the flowing water, causing the infant to sink to the bottom of the Nile. Or the basket could have leaked and filled with water causing the child to drown. Or an alligator could have swum to the basket and destroyed it with his massive jaws. Or the basket could have just continued to float downstream until it was completely out of sight and out of reach. Yes, anything could have happened to the child as he was placed in the waters of the Nile.

As the mother and the child's sister stand watching to see exactly what would become of the child, they witness a most remarkable sight. The Bible describes the scene:

> Then the daughter of Pharaoh came down to bathe at the river. And her maidens walked along the riverside; and when she saw the ark among the reeds, she sent her maid to get it. And when she opened *it,* she saw the child, and behold, the baby wept. So she had compassion on him, and said, "This is one of the Hebrews' children."
>
> Then his sister said to Pharaoh's daughter, "Shall I go and call a nurse for you from the Hebrew women, that she may nurse the child for you?"
>
> And Pharaoh's daughter said to her, "Go." So the maiden went and called the child's mother.
>
> (Exodus 2:5–8)

This is obviously a miraculous intervention of God. Have you ever considered that in order for Moses to have been rescued, Pharaoh's daughter had to be in just the right place at precisely the right time? Five minutes either way and Moses may have drifted down stream without anyone ever noticing.

Or, she could have seen the basket and simply ignored it. She was there to bathe in the waters of the Nile. Why should she pay any attention to a basket floating downstream past her? She could have simply busied herself with the task at hand and paid no attention at all to the basket. The entire episode was planned by God, and providentially carried out by God.

To make the story even more amazing is the fact that the child's sister, when she sees that Pharaoh's daughter has rescued her brother from the waters of the Nile, goes to her and offers to get an Israelite woman to care for the child. When the daughter of Pharaoh instructs her to get someone, the child's sister goes home and gets her mother, the baby's mother, to nurse and care for him.

Some would probably view all these parts of this amazing story as nothing more than coincidence. It was just by coincidence that the daughter of Pharaoh came out to bathe at just the right moment. Or it was just by coincidence that the basket floated safely on the surface of the water rather than filling with the water of the Nile causing the basket to sink. Or it was just coincidence that Pharaoh's daughter paid any attention at all to the object floating past. Just coincidence.

But the story makes it clear that none of this was by coincidence. These events did not happen by chance. It was directed by the invisible hand of God as He providentially cared for this child. What must have appeared to the parents of this small, three-month old baby to be a reckless, daring attempt to save the child's life, was actually the providential plan of God to protect His appointed deliverer for the entire nation of Israel.

So, the child was taken into the family of Pharaoh. He would have been reared in the prosperity of the ruler of the entire nation of Egypt. He would have been exposed to the best of the best: the best food, the best clothing, the best education, the best of everything. His adopted mother, the daughter of Pharaoh, would have made sure he would lack nothing. He lived a life of privilege and plenty.

The child grew into adulthood, living in Egypt forty years. When Moses was fully grown, he went out to make evaluation of the Israelite's circumstances as slaves to Pharaoh. It was then that he observed an Egyptian beating an Israelite. Upon seeing this, Moses intervened by killing the Egyptian. The next day, he again was out among the people, this time observing two Israelites fighting. When he intervened, he was asked sarcastically, "Who made you a prince and a judge over us? Do you intend to kill me as you killed the Egyptian?"

Moses then realized that his actions the day before were known. Realizing Pharaoh had been made aware of what had happened, Moses knew that drastic measures were in order. He fled Egypt, making his way as far as Midian. It was there that he took up residence, and where he spent the next forty years of his life.

Any of the events just described would qualify as a pothole. Moses' life, just as we saw in the life of Joseph, consisted of one traumatic experience after another. However, the pothole which will be considered in this chapter is the one which Moses experienced at the end of this forty years spent on the backside of the wilderness. The narrative of Exodus 2:23-24 says:

> Now it happened in the process of time that the king of Egypt died. Then the children of Israel groaned because of the bondage, and they cried out; and their cry came up to God because of the bondage. So God heard their groaning, and God remembered His covenant with Abraham, with Isaac, and with Jacob.
>
> (Exodus 2:23–24)

This is a beautiful example of God's faithfulness to His people. Long ago, hundreds of years prior to this event, God had entered into a covenantal relationship with Abraham. The covenant had been renewed with Isaac, and then with Jacob. But for all those hundreds of years since, the children of Israel had not enjoyed the benefits of the fulfillment of that covenant. As a matter of fact, they probably had begun to question the validity of the covenant as they witnessed generation after generation live and die without seeing the covenant fulfilled.

Try to imagine the significance of this series of events. I live in the United States of America. This country was birthed on July

4, 1776. The nation is now only 246 years old. Think of all that has happened in that time span. This country suffered through the years of the Civil War, as northern and southern armies fought for their respective political machines. Added to that is the participation in major world conflicts, World War I and World War II. Soldiers in America's armed forces also fought in the Korean Conflict, the Viet Nam war, Desert Storm, and others. We have witnessed great advancements in medical research, space exploration, healthcare, education, and so much more.

These are just a few of the major events in our history. Added to these are so many other historical events which have been long forgotten, perhaps only having a byline in historical records. And countless events have simply been forgotten. Historical records reveal only a fraction of everything that has happened in all those years. So much has been completely wiped from memory. Two and a half centuries is a long, long time. Many of the foundational principles upon which this nation was birthed have long-since been forgotten, or, if not forgotten, relegated to nothing more than a brief byline in our historical narrative.

The Israelites had been in Egypt long enough for several generations to be born and die. Think about all that could have been forgotten during those hundreds of years. If it were not purposefully and intentionally passed down family to family, generation to generation, century to century, then it would have long ago been forgotten.

The promises of God to their forefather, Abraham, were of such great significance that they were probably passed down faithfully, at least for a while. Some of the families may have become weary in striving to remember and pass down promises that were made so long ago. Some, perhaps, even lost any hope that those promises would ever be fulfilled. Still others may have lost hope in the promise that God had selected them to be His own special chosen nation. Four hundred years could even caused some to become bitter toward a God who would make such outlandish promises, only to watch the people who received them grow discontented and bitter while they languished as slaves in Egypt.

But God had not forgotten His covenant. Everything was happening according to His divine timetable, and the time had now come for Him to intervene on behalf of His people. And who was it that He would use to bring that covenant to fruition? Who was it that He would use to deliver His people from their severe oppression? The text reveals the plan God has for His people.

> Now Moses was tending the flock of Jethro his father-in-law, the priest of Midian. And he led the flock to the back of the desert, and came to Horeb, the mountain of God.
>
> (Exodus 3:1)

All attention is now focused on Moses. He would be the one whom God would use to deliver His people from their Egyptian bondage. But it is important to remember that Moses had fled Egypt forty years prior to this. Forty years is a long time. Not as long as four hundred, but a long time none-the-less. Perhaps he has forgotten the promises of God. It seems from the above text that he is simply minding his own business, doing what he has been doing for the last forty years. He is doing what any good shepherd would do: leading the flock to pastures that would provide a good supply of food for the sheep.

It is there, on the backside of the desert, that Moses is going to experience a divine encounter. It is there that God reveals His plan to Moses. After getting Moses' undivided attention through the miraculous burning bush, He tells Moses that He has heard the cries of His people and that He has a plan to deliver them from their present plight in Egypt. Moses may have been thinking to himself that it was about time God did something. After all, he had made an attempt forty years earlier to come to the aid of the Israelites, but that attempt blew up in his face, causing him to now have spent forty years on the backside of the desert.

It would be wise to take a moment to focus on the grave importance of something clearly implied in this story of God's providence. We need to guard ourselves against the tendency of getting ahead of God. We may sometimes feel that God is calling us to perform some task, or to begin some ministry, or to move to a new location. It is a common tendency to go full speed ahead, even before we get all the details of the new assignment. To do this usually ends in difficulty, if not total disaster!

It is extremely easy to get ahead of God. Moses seems to have sensed some sort of leadership or motivation from God when he intervened in the incident in which the Egyptian was beating the Israelite. I have heard so many young men who have felt the divine nudging to go into vocational ministry of some sort. They are striving to be obedient to that sense of calling, and they begin trying to make it all work out. Instead of waiting for God to clearly show the path He would have them follow, they jumped in before the timing was right, and found themselves struggling to make things work.

God doesn't want us to make things work – He wants to work things through us. If we busy ourselves trying to figure it all out, to work things out, force things to happen, then we will oftentimes find ourselves totally frustrated and looking for a way out. Moses ended up having to flee to the wilderness because he acted before God instructed him to do so.

This is such an important matter to remember. God's timetable is always perfect. His timing is impeccable. He is never early and never late. His punctuality is sheer perfection. I have known a few believers in my life who have tried to run ahead of God. They felt compelled to begin a new ministry, and in their excitement over the prospect of getting started they failed to wait for God's timing.

Moses had to learn this lesson the hard way as he tried to take matters into his own hands. He learned that getting ahead of God would result in extreme adversity, but once the timing is right the power of God will perform the task assigned.

So Moses has spent forty years in the wilderness. Forty long years tending the flocks of his father-in-law. He was probably elated to hear God reveal that He was about to do something on behalf of His chosen people. He speaks to Moses about His concern for His people:

> And the LORD said: "I have surely seen the oppression of My people who *are* in Egypt, and have heard their cry because of their taskmasters, for I know their sorrows. So I have come down to deliver them out of the hand of the Egyptians, and to bring them up from that land to a good and large land, to a land flowing with milk and honey, to the place of the Canaanites and the Hittites and the Amorites and the Perizzites and the Hivites and the Jebusites."
>
> (Exodus 3:7–8)

This must have brought a sense of great joy, excitement and anticipation to Moses as he realized that God was about to do what he had attempted to do forty years earlier. The time wasn't right then, but now, the timing is perfect. God has heard the cries of His people, and He now plans to deliver them from their oppression. But who will God use to accomplish this daunting task? Who could possibly bring such a huge assignment to completion? Moses will be the man. After God reveals to him that He has heard the cries of His people and that He now plans to deliver them, He then says,

> Come now, therefore, and I will send *you* to Pharaoh that you may bring My people, the children of Israel, out of Egypt.
>
> (Exodus 3:10 –emphasis added)

Everything had been just fine with Moses up to this point. He was probably nodding his head in absolute agreement and giving his hearty approval to everything God had revealed. But his hearty nods of approval now turned into woeful moans of argument as God tells him that he would be the deliverer. It would be all right as long as it was someone else doing the dirty work. But when it came down to Moses being the man, everything in him revolted. His response? Well, let's listen to Moses as he responds to God's invitation:

> But Moses said to God, "Who am I that I should go to Pharaoh, and that I should bring the children of Israel, out of Egypt?"
>
> (Exodus 3:11)

What had probably been sheer jubilation up to this point now turned into absolute horror! Perhaps in his mind Moses went back forty years to that fateful day when he had committed murder. Perhaps he envisioned going back to Egypt only to find that there was still a warrant for his arrest. Perhaps he thought that he would surely be executed for what he had done forty years earlier.

Or perhaps he just realized what an insignificant person he was. He had now been living in the wilderness forty years, tending the sheep that belonged to his father-in-law. He was not a person who would be readily recognized as a man of authority back over in Egypt. Perhaps that is what he was signifying when he asked who he was to take such a task upon himself. Perhaps Moses had been tempered over those forty long years, and he is no longer the arrogant young man who would try to take matters into his own hands and do things his own way. Perhaps this is at least part of the reason God allowed him to live in that wilderness for so long.

Regardless of his reasoning, Moses seems to be horrified at the thought of his personal involvement in such an overwhelming, seemingly impossible assignment. Thus, his cry, "Who am I that

I should go to Pharaoh?" This must have undoubtedly seemed like an incredible and insurmountable assignment.

But God was so gracious in His response to Moses. He says,

> I will certainly be with you. And this shall be a sign to you that I have sent you: When you have brought the people out of Egypt, you shall serve God on this mountain.
>
> (Exodus 3:12)

Note especially the first words: "I will certainly be with you." God is reassuring His chosen servant that he would not be going alone, but that God would be with him every step of the way. But even with this wonderful promise, Moses still found it impossible to accept such a challenge. It is at this point that he begins his argument with God. He offers all his excuses, which probably sounded pretty substantial to him. But God just brushed them off and continued to reassure Moses he was the man.

So, God assures Moses of His presence, and then even goes so far as to show him His power. But Moses is still not convinced. He offers God the petty excuse that he cannot speak eloquently, and then, in a last-ditch effort to convince God to change His mind, he actually asks Him to send someone else.

Moses had made his case. It is obvious that he did not want to go – he did not want this assignment. But try as he might, he could not convince God to appoint someone else for the job. God had been preparing Moses for this assignment for at least forty years. Whether Moses realized it or not, God had him right where he needed to be. And now, the timing was perfect for God to deliver His people. Still, Moses did not want to be the one.

Before we come down too hard on Moses for his reaction to God's assignment, it would be wise for us to consider the enormity of the task God was giving him. He was to go to Pharaoh, the ruler of Egypt, and demand the release of the entire Israelite population. This was no small band of nomads, but rather an enormous host of people, probably numbering in the millions! They were extremely profitable to Pharaoh, serving as slaves in his building projects. And here is this man who has been tending sheep on the back side of the wilderness for forty years who is supposed to go into the court of Pharaoh with the demand that this vast multitude be freed.

Would *you* want an assignment like that? It appears that Moses is indeed faced with a pothole of monstrous proportions. No wonder he offered all his excuses! No wonder he suggested that God send someone else!

Moses was not really all that different from most of us, was he? He evaluated the situation from his human perspective, realized that it was an impossible task, and kindly declined the offer to participate. It is not the natural human response to want to be involved in a work that is inevitably doomed for disaster. Rather, we want to make sure that those causes to which we give our time, talent and energy are causes which are guaranteed to work. We don't want to waste our time and efforts on causes which may prove futile in the end.

But aren't you glad that history is dotted with those who took the bull by the horns, even when the task seemed impossible, and accepted the challenge? Where would we be if there had not been those who looked the insurmountable challenge squarely in the eye, and charged ahead? Where would we be had it not been for individuals like Winston Churchill, or Abraham Lincoln, or the founding fathers of the United States, or Martin Luther, or John Calvin, or John Knox, or so many others who were willing to suffer in order to accomplish what they felt to be their personal assignment in life.

And of course, there are so many others who could be added to those named above, recording the names of those who have stood face to face with seemingly impossible situations, and accepted the challenge head-on. Moses' name would certainly be included in a list such as that above. Admittedly he went reluctantly: but he did go! He finally did accept the challenge. He finally said

"Yes" to God as He called him to do the seemingly impossible. And then, by the providential guidance of God, Moses was able to see the deliverance of an entire nation of people from bondage.

As we consider the rest of the story, of how God used Moses to miraculously deliver the people of Israel from their Egyptian taskmasters, it is obvious that God providentially led the way. Pharaoh saw an awesome display of God's power as Moses stood toe-to-toe with Pharaoh's magicians, performing the works of God. Moses had offered all of his excuses, but God oversaw all of his weaknesses. And it was in the weaknesses of Moses that God's power was displayed.

There are times when we may feel that God has placed an impossible task upon us. Looking at situations from the human perspective, we may begin to think that God has asked of us something which could not possibly be done. But when that happens, it is only that God is preparing His people for a marvelous, and even miraculous, display of His power. Moses witnessed the power of God in ways which are beyond our wildest imaginations. So wonderful were these displays of God's power that many today explain them away as being glosses to the original text of Scripture. But in reality, what we see is that God calls His people to perform impossible tasks, and then He actually does the work through those who will yield themselves to Him.

What we need to learn from this portrait of providence is the truth that God desires us to be people who will follow Him by faith, even when the task is far above and beyond anything we could ever accomplish. We live in a society in which we are taught from our very earliest age that we must attain for ourselves, that we must do it all, that we must depend on self. The Bible would teach us just the opposite. Those in the biblical record who attempted to do things their own way were those who failed miserably in their attempts. It was those who yielded themselves to God, and allowed Him to work through them, who were the real success stories. Moses learned that even though the task appears impossible from the human perspective, that all things are possible with God.

I remember quite well something that happened to me forty-five years ago. It wasn't long after I had been gloriously saved by God's amazing grace. I had been actively involved in every church activity available to me as a young believer. But as time progressed, I became a bit miserable in my Christian walk. At a men's ministry meeting, my pastor, concerned about the way I had been acting in recent weeks, asked if something was wrong that he might be able to help with.

After the meeting the pastor and I went into his study to pray together. He asked again about what might be bothering me. I tried to grin and make light of the heaviness I was feeling. I had not shared with anyone up to this point that I felt that God was calling me into pastoral ministry. I just shared with my pastor that I would appreciate his prayers, so he led us in a prayer that I thought would be the end of our conversation for the night. It was already getting late, and I'm sure he wanted to get home to his family. All I wanted to do was go home.

I cannot explain exactly what happened to me in the middle of the pastor's prayer. There was no blinding light that filled the room, no booming voice from above. It was in the stillness of the prayer, and the quietness of the pastor's study, that God spoke powerfully to my heart, soul, and mind. It was a still, small voice I heard in my spirit, but it was plenty loud enough to get my attention. That voice said to me what I had already felt – God was calling me into pastoral ministry.

I was terrified. Perhaps horrified would be a better word. Maybe even petrified. I can't think of a word that aptly describes what I felt. I just knew that I could not possibly do what He was calling me to do. How could I, an extreme introvert, ever stand before an audience of any number and preach or teach the Word of God? It was far beyond anything I could ever envision myself doing.

The pastor finished his prayer, looked straight into my eyes as if he were looking directly into my inner spirit, and said, "Do you feel as if God revealed anything to you as we prayed?" I lied. I'm not thrilled to make that admission, but the fact is, I lied. I simply said, "Nothing special."

At that point the pastor sat down behind his desk, took a small piece of paper and wrote himself a note. I had no clue what he might have written down, but it was of no concern to me. I just wanted to get out of there. I thought that if I could just get out of that room I could put this nonsense out of my mind. But I could not get it out of my mind, and it certainly was not nonsense.

The pastor then said that he knew something was deeply bothering me, and that he genuinely wanted to help with whatever it was. I then finally began speaking about my encounter with God during the pastor's prayer. I said, "Yes, God spoke to me, clearly and powerfully." He waited for me to share more, and when I didn't, he asked, "Well, what did He say?"

My response at this point in time, forty-five years later, makes me laugh because of the absurdity of my statement. I said, "If I say it, that means I accept it, and I don't want to accept it, so I'm not going to say it." Absurd, right? But I truly meant it when I said it. I was terrified because God was calling me to do something I knew I could not do. It was, in my estimation, the impossible task.

After sitting there in absolute misery for an unknown amount of time, I finally told him what I felt God had said to me. It was then that he picked up the piece of paper on which he had made himself a note, handed it to me, and asked that I would read it. I unfolded the small paper, and read the words, "God has called you to preach." I was completely stunned! How did he know? I had not mentioned this to anyone, not even my wife.

God revealed it to him so that he could affirm me. Yes, God was calling me to do what was an impossible task, but I soon learned that what He was actually calling me to do was to allow Him to work through me. Just as He had done with Moses, and so many others. And now, looking back on more than forty years in pastoral ministry, I see the providential hand of God that was at work from the beginning to the present.

There are so many lessons to be learned from Moses' experiences with the providential leadership of God. What I would leave us with as we come to the conclusion of this chapter is this: It is as we trust Him, and as we commit our ways to Him, that He works providentially through the potholes of life to bring glory to Himself.

QUESTIONS FOR THOUGHT AND DISCUSSION

1. Have your ever felt as if you were faced with an impossible task?

2. If you answered yes to #1, explain in your own words what the task was and how it turned out. Share this experience with a friend or family member.

3. Can you relate to Moses' arguing with God about his assignment? Have you ever argued with God over something you felt He was leading you to do?

4. Have you ever gotten ahead of God and experienced some sort of difficulty because of your impatience?

5. Can you relate to the author's choice of words – "terrified", "horrified", "petrified" – when thinking of a time in which you felt God's leadership to perform a task He has assigned? If so, share this experience with a friend or family member.

6. The testimony of Scripture relating to us these amazing stories of God's providence are to encourage us as we strive to follow God. So, we should share our personal experiences with others so that they might be encouraged by God's ongoing work in the lives of individuals today.

7. Will you make a commitment to share your own experiences with others? God can use you to encourage others to commit their paths to His leadership.

CHAPTER 4

JOSHUA

The Pothole of Leadership

After the death of Moses the servant of the LORD, it came to pass that the LORD spoke to Joshua the son of Nun, Moses' assistant, saying: "Moses My servant is dead. Now therefore, arise, go over this Jordan, you and all this people, to the land which I am giving to them—the children of Israel. Every place that the sole of your foot will tread upon I have given you, as I said to Moses.

"No man shall *be able to* stand before you all the days of your life; as I was with Moses, *so* I will be with you. I will not leave you nor forsake you. Be strong and of good courage, for to this people you shall divide as an inheritance the land which I swore to their fathers to give them. Only be strong and very courageous, that you may observe to do according to all the law which Moses My servant commanded you; do not turn from it to the right hand or to the left, that you may prosper wherever you go. This book of the Law shall not depart from your mouth, but you shall meditate in it day and night, that you may observe to do according to all that is written in it. For then you will make your way prosperous, and then you will have good success."

(Joshua 1:1–3, 5–9)

L ife presents us with some potholes that are horrible to even think about. There are problems of different types and different degrees of seriousness. There are potholes that concern our health, families, finances, neighbors, co-workers, etc. Our imaginations can run wild just thinking about all the possibilities.

But then there are other potholes that may not seem so bad when we first think about them. As a matter of fact, there are some that are desirable, even enviable. Think again, for example, about Abraham. God promised to make of him a great nation through which all other nations of the world would be either blessed or cursed. That is a pothole that would be envied by many. In all reality it would not even be considered a pothole by most.

One pothole that may be in that same category is that of leadership. Leaders are the trailblazers, the forerunners, the ones who are out front, leading the way, giving direction, coming up with the plan. The leader stands out in the crowd. They are confident in their abilities, willing to carry the responsibilities of leadership on their shoulders. They are not intimidated by being the one to whom all others look for guidance. They are leaders.

Joshua is just such an individual. He is a leader. He is one of those great Old Testament characters who can be studied from a wide variety of angles. It doesn't matter which of those angles one chooses to study his life, Joshua, consistently displays characteristics which are worthy of imitation.

Joshua was born into a nation which was experiencing great adversity. He was born in the land of Egypt, during the latter years of the Israelites bondage in that country. It would have been his lot in life to experience much of the oppression which was so prominent with his people in those latter years. The record makes it clear that the people of Israel were being oppressed severely by Pharaoh. In those waning years of their enslavement, Pharaoh had multiplied their workload, demanding from them enormous amounts of labor. Under his domineering hand, the people began to cry out to God and in response to their cries God had raised up a powerful deliverer, a man named Moses. It was through his leadership that God brought about the miraculous deliverance of His people from their Egyptian bondage. It was also through his leadership that God had provided for the people of Israel during the forty years that intervened between their exit from Egypt and their entrance into the promised land.

But Moses died, as do all great leaders. He had led the people faithfully during those forty years, but now he has passed from the scene. It would now rest upon Joshua's shoulders to take up where Moses had left off. It would now be his assignment to be the leader for the masses of Israelites as they prepare to enter the promised land, to take possession of that country long ago promised by God to Abraham.

There are some things we need to know about Joshua which will help us better understand why God selected him to succeed Moses. We are first introduced to him in Exodus 17, where he is portrayed as a military leader, perhaps even the general of all the armies of Israel. It was under his leadership, and more importantly by the grace of God, that the Israelites enjoyed an overwhelming victory in a battle with the Amalekites.

> Now Amalek came and fought with Israel at Rephidim. And Moses said to Joshua, "Choose us some men and go out, fight with Amalek. Tomorrow I will stand on the top of the hill with the rod of God in my hand." So Joshua did as Moses said to him, and fought with Amalek. And Moses, Aaron, and Hur went up to the top of the hill. And so it was, when Moses held up his hand, that Israel prevailed; and when he let down his hand, Amalek prevailed. But Moses' hands became heavy; so they took a stone and put it under him, and he sat on it. And Aaron and Hur supported his hands, one on one side, and the other on the other side; and his hands were steady until the going

down of the sun. So Joshua defeated Amalek and
his people with the edge of the sword.

(Exodus 17:8–13)

This story shows clearly that Joshua would prove to be a
great leader for the people. His willingness to follow the orders
of Moses shows that he was a leader who was willing to be led
by those in authority over him.

Later in the Exodus record (Ex. 24:13), Joshua is presented
as the assistant to Moses. The text shows clearly that he was
closely associated with Moses. He observed the leadership skills
and methods that made Moses a great leader, and by doing so he
would have learned much about how to be a great leader himself.
And, he witnessed Moses' dependence upon God when he and
the nation were faced with hardship and difficulty.

One of the great privileges of Joshua's life was the occasion
when he accompanied Moses onto the mountain where Moses
received the law from God. He did not go with Moses into the
cloud of God's presence where Moses personally conversed with
God, but he was privileged to be with Moses on the mountain.
What an awesome experience this must have been for Joshua as
God revealed His law to Moses. And how these experiences must
have molded Joshua into the leader he became.

However, it was there, as Moses was in the cloud of God's
presence receiving the law from God that would guide the
people of Israel in following God, that an awful sound came
from far below in the camp of the Israelites. Joshua heard the
sound of revelry coming from the camp. The Israelites had grown
impatient as they had waited forty days for Moses to return, so
they quickly began to take action that would result in a most
painful confrontation with Moses.

Joshua was with Moses as he descended from the mountain
where he had been in the presence of God, and where he received
the ten commandments. When Moses and Joshua had come
back into the camp and saw the people engaged in such revelry,

STEVE STEWART, TH.D.

Moses became angry and indignant. What he saw caused him to throw the stone tablets inscribed with the ten commandments violently to the ground. The tablets shattered into pieces, and Moses demanded from the people an explanation for their sinful behavior. Joshua was once again witnessing the actions of a great leader.

This would have added to Joshua's understanding of true leadership. He had been privileged to be with Moses, to observe Moses' actions, to hear his words of instruction to the people, to witness his judgments in those important cases which were brought before him. Joshua had seen and heard so much as he served in the role of Moses' assistant.

Now that the mantle of leadership had passed to him, all the knowledge he had received from being Moses' assistant would prove to be invaluable. The example of Godly leadership that he had witnessed in Moses would serve him well as he began his duties as Moses' successor.

Joshua had been appointed to succeed Moses before the death of Moses. It is imperative to note he was God's choice, and not just the personal choice of Moses.

> "Then the Lord said to Moses, "'Behold, the days approach when you must die; call Joshua, and present yourselves in the tabernacle of meeting, that I may inaugurate him.'"
>
> (Deuteronomy 31:14)

There are times when someone will presume to take matters into their own hands, which usually ends with less than desirable results. But when we wait for God's directives, we never go astray. He always has a plan, and if we will but wait for Him to show the way, He will make the path clear. Moses followed the Lord's instructions and Joshua was set apart to succeed him as leader of the nation.

So, when we come to Joshua 1:1-2 and hear God communicating

64

with Joshua that he would be the new leader, it did not take Joshua by surprise. But at the same time, we need to understand that it was still a shock as the previously announced plan of God became reality in Joshua's life. There may be certain events in life that we see coming from a distance, and we think that when they arrive, we will be prepared for them. Yet, when it does arrive, we suddenly realize that we are not prepared at all. There are certain things that come our way in life that seem to catch us off guard and ill-prepared.

This must have been the way Joshua now felt. Now, suddenly, Joshua finds himself in a huge pothole. We will call it the pothole of leadership. Again, many would not view this as a pothole, but as a most enviable position. But since leadership carries so much responsibility, and is accountable in so many ways, it would be wise to consider it as a pothole. By considering it as such we will be able to see how Joshua handled the pressures that were now his because of being appointed by God to succeed Moses as leader of Israel.

Have you ever found yourself in a position that demanded strong, assertive leadership? Perhaps it was on your job, or in the church, or in some aspect of community life. You found yourself thrust into a position which demanded leadership qualities which you really didn't know that you possessed. But still, you had to lead, you had to be strong, you had to be assertive. Everyone was depending on you to see them through. That is the position we find Joshua to be in as we come to the opening words of the book which bears his name. It is stated rather matter-of-factly:

> After the death of Moses the servant of the LORD, it came to pass that the LORD spoke to Joshua the son of Nun, Moses' assistant, saying: "Moses My servant is dead. Now therefore, arise, go over this Jordan, you and all this people, to the land which I am giving to them—the children of Israel."
>
> (Joshua 1:1–2)

Joshua is now thrust into the pothole of leadership. Yes, he has known this day was coming. And, yes, he had been tutored and mentored by Moses, the only leader the people had known. And, yes, he probably felt somewhat prepared for the task. But when the day arrives, and the mantle of leadership falls upon him, Joshua was probably overwhelmed with a sense of insecurity, and perhaps a feeling of inadequacy. To help us understand the magnitude of this pothole we must read between the lines a bit as we proceed through chapter one.

It would appear from the wording of this chapter that Joshua must have been experiencing a certain degree of fear and anxiety. It is of great significance to note that three times in the first nine verses God encourages Joshua with the admonition to be strong and courageous. We certainly do not want to do an injustice to Joshua by reading into those words more than we should, but it seems that Joshua may have been experiencing more than his share of anxiety.

Could God be encouraging him to be strong because he was displaying a degree of weakness? Could God be encouraging him to be courageous because he was displaying a certain degree of fear? Of course, there is no way we can be certain about it, but it would appear that Joshua recognized the tremendous amount of pressure that went along with this newly acquired position of leadership, and he was experiencing more than his share of second thoughts about accepting this new assignment. He had, after all, witnessed all the hardships Moses experienced as he led the people. He knew how obstinate the people had been under Moses' leadership and would probably prove to be now that he was their leader. He had to understand that the task before him was daunting, and without help from God he would never succeed. It's no wonder that God encourages him three times to be strong and courageous.

But to this admonition God also adds a wonderful promise. He assures Joshua that He would always be with him, just as He had been with Moses. This must have been exactly what Joshua needed to hear. God's promise of His abiding presence would give him the strength and courage he so desperately needed.

Perhaps some of us can relate to Joshua's experience. Perhaps some of us have been thrust into a position that demanded of us more than we ever imagined we could possibly give. I can relate very well to feelings of inferiority. I have always been an extremely shy, quiet individual. As a matter of fact, I was so shy during my high school years that I would never initiate a conversation, even with my best friends. Just the thought of raising my hand to ask a question in the classroom would cause me to break out in beads of perspiration. Can you imagine the horror I experienced when I felt God was calling me into pastoral ministry! I really wondered if He had not made His very first mistake. How could I ever stand before a group of people, regardless of the number in the group, and say anything? Terror gripped me, anxiety overwhelmed me, the enormity of the task seemed to be insurmountable.

As I think about being overwhelmed with these feelings of fear and anxiety, it recalls something that happened to me in the years before being called into ministry. I was working for an electronics firm, when my supervisor, the chief engineer of the company, approached me about going to Toastmaster's International so that I might learn to speak in public. After attending the meetings for a couple of weeks, we were all given our first speaking assignment. We were to prepare a five-minute speech on a subject of our choice. I chose my topic and worked frantically in preparation for the presentation of the speech at the next meeting.

When it came my turn to speak, I walked to the podium, stood there for what seemed like forever, trying to force words to come from my mouth. After the passage of an unknown amount of time, I burst into tears, after which I returned to my seat in humiliation. I was twenty-four years old at the time and have never forgotten the embarrassment of that moment. So again, it should be quite clear that when I sensed God calling me into pastoral ministry I felt completely and absolutely that it would be beyond anything I could ever do.

STEVE STEWART, TH.D.

I have talked with so many others in pastoral ministry who have related the same feelings of inability, inadequacy, and insecurity. I have heard testimonies of those who ran from God's calling upon their lives for certain periods of time – some longer than others – because of the tremendous responsibility which is part of that calling.

These feelings of inadequacy are not only experienced by those whom God sovereignly selects to be in leadership positions in the church, but they are also experienced by individuals in other areas of life as well. There are those who find themselves in positions which demand more than they think they have to offer.

So how was Joshua supposed to handle the enormity of his newly assigned task? And how are we to handle the demands of leadership when they come to rest upon our shoulders? We find some answers to that question as we consider the record of Joshua. We have in this book a powerful display of what God can do through those individuals who will follow His guidance and accept His call to leadership.

We need to realize first that those three admonitions given by God to Joshua to be strong and courageous were not empty words but were words packed with significance. God knew that the responsibilities that would come to rest on Joshua's shoulders would be more than any one person could handle alone, so He gives him a reassuring promise:

No man shall be able to stand before you all the days of your life; as I was with Moses, so I will be with you. I will not leave you nor forsake you.

(Joshua 1:5)

God knew that Joshua could not handle this enormous responsibility alone, and He promised that he would not have to. He gives Joshua one of the most reassuring words of promise anyone could ever receive. "As I was with Moses, so I will be with you."

68

Can you imagine what that statement must have brought to Joshua's mind? He had witnessed the miraculous omnipotence and omnipresence of God as He revealed His power and presence through Moses. And now, God promises that just as He had been with Moses, He would be with Joshua. Joshua had witnessed God's power through Moses in the confrontation with Pharaoh. And now, God promises to be with him just as He had been with Moses. Joshua had witnessed the power of God in the parting of the Red Sea. And now, God promises to be with him just as He had been with Moses. Joshua had witnessed the wonder of God's presence and power upon Moses' life through that forty-year period of wandering in the wilderness. And now, God promises to be with him just as He had been with Moses. I purposely repeat the phrase over and over simply because it is something every follower of the Lord needs to be reminded of over and over. We tend to sometimes forget God's promise to be with us as we go through life. We are sometimes faced with a situation where we feel we have to handle the pressures all alone, and we find ourselves overwhelmed with the responsibility it presents. It is in those times that we desperately need to remember the promise of the Lord to be with us – always.

Think about what God was communication to Joshua in that promise. God was reiterating to Joshua some wonderful truths that we would all do well to remember. First, God was telling Joshua to remember the past. When God reminded him of how He had been with Moses, this would have been a reminder of how God had worked in those years of the immediate past through the leadership of Joshua's predecessor.

Moses had been a conduit of God's presence and power as he led the people through all those years of wilderness wanderings. Food had been miraculously provided in the form of manna from heaven. Their clothing never wore out during those long years. Water had been miraculously provided from a rock on two occasions. Time after time Joshua witnessed these amazing feats of God performed through Moses. And now, God assures Joshua that He would be with him just as He had been with Moses. This must have been a most reassuring thing for Joshua to hear from God. What greater word of encouragement could anyone hear than this? God was reminding Joshua of His miraculous works through Moses and assures him that he will experience the same presence and power of the Lord in his life.

But there is much more to it than that! There is also the present tense aspect of God's message. God tells Joshua that He will be with him just as He was with Moses. That must have been such an uplifting word for Joshua. God says, "As I was with Moses, I will be with you." I was, past tense, and I will, present tense. A lesson from the past, and a promise for the present. Joshua would have put these two together and thanked God for this amazing word!

And there is an invaluable lesson for us to learn from that promise as well. God was communicating to Joshua that he need not live in the past. Yes, it is good and proper to remember the workings of God in the past, but don't get bogged down in reliving past events. God wants us to progress, to move forward. If Joshua had decided to just live in the past, then nothing of any significance would have been accomplished through his leadership. As a matter of fact, he would not have even qualified as a leader if he just sat around, remembering the past, and reminding the people of what God had done in by-gone days. God wants him to move ahead, and that is the reason He promises to be with him just as He had been with Moses.

Joshua could have called the leaders of Israel together and offered a plan by which they could memorialize Moses and the word he had received from God. He could have suggested that they erect a statue of Moses and build an altar at the statue so that homage could be paid to their great leader, now deceased. He could have suggested that they remain where they were, because to cross over the Jordan River into the promised land would present far too many obstacles, and since Moses was no longer with them, they need not rush over. He could have allowed his fear and anxiety to cause him to stay right where he was. But God gave him this present tense promise: He would be with Joshua just as He had been with Moses.

This is one of the most amazing promises that can be found in all of scripture. God promises His children that He will be with us, and that He will never leave nor forsake us. We can never, for any reason or under any circumstance, be separated from the love of God which is in Christ Jesus our Lord. No matter what comes our way in life, we can rest assured that He is always present. So, there is a past aspect of God's promises to Joshua, and there is a present aspect of the promise.

Then there is a future aspect of this statement as well. God reminds Joshua of how He had been with Moses; He then promises to be with him as He had been with Moses; and He further makes a promise to Joshua that he will lead the people to inherit the land which had long ago been promised by God to the forefathers of the nation. Joshua would be the one whom God would allow to lead the people into the land, conquer the land, and divide the land among the twelve tribes of Israel. No wonder God assured him of His continued presence.

And how encouraging it must have been for Joshua to hear these powerful promises of God. He had no need to be afraid but could be strong and courageous because God promised His continued presence, His continued power, and His continued protection. He could go with confidence knowing that God would continue to manifest Himself among the people through the leadership of Joshua.

We need to take these promises to heart and live by faith in the encouragement they offer. There are countless multitudes of people who seem to live in the past. Perhaps it is because there were bright, prosperous days of old which they now have come to cherish. Of course, there is nothing wrong with that, as long as we don't get trapped in the past. Perhaps you know someone who pretty much dwells in the past. All they talk about is what happened back then. When you hear some professional sports figures being interviewed, oftentimes the conversation will constantly be drawn back to the past.

I have heard church members who talk about nothing but the past. It is as if God has taken a long vacation because the only thing they talk about is what God did, past tense. It is good to remember the past, and even celebrate the past, but let us also remember that God has promised to be with us just as He was with those in the past. So, let us move on into a bright and glorious future by faith in God who continues to work even today.

Even with these great promises God gave to Joshua, his task of leadership was still overwhelming. So, how is he to accomplish the job God has assigned? Chapter one gives us three insights which will help us face the formidable task of accomplishing what appears to be an impossible assignment.

First, this promise of God to Joshua would have given him confidence. In verse five God promises Joshua that no man shall be able to stand before him. This amazing promise is coupled with the reminder that God would never leave nor forsake him. God is teaching Joshua that he can face his task with confidence, not in what he can accomplish himself, but in what God can accomplish through him. It would be well to remember the words of the apostle Paul: "I can do all things through Christ who strengthens me." That doesn't mean that there is nothing I can't do. There are multitudes of things I could never do because I don't have the skills required to do them. But it does mean that I can do anything and everything God desires of me as I rely on His presence and power in my life.

Confidence in the life of a follower of the Lord comes from our dependence upon Him. I am not to have confidence in what I am capable of doing, but I can have confidence in what He can do through me. This is a comforting promise, but it is also a challenging reminder. We are not to develop an "I can do this" mentality, unless it is "I can do this by the strength and grace of God." Joshua was not to become presumptuous in thinking that he could now lead the people on his own, by his own ingenuity and expertise. He had to maintain an attitude of total dependence upon God to work through him.

Second, Joshua will perform the impossible by living according to strong convictions. God commands Joshua to be a student of the Word of God. Listen carefully to these words:

> This Book of the Law shall not depart from your mouth, but you shall meditate in it day and night, that you may observe to do according to all that is written in it. For then you will make your way prosperous, and then you will have good success.
>
> (Joshua 1:8)

It is of great interest to note that this verse is the only place in the Bible where we find the word 'success'. If we want to be a success in life, then here is how to attain it: learn the word of God and live according to that word. We must have convictions based upon the absolutes of the Bible. We must make the Bible a matter of daily meditation, learning it and then living by its teachings.

This is becoming more of a struggle in the present day because the Bible is becoming less and less important in the eyes of the world at large, and also in the eyes of modern-day believers and the modern-day church. Biblical principles which were at one time embraced as absolute truth and given highest priority in striving to live a disciplined life are now viewed as outdated. They have now been replaced by a more progressive mindset in which pretty much anything goes. What may be deemed as right behavior by one may be viewed as wrong behavior by another. Everyone is left to himself to decide what is right for him. To live a successful life, according to this passage, is to live life in accordance with the teachings of God's word.

And third, we need to have courage. There is much in our world which would rob us of our courage, and this was true of the world in Joshua's day as well. So how was he to have the courage which would be necessary to be a success? Three times

God tells him to be strong and courageous. This was something Joshua would need to be constantly reminded of. He was about to lead the people into the promised land, where they would inherit what had been promised long ago to Abraham. But there was a problem: the land was already occupied! Fortified cities would have to be conquered. Scores of people would have to be driven out or destroyed. The task before Joshua was daunting. He would have to be a man of confidence, courage, and conviction in order to see the fulfillment of God's commands.

We need to heed this same admonition, because it is in the confidence, courage, and convictions we have by living in fellowship with God that we are able to ultimately have victory in the world. How are we to do that? By remembering!

We need to remember that God's promises to Joshua are still valid today. He will be with us; He will strengthen us; He will give us good success: IF! If we abide in His word, practice His word, and follow His orwd's teachings on living a life committed to fulfilling His will. This is becoming more and more difficult as there are so many opposing "voices" in our contemporary cultural setting. The demands of the "woke" movement and the LBGTQ community call into question the clear teachings of scripture. The contemporary church seems to be struggling with its identity, and how it should present itself to an unbelieving world. The belief in any form of absolute truth is being attacked vehemently from so many sides.

If we are to be successful in representing God to such a godless environment, then we must claim the promises God made to Joshua long ago. He will be with us to strengthen us for the daunting task we face in being the salt and light our world so desperately needs.

QUESTIONS FOR THOUGHT AND DISCUSSION

1. Joshua was thrust into a position which may have caused him to experience anxiety and fear. Have you ever felt this way when put into a position of leadership?

2. There are three different aspects of God's promise to Joshua: past, present and future. Do you feel these promises are still valid today?

3. If you answered yes to #2, identify an experience in your life from the past where God was with you in some time of difficulty.

4. Share your experience from #3 with a friend or family member.

5. Has God proved His faithfulness to you in a recent experience? If so, describe the experience.

6. Share your experience from #5 with a friend or family member.

7. God admonishes Joshua to be strong and courageous. Do you feel God still strengthens us to face obstacles that we come across in life?

CHAPTER 5

NAOMI

The Pothole of Grief

Now it came to pass, in the days when the judges ruled, that there was a famine in the land. And a certain man of Bethlehem, Judah, went to dwell in the country of Moab, he and his wife and his two sons. The name of the man *was* Elimelech, the name of his wife *was* Naomi, and the names of his two sons *were* Mahlon and Chilion—Ephrathites of Bethlehem, Judah. And they went to the country of Moab and remained there. Then Elimelech, Naomi's husband, died; and she was left, and her two sons. Now they took wives of the women of Moab: the name of the one *was* Orpah, and the name of the other Ruth. And they dwelt there about ten years. Then both Mahlon and Chilion also died; so the woman survived her two sons and her husband.

(Ruth 1:1–5)

There are very few things in life – if any at all – that cause more of a personal crisis than times of sorrow and grief. While serving churches as pastor for forty years, grief counseling outnumbered all other types by far. If statistics had been kept, grief counseling would have probably occurred more than all other types of counseling combined.

Grief is debilitating, paralyzing, and can be totally destructive if left unchecked. Grief can cause one to withdraw, to live in self-imposed isolation, not wanting to face the harshness of life. It may cause others to live in anger and resentment for the remainder of their lives, looking for someone to blame for the death of their loved one. Grief can bring about so many different and varied responses from different individuals.

There is no "right way" to handle grief. Every individual must go through the process as best they can, and there is no "one size fits all" method. There are programs one can go through to help with the grieving process but again, it is different for each one. One person may be able to move on with life after a relatively short grieving experience, while others might need months, or even years to work through their personal grieving process.

The book of Ruth is a virtual textbook on grief. There are so many lessons to be learned from this book that will prove to be of great help for those going through the grieving process. The book of Ruth is one of the most beautiful, tender, touching stories to be found in all human literature. It presents us with the poignant portrait of Ruth, a Moabitess woman who marries a young man from Bethlehem of Judah. Without question she is the main character in the narrative, and for that reason we oftentimes overlook, or relegate to a secondary position of importance, another key figure in the story: Naomi.

Naomi is Ruth's mother-in-law. She is the wife of Elimelech, and they have two sons, Mahlon and Chilion. The narrative informs us that she and her family are forced to leave their homeland due to a severe famine. They left their home in Canaan and settled in Moab. Even though the story leaves many details to our imagination, it does seem obvious that they prospered, at least to some degree, for some brief period after arriving in Moab. All seemed to be going well. The text informs the reader in the brief introduction that their needs were being met, and they were developing meaningful relationships with the residents of Moab. But then, the unexpected happened. Elimelech died. The text states rather tersely:

> Then Elimelech, Naomi's husband, died; and she was left, and her two sons.
>
> (Ruth 1:4)

What a tragedy! What in the world was she to do now? They had left home, family, friends, all that was familiar and comfortable. They had settled in a foreign land, hoping to find a home where their needs would be met and where they could settle into a life of fulfillment and joy. And now, suddenly, Naomi is left with two sons, in a foreign land. Her only means of support after Elimelech's death was to rely on her two sons.

Sadly, however, that is not the entirety of the story. After the initial shock of the death of Naomi's husband and the father of their two sons, it appears that they once again strive to make the best of a bad situation. Naomi's two sons, Mahlon and Chilion, are still with her, and undoubtedly making every effort to take care of her. The text goes on to inform the reader that both Mahlon and Chilion were married to Moabite women: Orpah and Ruth. Then, they continue to live in Moab for ten years. Obviously, they are making every effort to make the best of a very bad situation, even though they must have been anything but content.

But then, the unexpected happens. Again, the text is painfully blunt:

Then Mahlon and Chilion also died; so the woman survived her two sons and her husband.

(Ruth 1:5)

Naomi's life is one episode of grief followed by another episode of grief. Grief added to grief. Grief multiplied by grief. She had already suffered a form of grief years earlier when she was forced to say good-bye to friends and family. That would have been a traumatic, excruciating experience. To have to leave home, and travel to a distant country because famine had ravaged the land, would have caused grief to run deep. To realize that they would perhaps never see the family and friends they left behind would have left deep emotional scars they would carry for the rest of their lives.

Then, if it wasn't enough to experience that horrific loss, her husband dies. Naomi then must pick up the pieces and strive to make the most out of the pain and anguish she was experiencing. She had two sons, after all, that would need her love and care, so she probably felt as if she could not spend a lot of time grieving the loss of Elimelech. The demands of life continued, and she must do whatever is necessary to carry on.

But then, after trying to put the pieces of her broken life back together after Elimelech's death, her first son dies. Grief added to grief. The grieving process begins yet again. The wounds are still fresh from her husband's death, and now she is plunged into the depths of the despair of grief yet again.

Then, as if that were not enough, her second son then dies. Grief multiplied by grief. Sorrow upon sorrow. What suffering! What sadness! What sorrow! No one should ever have to live through such a grueling series of horrific events! Blow after blow. Wave after wave of crashing grief was her constant companion. Naomi never had time to rebound after each succeeding loss. First, her home. Then, her husband. Then, her first son. Finally, her second son. Loss after loss. Blow after blow. Wave after wave. Grief was Naomi's constant companion.

But the sad reality of life is that many must live through just such an ordeal as this. As I write this chapter, I have just returned to my office from the hospital where I sat with a brother and sister who had been forced to make the decision to cut off life support for their mother. Earlier in the day, I had sat in my office with another young man as we made arrangements for his mother's funeral service. Grief is a shocking reality of life. It seems that none of us live very long before we are touched with the reality of death, and the sobering shock of grief.

Naomi had to live through it. We might wonder how she ever survived. How could she carry such a heavy burden How could she bear up under such tremendous grief? The narrative graphically displays her struggle with grief. It makes clear the fact that Naomi had a difficult time facing the reality of losing her husband and sons in death. We don't have nearly as much recorded for us as we would like, but we do have some strong statements, directly from the mouth of Naomi, that reveal her overwhelming struggle.

The intensity of her struggle with grief is seen as she decided to move back to her home. She decided to return to Bethlehem because she had heard a report that the famine was over and God had visited His people once again (see Ruth 1:6). As she prepared for her journey, her two daughters-in-law reveal their desire to return with her. Naomi instructs them to remain in their homeland with their people. Her reasoning for telling her daughters-in-law to remain is expressive of her deep feelings of loss and hurt. She says matter-of-factly:

> No, my daughters; for it grieves me very much for your sakes that the hand of the Lord has gone out against me.
>
> (Ruth 1:13b)

It is obvious that Naomi was having a difficult time dealing with the deaths of her husband and sons, and rightly so. She even appears to have developed somewhat of a bitter spirit through the ordeal. This is an unusually common reaction to the death of a loved one. In Naomi's experience, it wasn't just one death, but three. Husband, and then a son, and then another son. The text doesn't reveal exactly how much time elapsed between the deaths, but no matter how much time transpired it would not have been nearly enough. Naomi was crushed time after time after time. Grief came like waves crashing on the shore – relentless in their assault, never pausing, never giving time to recover.

No wonder Naomi sais to her daughters-in-law that the hand of the Lord had been against her. When she informed Orpah and Ruth that she had decided to return home, they both tell Naomi that they will go with her. Naomi, however, tells them to stay in their homeland, with their family. Orpah took Naomi's advice and returned to her home, but Ruth told her that wherever she went she would go also. Ruth made a total commitment to be with Naomi, and that Naomi's people would be her people, and Naomi's God would be her God.

The two of them set out for Bethlehem. Naomi is a broken woman still dealing with the weight of her enormous loss. As they arrive in her hometown her family and friends who haven't seen her in many years come to greet her and welcome her home. Naomi's response to their greeting is painful to read, but it shows the deep hurt and the emotional scars that still linger in her heart. Listen to her pain as she reacts to those who would welcome her home.

> Now the two of them went until they came to Bethlehem. And it happened, when they had come to Bethlehem, that all the city was excited because of them; and the women said, "Is this Naomi?" But she said to them, "Do not call me Naomi; call me Mara, for the Almighty has dealt very bitterly with me I went out full, and the Lord has brought me home again empty. Why do you call me Naomi,

since the Lord has testified against me, and the Almighty has afflicted me?"

(Ruth 1:19–21)

Naomi's bitterness is obvious as she returns to her homeland and is met by the residents of Bethlehem. She doesn't hold back in sharing her bitterness. She is wearing her hurt openly for all to see. She isn't trying to hide her deep emotional pain. She just simply reveals the personal grief and sorrow she had experienced while in Moab. And from these statements, it is obvious she felt as if God had dealt her an unkind, if not unfair, hand.

I am so thankful that God inspired the writer of this book to reveal her struggle. So often we feel that we are not allowed to grieve the death of a loved one, especially in light of the fact that Christians have hope that takes us beyond the grave. We feel that to show any sign of grief or sadness is to display a spirit of hopelessness. But as I have shared with many grieving families, God created us with the ability to grieve. This is such an important aspect of our humanness. God created us with the ability to work through the process of grief so that we could mourn the loss of a loved one in our own personal way and in our own time. Grief is real, and each individual must work through it in their own way.

But there is a word of hope and encouragement we need to remember. Paul admonishes his friends in Thessalonica that they should not grieve as others who have no hope, but that they could and should grieve. He doesn't imply that we should not grieve, but only that we should not grieve as if we had no hope. What a tremendous difference!

But I do not want you to be ignorant, brethren, concerning those who have fallen asleep, lest you sorrow as others who have no hope. For if we

believe that Jesus died and rose again, even so
God will bring with Him those who sleep in Jesus.
(1 Thessalonians 4:13–14)

According to Paul's instruction it is perfectly right for a
believer to grieve the loss of a loved one. Those left behind in the
wake of death are hurt, deeply and painfully, with anguish of
heart, mind and emotions. And Paul informs us that it is perfectly
legitimate and within God's will for us to grieve, just not as those
who have no hope beyond this life. I have often shared with those
who have just lost a loved one to death that God gives us a form
of spiritual anesthesia. By His grace we don't experience the full
impact of the loss immediately. If we did it would be difficult
for any of us to survive the weight of losing a loved one. But He
allows the full impact to come upon us gradually, so we are able
to deal with the harshness of death. We still have to deal with it,
but His grace enables us to process it over time.

But what is involved in the grieving process? Wouldn't it be
great if we had a manual which revealed to us exactly what to
expect when we find ourselves in a situation like Naomi's? But
the reality is, we don't. And for good reason. We are all different.
The grieving process through which one individual may work
could be vastly different from that through which another works.
There is no four- or five-point formula which can be used by all.

Many have attempted to classify the grieving process by
describing various stages through which one must go as they
work their way through their grief. The process of grief has been
described as ranging from as few as three stages to as many as ten
or more. One psychologist has suggested three stages: the stage of
shock, the stage of intense grief, and the stage of reestablishment. A
minister, after counseling with many persons going through grief,
suggested seven stages: shock, disorganization, volatile emotions,
guilt, loss and loneliness, relief, and finally reestablishment.

The most obvious problem with such lists of stages of grief
is that we begin looking for each of the stages. For example, lets

imagine the case of a young woman whose mother dies. The young woman's husband has read one of these theories which include the various stages of grief and begins trying to help his wife work her way through them. However, his wife may not fit the model. She may display five of the seven stages as depicted by the pastoral counselor, but the other two may not be part of her individual grieving process. The husband could make matters worse by trying to force his wife to work through one or more of the stages when in actuality they may not pose any problem for her whatsoever. However, if we can keep in mind that the lists of stages are only for our help and consolation, then they may prove to be of benefit when we, as Naomi, must stand by the freshly dug grave of a loved one.

As we look at the painful story of Naomi's extreme loss, how do we see a portrait of God's providence? Where was God when she was faced with all this tragedy?

God was with her and her family at every stage of the journey. That may sound rather glib and unrealistic to some, but the reality is that God's grace sustained Naomi through some of the most difficult experiences one could imagine. Perhaps you have been one of the multitudes who have stood by the graveside with a friend who has lost someone extremely close, and you have thought to yourself, "I could never handle this. I could never stand where he is standing. I could never be as strong and courageous as he is being." But then, a few weeks, or months, or years, later, you did stand in that same place. And you found yourself being able to stand, not by your own strength, but by the strength of God. God's grace is given in amounts that are commensurate with the need.

Some might argue that His grace would have been much better if it had protected Naomi from the many losses she suffered. Would that not have been a greater display of grace in Naomi's life? Why does God not just protect us from the ravages of death instead of giving us grace to face it?

We must remember that death is a part of the human

experience due to the presence of sin in the world. Death came about as a result of Adam and Eve's act of disobedience in the garden. Every human will experience death if the Lord tarries in His coming. We will all pass through the darkness of that valley. It is a reality that we must all face. Therefore, knowing that we will all face this enemy, God has provided grace to deal with it when it becomes our personal experience. Instead of leaving us to deal with it as best we can, He extends to us grace that will get us through this most horrific of human experiences.

That is what Naomi experienced. She experienced grace and peace. Grace that sustained her throughout the entire ordeal that lasted several years. And as she worked her way through her anger and bitterness, she once again found her peace in God. It was that peace that the apostle Paul described as being beyond explanation.

The Bible teaches us an amazing thing about peace. It teaches that we can experience peace in two ways. First, we can experience peace with God. Peace with God is established through a personal relationship with God. It is the peace of being forgiven; the peace of being restored; the peace of being made whole. This peace takes place when one comes to anchor his or her faith in God as their source of help and hope. In the New Testament perspective, it takes place when one receives the Lord Jesus Christ as their personal Lord and Savior. Christ has made it possible for reconciliation to take place between a holy God and unholy man. Naomi was one who had experienced that peace with God through her relationship with Him as she had placed her faith in Him.

But in the face of the shocking reality of death, she needed to experience more than peace with God: she also needed to experience the peace of God. Paul describes the peace of God as being of such great magnitude that it exceeds understanding. Read carefully these insightful words from Paul:

> And the peace of God, which surpasses all understanding, will guard your hearts and minds through Christ Jesus.
>
> (Philippians 4:7)

After working her way through her grief by the grace of God, she then came to experience the amazing peace of God.

When we are faced with the shocking reality of death, the anchor which will keep us steady in that overwhelming, relentless storm of life is the anchor of peace with God which will result in the peace of God. Naomi, along with countless others who have stood by the grave of a loved one, experienced this wonderful peace of God. It is a peace that settles us in the storm, and a peace that enables us to make it through the storm. God is, indeed, that ever-present help in time of trouble, and when overwhelming troubles arise, God is ready and able to keep us steady through the storm.

My wife suffered a health crisis in which God's peace became a personal reality in my life. I was awakened at three o'clock in the morning by her violent shaking as she experienced a gran mal seizure. She had never had one before, and thankfully she hasn't had one since. As she convulsed, our daughter called 911 for help. While awaiting their arrival, my wife suddenly quit convulsing and became deathly still. I tried to find a pulse to no avail. I then tried to detect her breathing, again to no avail.

I lifted one of her arms and let it drop back to the bed. It dropped with a thud. There was no sign of life. None. As I stood by the bed holding her hand, trying to get a response from her, I thought that she had passed from this life. Once the paramedics arrived on the scene, they, too, began trying to detect a breathing pattern. They could find none. They searched for a pulse, again with no success. As I watched them working with her, I could see the look of concern on their faces.

They began to prepare her for transport to the local hospital, all the while with no signs of life being detected. They constantly looked back and forth at each other, their concern for the seriousness of my wife's condition etched deeply on their faces. I watched as they carefully placed her in the emergency vehicle. I had started the engine on my truck and pulled up directly behind them. Then, I waited. And waited. And waited. The emergency vehicle made no move.

Finally, the door of the emergency vehicle opened and one of the paramedics stepped back to my truck. I opened my door and stepped out. He came over to me and said, "We have found a pulse and are ready to transport."

I share that experience to testify to the wonderful peace of God that passes all understanding. As I stood by the bedside, and as I tried to no avail to find a pulse and to detect breathing, and as I waited for the paramedic to tell me anything about her condition, I was overwhelmed with a settled sense of peace. It washed over me like a flood. I cannot explain it, for there is no explanation for it. But it is real, and it is enough.

On that occasion it did not end with a grave. But I know that one day it will. Either I will die first, or Teresa will, but we know that it is inevitable. We will all die. And the survivor will find that God's peace will settle them through the ordeal.

If you have not already stood by that freshly dug grave and saw that closed casket slowly descend into the earth, then please know that you will. At some point in your life you will lose that family member, that friend, that acquaintance, and you, along with others, will gather for a memorial service, remembering the life of the one now gone. It is then, there, and in the days that follow, that you will desperately need the all-sustaining grace and the ever-present peace of God. And, as with Naomi, we will be able to stand firm in and through the storm.

QUESTIONS FOR THOUGHT AND DISCUSSION

1. Grief is one of the most devastating experiences in all of life. If you have lost a loved one to death, explain how you went through the grieving process.

2. Did you recognize any of the stages of grief suggested in this chapter?

3. The Book of Ruth presents the very real struggle Naomi experienced as she lost her husband and sons. Is it wrong for a Christian to grieve?

4. Paul makes the statement that we should not grieve as others who have no hope. Explain in your own words what you think he meant by this statement.

5. Do you feel that grief is a lack of faith? Why or why not?

6. Do you feel that God is angered by a believer grieving over the death of a loved one? Why or why not?

7. What do you think Paul meant when he referred to the peace of God as being beyond explanation?

CHAPTER 6

JOB

The Pothole of Suffering

There was a man in the land of Uz, whose name *was* Job; and that man was blameless and upright, and one who feared God and shunned evil. And seven sons and three daughters were born to him. Also, his possessions were seven thousand sheep, three thousand camels, five hundred yoke of oxen, five hundred female donkeys, and a very large household, so that this man was the greatest of all the people of the East.

Now there was a day when the sons of God came to present themselves before the Lord, and Satan also came among them. And the Lord said to Satan, "'From where do you come?'"

So Satan answered the Lord and said, "'From going to and fro on the earth, and from walking back and forth on it.'"

Then the Lord said to Satan, "'Have you considered My servant Job, that *there is* none like him on the earth, a blameless and upright man, one who fears God and shuns evil?'"

So Satan answered the Lord and said, "'Does Job fear God for nothing? Have You not made a hedge around him, around his household, and around all that he has on every side? You have blessed the work of his hands, and his possessions have increased in the land. But now, stretch out Your hand and touch all that he has, and he will surely curse You to Your face!"

(Job 1:1–3; 6–11)

With the invention, introduction, and development of the internet we have become accustomed to having information at our fingertips. We can upload instruction and service manuals for pretty much anything in our possession. I have personally gotten information for repairs on my car, my travel trailer, my water heater, my refrigerator, and so many others, right in the comfort of my home. I have been able to accomplish this without involving any repairman. It is a wonderful tool we have at our disposal and used countless times every day around the world. There are very few topics that cannot be researched, and very few problems for which we can't find a solution, by simply taking time to search it out on the web.

There are some solutions to some problems, however, that cannot be found on the internet. There are certain problems that can't be solved. Most people seem to have a strong tendency to want to categorize everything, to make stereotypes of every situation, to find patent answers to all the perplexities and difficulties of life and be able to come up with a patented solution to every circumstance we could ever possibly face.

And how wonderful it would be if that was the way life worked. It would be so helpful to have a manual, and in that manual have an alphabetical listing of every possible eventuality of life, and underneath that alphabetical listing find printed a patented, guaranteed solution to every problem. But we don't have such a manual, and the reason for that is simple: we are all different, and even though we may face somewhat the same dilemmas and difficulties, how we react to those situations may be totally different. Problems relating to life and livelihood are far different than looking at a schematic of the electrical wiring on a refrigerator and deciding what needs to be done to correct the problem. There is no manual for the problems faced as we just live life.

There is a book of the Bible in which we have what we might describe as a catastrophic collision of opposing world views. A world view is, to be overly simplistic, how one views the world.

91

It is the personal lens through which one interprets world events. It is the method of explanation one offers for those situations in life which seem to be unexplainable. How one views the world will in large part determine how he understands the world, and personal events, situations, and circumstances.

Your personal world view will guide you either consciously or unconsciously as you strive to understand your personal experiences. We all have presuppositions that are guided by our personal world view that serves as the lens through which we view those experiences. Those presuppositions may be true or false, and we may adhere to them consistently or inconsistently, but they determine how we view the basic make-up of the world. Some, for example, believe the world to be flat. They sincerely hold to this presupposition even though it has been proven beyond doubt to be false. However, how they view the world will be determined in large part by this belief.

Think about the person who professes to be an atheist. His presupposition is that there is no god. So, based on this belief, he believes that the universe came into existence through the process of evolution. All forms of life on Earth, according to the evolutionist, have evolved from a single-celled amoeba, which would mean that there is no distinction between the varied forms of life on the planet. Therefore, he will view life as a relatively meaningless duration of time and succession of events.

The true evolutionist, who believes that the world came into existence through some cataclysmic explosion billions of years ago, and who believes that human life is just one of the mutations of the ongoing development of the overall life cycle, will see little importance in striving to find ultimate value in human life. Human life, to the evolutionist, is no different than animal life. Therefore, a hunter who sits in a deer stand for hours, waiting patiently for that huge, ten-point buck to step into his line of fire, would be no different than the sniper who positions himself in a strategic position to fire upon unsuspecting persons as they walk past. Life, after all, is the same in all its varied forms: human, animal, reptile, bird, or fish.

However, the Bible teaches something far different than that. Human life is very much different than animal life. Humans are created in the image of God. Those who embrace this belief would have a totally different view of the world than that of the atheist. Whereas the evolutionist would look at the world through the lens of evolution, the Christian would look at the world through the lens of Scripture. This would result in a vastly different means of interpreting the events and eventualities of life. This is referred to as a theistic world view – an understanding of the world with God at the center.

But further clarification needs to be made, as there are many different theistic world views. This book is written from a very specific, theistic world view. It is written from a Biblical world view. And then even more specifically it is written from a Biblically conservative world view. The reason I point this distinction out is because there are so many different interpretations of scripture under the umbrella of conservative Christianity. For example, the world view of the fundamentalist evangelical will be vastly different from that of the liberal or moderate student of the Bible. And to make it even more confusing, even within the ranks of one branch of the theistic world view there is still debate as to how certain issues should be addressed, understood and explained.

This is perhaps the reason that one particular book of the Bible was inspired by God. In this book of the Bible, we see five people who all hold to an extremely dogmatic theistic world view. If we could question each of these five persons individually, we would hear each of them give testimony to their belief in God, and to their belief in God's ongoing personal activity in the world. We would hear each of them speak of their personal faith in this personal God. But when it came down to their speaking about one certain subject, we would hear them disagree vehemently, adamantly, and dogmatically. None of them would be willing to give an inch of ground to the others in their arguments which justified their personal opinions.

The reason for that is because this book of the Bible, and this Biblical character, deals with a problem which is the common lot of humanity. It is not only experienced by those who would describe themselves as being adherers of the theistic world view, but also within the ranks of every other world view known to man. As a matter of fact, many who adhere to the atheistic world view do so because they can't bring themselves to believe the claims of the theistic world view concerning this subject.

The subject to which I refer is that of human suffering, and the person under consideration is Job. Most theologians agree that this is the oldest book in the Bible. If that is true, then it teaches us the simple yet profound truth that this is one of the oldest and most perplexing problems which has ever confronted man in his attempt to understand the world. It continues to be just as perplexing today as it was when this book was written.

There is very little known about Job. From all indications, it appears that he lived in the patriarchal or pre-patriarchal period, which would again give evidence that it could be the oldest book in the Bible. There is really no way of telling what part of the world he lived in, and again this was probably done purposely by God, driving home the fact that this is a universal problem.

Job focuses on one subject: suffering. The mention of this subject brings certain theological and philosophical issues to mind. Why does suffering exist? What is the cause of human suffering? Why does one individual experience significant suffering all through his life while another suffers almost none? These are questions that have been debated and discussed for millennia and will continue to be debated until the Lord returns.

Then, to these basic questions are added questions aimed more specifically at God. Isn't God powerful enough to eradicate all human suffering? Doesn't He care about His human family? And, even more specifically, doesn't He care about those who are striving to follow Him? How could an all-powerful God allow such awful suffering when He is perfectly capable of eradicating it?

Also, how are we to understand the reality of suffering in light of the fact that God is a good God? If He is good, and has all power, then how are we to understand the existence of suffering? These realities just don't seem to make sense. They seem to be irreconcilable to the human mind. They seem to be inexplainable as they appear to be contradictory, making no sense at all.

We would love to have answers to these problematic questions. We would love to have the fog of confusion lifted, and the mind-boggling perplexity of these seeming contradictory subjects explained, but no one has been able to come up with definitive answers to these dilemmas of life.

So, we turn to the one book of the Bible that focuses solely on this subject. We go there with the hope that we will find satisfactory answers. We scour the pages of this book with the hope that we will finally be able to make sense of the sufferings we all experience. We look and look, read and read, pray and pray.

Finally, we reach the conclusion and must admit that the book of Job does not answer those probing questions to our satisfaction. However, what it will do is teach us invaluable lessons that will help us when the suffering is ours.

The description of Job's suffering is found in the last verses of chapter one:

> Now there was a day when his sons and daughters *were* eating and drinking wine in their oldest brother's house; and a messenger came to Job and said, "The oxen were plowing and the donkeys feeding beside them, when the Sabeans raided *them* and took them away—indeed they have killed the

servants with the edge of the sword; and I alone have escaped to tell you!"

While he *was* still speaking, another also came and said, "The fire of God fell from heaven and burned up the sheep and the servants, and consumed them; and I alone have escaped to tell you!"

While he *was* still speaking, another also came and said, "The Chaldeans formed three bands, raided the camels and took them away, yes, and killed the servants with the edge of the sword; and I alone have escaped to tell you!"

While he *was* still speaking, another also came and said, "Your sons and daughters *were* eating and drinking wine in their oldest brother's house, and suddenly a great wind came from across the wilderness and struck the four corners of the house, and it fell on the young people, and they are dead; and I alone have escaped to tell you!"

Then Job arose, tore his robe, and shaved his head; and he fell to the ground and worshiped. And he said:

"Naked I came from my mother's womb,
And naked shall I return there.
The Lord gave, and the Lord has taken away;
Blessed be the name of the Lord."

(Job 1:13–21)

We can't begin to imagine what Job must have felt as these reports were brought to him, one after the other. Everything Job had was now lost, except his life and the life of his wife. All else was gone – destroyed or dead.

Each year we see the devastating destruction of hurricanes, tornadoes, floods, and earthquakes. Hurricanes cause horrific damage and destruction to coastal cities as they make their way onshore. Sometimes they have wind speeds surpassing 150 miles per hour. These cause billions of dollars in damage, and cause death and destruction on a massive scale. Forest fires rage through our forests, destroying vegetation and animal life, as well as any man-made structures that are in the path of the flames.

Our world is still coping with the on-going pandemic, Covid-19. Each time one strain seems to be declining in its spread, another strain mutates and begins the fight all over again. The numbers of those who have suffered and died because of this pandemic continues to stagger the imagination. There are very few who do not know someone who has suffered from this disease and others who have died because of contracting it.

How do we fit these events into our cozy Christian faith? How does all this tragedy fit into a biblically conservative theistic world view? Is there any way to reconcile belief in a good and all-powerful God with the existence of suffering?

We are stuck with the same dilemma which faced Job and his friends. How do we explain the seemingly needless suffering in the world since the Bible teaches us about a loving God who cares deeply for His creation, especially His human creation? The pieces of the puzzle just can't seem to be forced together!

And there is something which makes this dilemma even more difficult to comprehend. The book of Job makes it unquestionably clear that God providentially allowed Job's suffering. This shakes us to the very foundation of our Christian belief, our theistic worldview. This is a spiritual earthquake of enormous magnitude. It far surpasses 10.0 on the spiritual Richter scale.

The dilemma is this: Job and his friends are now struggling with the task of giving a reasonable explanation to the reality of suffering from their personal, individual, theistic worldview. They are all in agreement that God is somehow involved in all this devastation, but how? So, within the confines of a solid theistic worldview, we see five men struggling to give a justifiable solution to the reality of human suffering and tragedy.

The two opposing views are easily discernible. Eliphaz, Bildad, Zophar and Elihu present lengthy discourses on the subject, but in essence they all say basically the same thing, only differing in emphasis. They all agree that suffering is a direct result of personal sin, and that Job undoubtedly has committed some atrocious act of grievous sin against God. Therefore, the solution is simple: repent and be restored to fellowship with God.

There you have it! Point one, you have sinned. Point two, you need to repent. Point three, if you repent, God will forgive. And point four, upon your repentance and restoration, you will be absolved of any and all wrongdoing. It's just that simple! We become judge and jury and can pronounce judgment in short order every time we see someone suffer.

However, in reality it is not that simple at all. There are times when God allows suffering to consume us, and it is not necessarily because of some act of personal sin we have committed. Of course, we need to understand that there are indeed times when our suffering is a result of personal acts of sin, but the book of Job teaches us in no uncertain terms that there are times when God allows suffering for reasons known only to Him.

We have all probably known someone who has suffered greatly for no apparent reason. Irene Kennington is one such individual. Mrs. Kennington certainly had her share of grief and tragedy. One of her children was killed in an automobile accident. Her first husband was killed when struck by lightning. The ironic thing about his death is that he was struck by that lightning bolt as he stood in the doorway of their home giving thanks to God for sending some much-needed rain. Mrs. Kennington then became gravely ill, with the doctors giving her very little hope of recovery. She did, however, recover from that illness, only to witness the death of her second husband as he suffered a massive heart attack.

Was this woman a grievous sinner? Was her life characterized by wanton, reckless disregard for the things of God? No! Irene Kennington was a Godly lady, who served her Lord faithfully through all those years and all those tragedies. She never lost faith in God and trusted Him to carry her through her awful succession of tragedy and loss. Mrs. Kennington knew all about human suffering. But the question remains: Why? Why did God allow Job to suffer as he did? And why did He allow Mrs. Kennington, along with countless others to suffer so horrifically?

This pothole is by far one of the most devastating and destructive that can invade the experience of any human being. I have witnessed some who have become cold and callused toward God because He allowed suffering to come into their life. I have heard some even question the existence of God because of the suffering which is so prevalent in the world.

I remember one such individual in particular. His wife was a faithful member of the church I was serving as pastor. She told me about her husband and asked if I could go speak with him and try to answer some of his questions that she felt were hindrances to him committing his life to the Lord. During the conversation he shared with me some of his experiences on the battlefields of Viet Nam. He described, in graphic detail, the things he had seen – things that continued to cause him to be awakened with sounds of his own screaming.

After sharing with me all those details of his personal experiences with suffering and evil in the world, he said, "How could I ever believe in a God who allows such evil and suffering to exist when He has power to eradicate it?" The existence of suffering was his excuse for rejecting God.

I have seen others, such as Irene Kennington, come closer to God through the tragedies of life. She lived quite a few years after the death of her second husband and remained faithful to God until the end of her life.

What determines the difference? When we consider the case of Job, it is beyond question that everything that happened to him and his family was a direct result of the providential involvement of God. Of course, Job did not realize all that was happening in the spiritual realm. He was totally oblivious to the conversations between God and Satan. He was completely unaware that he was the subject of a conversation in the heavenly counsel room of God. He, along with his three friends, were all just trying to make sense of a seemingly senseless series of events.

Then, added to the perplexity and confusion of their struggling to understand and explain Job's suffering, there was that period in which Job felt totally abandoned by God. There are times of extreme suffering that may cause even the most committed believer to struggle with the existence of suffering, and more specifically the exitence of their personal experience with suffering. Job's personal struggle with his suffering is clearly seen in this statement:

> Look, I go forward, but He is not there, and backward, but I cannot perceive Him; when He works on the left hand, I cannot behold Him; when He turns to the right hand, I cannot see Him.
>
> (Job 23:8–9)

This is a powerful profession of Job's faith in God. Job did not know where God was during all his suffering, but even amid that uncertainty, Job was still certain of God's intimate and personal participation in the events of life. He continued to maintain his personal integrity, and his unwavering belief that God would see him through the awful tragedy and loss he had now experienced.

Have you ever felt this way? Have you ever wondered where God was during a period of personal suffering? Maybe it was because of a personal time of loss – the death of a spouse, parent or child – and you were completely baffled as to why it happened. Or maybe it was your bewilderment about world events, as you watched news broadcasts giving information about a devastating hurricane that had left a path of death and destruction. You watched and wondered why God had not intervened.

We all experience suffering of some kind as we go through life. For some, suffering seems to be their lot in life. And we are left to understand it as best we can considering our personal worldview.

As much as we might wish there existed a manual with detailed instructions on how to get through, we know that no such manual exists. Even the book of Job, which focuses in its entirety on suffering, does not offer us such a manual which gives solutions to the difficulties of life. But this timeless book does offer us some wonderful truths which will help us face the realities of life when they overwhelm us.

First, the book of Job teaches us some powerful lessons on the subject of man's faith in God. There is no justifiable reason to dispute the reality and consistency of Job's faith. Even in the midst of all his suffering, he can say,

> I know that my Redeemer lives, and He shall stand at last on the earth; and after my skin is destroyed, this I know, that in my flesh I shall see God, whom I shall see for myself, and my eyes shall behold, and not another.
>
> (Job 19:25–27)

Job had an unwavering faith in God, and nothing could take that faith away. Yes, we see clearly displayed throughout this book the struggle Job had in holding onto his faith, but he never lost his faith. He tenaciously held onto his belief in God. This is absolutely crucial in the life of every believer as he suffers the different types of tragedies this life throws at us. It is our faith that gives us the victory in this world.

Faith is the one thing that enabled Job to see beyond his horrific circumstances. Faith provides sight to see what cannot be seen with the human eyes. It is faith that facilitates our belief in the fact that God is indeed a good God and is always working for good. Regardless of how things look from this earthly perspective, God sees from a totally different perspective. We can only see the moment, whereas God sees the whole story. We can only experience the here and now, whereas God sees the end from the beginning. Faith enables the believer to embrace the goodness of God even in the midst of the bad things that come our way.

For the gentleman I spoke of earlier who could not bring himself to believe in a God who would allow such horrific suffering and evil as he had personally witnessed on the battlefields of Viet Nam, faith was what he needed to see beyond. However, he could not embrace the idea of faith, and could not believe in a God who did nothing to alleviate this awful evil. Mrs. Kennington, on the other hand, was able to see beyond the suffering she and members of her family experienced. How? Faith that allowed her see the unseeable, to believe the unbelievable, to embrace the fact that God is good, even when He allows bad things to happen.

A second truth we can learn from this book that perhaps will revolutionize our way of handling suffering when it comes our way is God's faith in man. Have you ever stopped to meditate on what is transpiring in that heavenly counsel between God and Satan? God, in essence, is telling Satan to do as he wishes to Job. And why? Because God has faith that Job can handle it.

Now I realize that in one sense God doesn't have to have faith in us. He knows already exactly how everyone will react to any situation they may encounter. But it does show us that when God allows suffering to enter our experience, it is testimony that He believes we can handle it by His grace. This insight should help us all face our problems in life from a completely different perspective. To think that God believes in us to the degree that He is confident we can handle the problems he allows us to face should give us confidence amid those problems.

Think about how truly amazing this insight is. There are approximately eight billion people populating planet earth. That number is far too large for my extremely simplistic, finite mind to comprehend. But think about the fact that this large number does not in any way confuse God. He knows each one intimately and personally. He distinguishes one from another and never gets them confused. You are a matter of great importance to God. His eye is on you! Just as it was with Job, He has faith that you can handle whatever He allows to come your way in life.

I have yet to meet anyone who testified to how much they thoroughly enjoyed suffering. And yet, if we could develop the right mentality about the subject, it could very well revolutionize the way we understand it and handle it when it invades our personal arena of human experience. If every believer in Jesus Christ could determine that they would use their suffering as a vehicle through which they could glorify God what a powerful testimony it would be to an unbelieving world.

That is, by the way, exactly how we are to understand those periods of suffering. We are to use everything that comes our way in life to glorify Him. And Paul reminds us that the sufferings of this present life are not worthy to be compared with the glorious future we have in the presence of God. Faith is what enables us to live in such a way in the face of our sufferings.

A third lesson we can learn about how handling adversity when it comes is to consider Job's faithfulness to God. Job gives this powerful word of testimony:

> As long as my breath is in me, and the breath of God is in my nostrils, my lips will not speak wickedness, nor my tongue utter deceit. Far be it from me that I should say you are right; till I die I will not put away my integrity from me. My righteousness I hold fast and will not let it go; my heart shall not reproach me as long as I live.
>
> (Job 27:3–6)

Oftentimes we see individuals who use adversity as an excuse to turn away from God and to live a life of rebellion against Him and His word. They become bitter against God and against man, and they live an embittered life from that point on. Job refused to give the devil a victory in his life by turning away from God, but rather he held tightly to his faith in God and continued to maintain his integrity. He proved to be faithful to God, even when he was struggling to know where God was in relation to his problems.

Faith in God and faithfulness to God go together. It is faith that enables faithfulness, and it is faithfulness that fuels faith. Our faith in God empowers us to remain committed to God even when He allows adverse circumstances to invade our lives. As we go through those adverse circumstances, it builds our faith in God as we can look back on those experiences and see how God's invisible hand has been at work all along. This, in turn, reinforces our faithfulness to God as we continue to trust in Him even in those periods of darkness in which we may, as Job, feel abandoned by God. Through eyes of faith we see through the darkness and continue to faithfully follow Him and live for Him.

This leads to a final lesson we can learn from Job's experiences. We need to constantly remind ourselves of God's faithfulness to man. God never let Job down. He was always right there, ready to intervene if things got out of hand. Remember, it was God who set the limits on how much suffering Satan could unleash on His servant. God always holds Satan's reigns tightly in His omnipotent hands, and He never allows things to get out of control.

It probably appeared to Job that things were out of control. From our limited, finite understanding of how the complexities of the universe work, and why things happen the way that do, we might see nothing but chaos and confusion. It may cause some to doubt the existence of God, or the goodness of God, or the care and compassion of God. If Satan could only do what God allowed him to do, then why did God not allow him to do anything? Certainly that seems to be a very real possibility.

One of the major things to remember is that all forms of suffering and evil are a result of the fall of man. God is not to be blamed for the existence of suffering, but He does allow suffering. The underlying cause of all suffering is sin.

However, we must also remember that all suffering is not

necessarily a result of personal acts of sin. The person who contracts terminal cancer is not necessarily the cause of the disease. The disease is a result of the curse of sin. But, it is possible that an individual's cancer is the result of lifestyle habits that are known to cause cancer. The existence of cancer is the result of the fall of man, but the contraction of cancer in an individual may or may not be the direct result of personal choices they have made.

Perhaps you are thinking that things are getting out of hand with your personal experiences. Perhaps you are thinking that God could have, and should have, given us more insight and explanation into this perplexing matter. But then faith would be unnecessary. If we could fully understand these perplexities of life then we would never be able to experience God's faith in us and His faithfulness to us.

It should be a matter of tremendous gratitude in the life of every believer to realize just how much God believes in us, and it should motivate us to believe more in Him.

QUESTIONS FOR THOUGHT AND DISCUSSION

1. Suffering is a reality in life. Think about a time of suffering in your life. Write the experience in a journal. Then, share it with a family member or friend.
2. How were you able to use the experience you wrote about in #1 for God's glory?
3. The author spoke of four lessons we could learn from Job's experiences. How would you explain these to someone who is going through a season of suffering:

   a. Your faith in God.
   b. Your faithfulness to God.
   c. God's faith in you.
   d. God's faithfulness to you.

4. If someone questioned God's goodness on the basis of suffering in the world, how would you respond?
5. How would you explain that God's goodness is not to be equated with the good things God does?

CHAPTER 7

ESTHER

The Pothole of Prominence

Now when the time came for Esther the daughter of Abihail the uncle of Mordecai, who had taken her as his daughter, to go in to the king, she requested nothing but what Hegai the king's eunuch, the custodian of the women, advised. And Esther obtained favor in the sight of all who saw her. So Esther was taken to King Ahasuerus, into his royal palace, in the tenth month, which is the month of Tebeth, in the seventh year of his reign. The king loved Esther more than all the other women, and she obtained grace and favor in his sight more than all the virgins; so he set the royal crown upon her head and made her queen instead of Vashti.

(Esther 2:15–17)

There are moments in life in which we feel as if God has totally and completely forsaken us. There are times in which we might think that we are on our own, left to get by as best we can. There are times in which we might easily identify with Job, when he said that he had looked in all directions for God's presence but had not found Him. It is in those times that we are tempted to question the validity of the promises of God. It is in those times that we are tempted to question the goodness of God. It is in those times that we are tempted to question the love of God.

With Job it was a time of personal loss, tragedy, and suffering. But there are times when the difficulties go far beyond one person, or one family. There are times in which suffering affects a larger number of people. Perhaps a tornado destroys an entire city, or an earthquake completely swallows a village, or a tsunami kills a quarter of a million people. There are times when suffering is on a much larger scale than we have seen in the book of Job.

The Book of Esther records a historical period during which all Israelites felt that God had abandoned and forsaken them. The book focuses on a young woman named Hadassah. She lived during the days of Persian rule - days in which the nation of Israel was still in captivity following the Babylonian's invading and destroying the city of Jerusalem and taking the people into bondage. After the fall of the Babylonian empire at the hands of the Persians, the people of Israel were scattered throughout the land of Persia. Even though they were not actually in slavery in this foreign land, they were still in exile from their homeland of Israel.

Probably, most Israelites thought that God had indeed forsaken them. And it is during the lifetime of Hadassah that they will come to believe more than ever before that God had truly abandoned them.

Hadassah lived during the reign of Ahasuerus, a powerful Persian ruler who reigned over a vast kingdom which extended from India to Ethiopia. We are informed that there were 127 provinces under his direct rule. He was one of the most powerful men in the world at this point in history.

In the third year of his reign he gave a feast for all of his officials and servants, from each of the 127 provinces. The feast was an extravaganza, lasting for 180 days. At the conclusion of the 180 days of celebration and festivity, the king gave a seven-day feast for all the people who were in the capital city of Susa. It was at the conclusion of this seven-day feast that Ahasuerus ordered the queen to present herself before all his intoxicated guests.

Queen Vashti politely refused this request of the king. This act could have been viewed as an act of extreme courage, or of complete insanity. When the king gave an order, he would expect it to be carried out without hesitation. There would be no room for discussion or debate. The king had spoken, and now he should be obeyed.

When Queen Vashti made her decision to disobey the king's command, he called his counselors together and asked what should be done in response to her insolence. They reasoned together and decided that if the king took no action, it would cause all the wives in the kingdom to become rebellious against their husbands. After deliberating on Queen Vashti's action, the decision was made that she would be dethroned.

After the deposition of Queen Vashti, the king's anger finally subsided, and a search was begun to find a new queen. Young women were brought into the palace, and one by one they were brought before the king. Out of this large number of potential candidates the king would choose one to sit beside him on the throne. At this point in the story, we are introduced to the heroine, Hadassah. She is one of a host of women who are brought before the king. Hadassah is of Jewish descent. She is an orphan, having been raised by her cousin, Mordecai.

Out of this host of women, Hadassah is the one selected by King Ahasuerus to be beside him on the throne. Hadassah is given the name Esther, a Persian name meaning "Star", and begins her reign as queen. At this point in time she has no idea that a gaping pothole loomed just ahead.

Granted, this may not seem to be much of a pothole at first glance. I mean, who would not like to be elevated to such a position? This common Jewish girl, who had lost her parents, and had been raised by a relative, comes out of virtual obscurity and is cast into the highest position a woman of her day could attain - Queen of Persia. From a life of mediocrity to a position of prominence. From a meager existence to queen of an entire country, a world dominating empire. What possible pothole could this be?

It is the pothole of prominence. The pothole of being cast into a position of prominence, power, and prestige. Esther is taken out of the shadows of obscurity and cast into the limelight of world renown.

Again, some of us may be wondering why this is a pothole. How would this be a difficult position for Hadassah? Most of us are probably working to attain a position of prominence. Most of us are probably aiming at goals of success which would earn us the respect of others. Most of us are probably desirous of being famous, of being known, of being recognized and respected by others. Most of us would probably love to have a prominent position such as the one awarded to Hadassah.

There are those who handle this type of success well. They do not become proud or arrogant or egotistical as they move up in the world. They become great philanthropists, remembering their humble beginnings, and giving generously to those who are much less privileged than they.

But there are also those who can't handle the success. They become proud, conceited, arrogant, boastful. The more they get, the more they want. They never seem to be satisfied with what they have. They may come to the place that they could never, in their lifetime and the lifetime of their children and their children's children, be able to spend all they have come to possess. But still, they want more.

And they tend to forget their friends - those who had been so close to them in previous years. They tend to forget the little people who have helped them so much along the way. They tend to forget so many things, and so many people, from their past.

That, for so many, proves to be a pothole of disastrous proportions. Hadassah sat in the position of Queen over the vast empire of Persia. She could have easily forgotten her meager beginnings. She could have easily divorced herself from her past. She could have so easily forgotten, and forsaken, her people. Prominence and prestige have the tendency to cause us to develop an entirely different perspective on life.

It seems very possible that Hadassah was faced with these temptations. We certainly don't want to read more into the text than is there, but in chapter four of the book of Esther, it seems reasonably clear that Esther was having a difficult time deciding what she must do.

That, however, is getting a little ahead of the story. In the third chapter of the book, we are introduced to Haman:

> After these things King Ahasuerus promoted Haman, the son of Hammedatha the Agagite, and advanced him and set his seat above all the princes who were with him. And all the king's servants who were within the king's gate bowed and paid homage to Haman, for so the king had commanded concerning him. But Mordecai would not bow down or pay homage.
>
> (Esther 3:1–2)

Haman is obviously one of those individuals who allowed his promotion to cause him to become proud, arrogant, and egotistical. In his newly acquired position, he expected all those below him to bow down to him when they came into his presence. And it seems that everyone complied with this requirement.

Everyone except Mordecai, who refused to bow down and pay homage.

Mordecai's lack of respect infuriated Haman. He could not get Mordecai's insolence out of his mind. It seems he was haunted by Mordecai's lack of respect for him and his newly acquired position in the court of the king. He was completely obsessed with his desire to see Mordecai suffer. As a matter of fact, he was so deeply moved with hatred toward Mordecai that he decided it would not be enough to punish just him. His hatred consumed him, so Haman came up with a plan through which he could not only get rid of Mordecai but all Jews throughout Persia. He goes to the king with his scheme:

> Then Haman said to King Ahasuerus, "There is a certain people scattered and dispersed among the people in all the provinces of your kingdom; their laws *are* different from all *other* people's, and they do not keep the king's laws. Therefore it *is* not fitting for the king to let them remain. If it pleases the king, let *a decree* be written that they be destroyed, and I will pay ten thousand talents of silver into the hands of those who do the work, to bring *it* into the king's treasuries."
>
> (Esther 3:8–9)

How unbelievable and unthinkable! Haman is so incensed because of Mordecai's display of disrespect toward his position that he concocts a plan through which all of Mordecai's people would be destroyed. The plan presented to the king was that on a certain day all Jews scattered throughout the vast kingdom of Persia would be annihilated. Then, to make the scheme even more amazing, the king gave permission to go through with this evil plot.

Haman clearly appealed to a weakness in the king's character. It is obvious that the king was moved by the accusations Haman brought against the Jews living throughout his vast empire. Perhaps he thought that to allow the Jews to continue living by their laws, and purposefully disrespecting the laws of Persia, would undermine his rule as king. Perhaps he felt that ridding his empire of all Jews would protect Persia from division.

Regardless of the king's reasoning, he concluded that Haman's plan needed to be carried out. Mordecai discovers the plans of Haman and displays his consternation by wearing sackcloth and ashes, a sign of deep grief and remorse. When Esther is informed about Mordecai's public display, she sends clothes to Mordecai hoping that he would remove the sackcloth. Mordecai refused to comply. He would not be comforted in this time of trouble for his people. How could he be? The entire Jewish population had just been sentenced to die!

At this time Esther did not know the reason for Mordecai's unusual behavior, so she sent one of her servants to ask Mordecai what had prompted him to act in such a way. Mordecai sends word back to Esther, informing her of Haman's wicked plot. He gives her all the sordid details of the edict that had been signed by the king and sent to all the provinces: an edict pronouncing a day of death for all Israelites. He then asked that she go to the king and make an appeal for her people, and she responds by saying,

> All the king's servants and the people of the king's provinces know that any man or woman who goes into the inner court to the king, who has not been called, *he has* but one law: put *all* to death, except the one to whom the king holds out the golden scepter, that he may live. Yet I myself have not been called to go in to the king these thirty days.
>
> (Esther 4:11)

Esther would have been placing herself in grave danger if she went into the king's presence without first being summoned by the king. She understood the protocol of going into the king's presence, knowing that when he was on his throne he would be about the business of the kingdom. She had to give serious thought about bursting into his presence without the proper invitation. So, in one sense she was perfectly justified in her hesitation to simply present herself before the king. After all, it had been quite a while, thirty days, since last being invited to come to the throne.

However, it sounds almost as if she was thinking only of herself. It appears, at least for the moment, that the news of all the people of Israel being annihilated had little bearing on her. She was seemingly more concerned about her own safety and welfare than she was about the plight of all Jews spread throughout the vast empire ruled by King Ahasuerus. Esther was faced with a dilemma. Would she act out of fear, or would she act out of faith?

Esther finds herself in a most unenviable position. It would be an extremely difficult thing for anyone to put their life on the line for someone else. Does anyone really know how they would respond if confronted with such a decision as this? We would like to think that we would without hesitation take a stand for others, regardless of the personal cost. But one cannot possibly know unless they are placed in the same type of situation. Esther was obviously wondering if it was really worth the possibility of losing her life. Or, perhaps she was wondering if it were worth giving up this position of prominence she had now come to occupy and enjoy.

It would have certainly seemed wise for Esther to keep her true identity a secret rather than letting it be known that she was a Jew. The decree that all Jews would be killed had been signed by the king and delivered to the provinces. Esther realized that she would not be able to keep her Jewishness a secret when the decree was carried out.

We can apply this same truth to our lives as Christians. We may never find ourselves in the same dire situation as Esther, where making our identity as a believer in Jesus Christ known would cost us our life, but we may suffer in other ways. As our society becomes more and more anti-Christian, and we find ourselves in a diminishing minority, then we may find that it costs us something to identify ourselves with Christ. And, considering what is happening in other parts of the world, with Christians being executed just for identifying with Christ, it is not too far-fetched to think it may happen in America at some time in the future.

It is impossible to imagine the inner turmoil Esther must have been experiencing. She is faced with decisions that could be a matter of life or death for her. If she goes into the king's presence without being invited, she stands a very real chance of being executed. But if she does nothing the entire Jewish population will be completely destroyed by order of the king. Further, if she identifies herself as a Jew, she will suffer the same fate as all other Jews on the appointed day for their mass annihilation. Either way, she would be put to death by the simple process of identification.

Her only alternative was to strive to keep her Jewishness a secret from the king, and thereby hold onto her position, and to her life. Mordecai undoubtedly recognized from her reply that she was experiencing a great deal of anxiety over the news he had shared, so he sent her a second message. It was brief and to the point:

> Do not think in your heart that you will escape in the king's palace any more than all the other Jews. For if you remain completely silent at this time, relief and deliverance will arise for the Jews from another place, but you and your father's house will perish. Yet who knows whether you have come to the kingdom for such a time as this?
> (Esther 4:13–14)

No mincing words with Mordecai! If you keep silent, you will die with all the rest of us. Your only way of escape is to plead our case before the king. Your only hope is to identify yourself with your people. It may cost you dearly to do it, but this is your only reasonable course of action.

Again, we may never find ourselves in such a serious set of circumstances, but we may at some point be in a position where our speaking up for our faith will cost us dearly in some other way. What are we to do? Well, Jesus was no mincer of words either. He said pointedly that if we deny our Father before men, then He will deny us before the Father. Those are extremely serious words, aren't they? If we deny knowing Him here, then He will deny knowing us there. If we put friendship, or position, or prestige, or wealth, or anything before Him here, then He says He will deny us there.

So, what did Esther do? She went before the king, pleaded for the lives of her people, and God providentially intervened through her as the Jews were delivered from the wicked plot of Haman. The providence of God is further seen in the king's decision to have Haman executed.

In a frantic effort to save his own life, Haman goes to Esther to beg for her to ask the king to spare him. When the king comes back into the chamber where Haman is pleading with Esther, Haman has fallen on his knees before Esther as she sits. The king recognizes this as an act of assault against Esther, and he immediately issues the sentence of death for Haman. The king then had Haman executed on the gallows he had erected for the purpose of executing Mordecai. God certainly has His way of bringing about His plans, of providentially protecting His people, and will do whatever is necessary to bring it to pass.

Sometimes our faith may call for us to put everything on the line. Sometimes it may appear that it would be more profitable, or safer, for us to keep our spiritual identity in the Lord a secret. But we need to learn from Esther's experience that God will work providentially to bring us through.

An interesting side note that should be pointed out is that there have been those who have argued that this particular book should not be in the Bible. The argument is centered around the fact there is no reference to God anywhere in the entirety of the book. But what if God did that for a specific purpose? What if God purposely had any reference to Himself omitted to emphasize the point that Esther could not sense the presence of God in her ordeal, but that He was there all along?

There may be situations that arise in our lives that cause us to question God's presence, His love, and His concern. We may feel that, as Job, we have been abandoned by God personally. Or, as Esther, we may feel that we live in a nation that has been abandoned by God. What do we do in those moments of the plague of doubt, when we are questioning everything we have ever believed about God? How are we to react to those things we experience that can't be forced into a cozy, clean, Christian understanding of God's goodness?

We need to learn that sometimes we may feel all alone, that God has left us, and that we must remain faithful to God in face of the situation. But remember, He is always there, always working, even when we can't detect His hand. And He will see us through.

There are so many lessons to be learned through the experiences of Esther. It is obvious that the providential guidance of God was working through the entirety of her experiences. What other explanation could be offered for the astounding events recorded in this amazing record of God's protection. And it was protection not only for Esther as an individual, but through her for the entire Jewish population.

Esther found herself in a pothole that called for drastic, dangerous measures. It is clear that she struggled fiercely with her decision to do as Mordecai asked, or to try to protect herself by doing nothing. She had the option to simply ignore Mordecai's instructions and hopefully have her life spared. But Mordecai tells her that she could very well be where she was and who she was for "just such a time as this". Even though God is not mentioned in the book, His guiding hand of providence is evident throughout. And it is nowhere clearer than in this statement.

Have you paused lately to ponder that truth in relation to your life? You are where you are for just such a time as this. All Christians are desperately needed in our present post-Christian culture to shine the light of God's love and grace into a world steeped in spiritual darkness. We are not here by chance, or coincidence, but by divine appointment to be bearers of the Gospel of our Lord Jesus Christ.

We are here for just such a time as this.

QUESTIONS FOR THOUGHT AND DISCUSSION

1. Esther was providentially placed in her position as Queen through the deposition of Vashti. Do you see this as happening by chance/coincidence, or do you see the hand of God at work? Explain your answer.

2. How do you view Mordecai's actions toward Haman – as an act of arrogance, or as an act of commitment to God? Explain your answer.

3. The story of Haman is remarkable. It reveals how dark the human heart is without God. Can you think of others throughout history who have shown this depth of darkness? Name them and explain your answer.

4. Do you see yourself as being where you are for "just such a time as this"? Why or why not?

5. Think about your personal routine. Can you identify ways in which you could have an impact on those with whom you have regular contact? Can you identify things you can do to shine God's love into your environment? Make a list of some things you can begin doing that would make this a reality.

6. God is not mentioned in the Book of Esther. How would you explain that to someone who had just read the book for the first time?

CHAPTER 8

SAUL

The Pothole of Jealousy

But you have today rejected your God, who Himself saved you from all your adversities and your tribulations; and you have said to Him, "No, set a king over us!" Now therefore, present yourselves before the Lord by your tribes and by your clans.

And when Samuel had caused all the tribes of Israel to come near, the tribe of Benjamin was chosen. When he had caused the tribe of Benjamin to come near by their families, the family of Matri was chosen. And Saul the son of Kish was chosen. But when they sought him, he could not be found.

So they ran and brought him from there; and when he stood among the people, he was taller than any of the people from his shoulders upward. And Samuel said to all the people, "'Do you see him whom the Lord has chosen, that *there is* no one like him among all the people?'

So all the people shouted and said, "Long live the king!"

(1 Samuel 10:19–21; 23–24)

S ome people just seem to have been born with leadership skills. As they grow into maturity, it becomes obvious to everyone that they are natural born leaders. They are able to make wise decisions, be assertive when necessary, take immediate action when the situation dictates, and do whatever is necessary to bring about the desired results.

Just the mention of this type of person has probably brought certain individuals to your mind. There are those in high school who are elected as class presidents because of their natural ability to lead (at least sometimes – at other times it is just a popularity contest!). There are those in college who really stand out from others because of this quality of leadership. There are those in the work world, the business world, the political world, the military, and other fields who are the natural born leaders.

Others seem to naturally follow these leaders. Why? Because they exhibit leadership skills with confidence and conviction. It is obvious that they have those special characteristics which set them apart. Leaders lead, and others are glad to follow when their leaders lead with confidence and clarity.

Our country has been blessed with an abundance of natural leaders through the years of its existence. From what we read in our history books, we are led to understand that men such as George Washington, Benjamin Franklin, Patrick Henry, and countless others were of this special caliber. Others were willing to follow them wherever they went and whatever they were doing. Presidents lead nations. Generals lead armies. Corporate managers lead mega-corporations. Pastors lead churches.

The Bible is replete with examples of this type of individual as well. One such individual was a prominent figure in the history of Old Testament Israel. He was born in the tribe of Benjamin, one of the smallest of the Israelite tribes. He was from the small village of Gibeah, located in the hill country just a few miles north of Jerusalem. He never traveled far from that homeland, except during his military exploits, which were many. He married a woman named Ahinoam, and they had five children - three sons and two daughters.

This man lived during a rather troublesome and tumultuous time. It was during his lifetime that the Philistines had settled along the Mediterranean coast. They had become a rather powerful people, and their plans were to move inland from the coast, extending their boundaries. However, in order to accomplish this military maneuver, they would have to defeat and drive out the Israelites, who stood in the way of their eastward expansion.

The Philistine army attacked the Israelites, handing them a sound defeat at Ebenezer. This victory accomplished two things for the Philistines. First, it gave the Philistines almost complete control over the Israelite territory west of the Jordan River. This was a major step toward their ultimate goal of eastern expansion. Second, it made the Israelites vulnerable to other nations on their surrounding borders. One of these nations was Ammon, situated to the east of the Israelites land in Transjordan. The Ammonites decided to take advantage of the Israelites defeat at the hands of the Philistines by attacking them from the opposite side. It was in response to this attack by the Ammonites that this natural born leader arose.

A young man named Saul summoned an army of volunteers and defeated the marauding Ammonites, giving the Israelites a significant boost in morale. Taking advantage of this obvious willingness of the people to follow his leadership, Saul led the Israelites in fighting against the Philistines, winning major battles at Gibeah and Michmash. It was at this time that Saul was appointed as king over Israel. As king he was continually faced with the ongoing tension between the Israelites and the Philistines, which continued throughout Saul's reign as king. As a matter of fact, it would be at the hands of the Philistines that Saul and his sons would die in battle.

During his reign, Saul displayed some characteristics which were befitting a king. However, he had at least one major character flaw which resulted in his downfall. Saul proved to be capable of displaying jealousy to the degree of total insanity. It was this pothole, the pothole of jealousy, which ultimately destroyed this man.

Saul's downfall actually began during one of Israel's battles with the Philistines. The armies of Israel and Philistia were in battle formation, with a valley separating them. This proved to be more of a staring down contest than a physical altercation between the armies of the two nations. First Samuel 17:1-3 describes these events:

Now the Philistines gathered their armies together to battle, and were gathered at Sochoh, which belongs to Judah; they encamped between Sochoh and Azekah, in Ephes Dammin. And Saul and the men of Israel were gathered together, and they encamped in the Valley of Elah, and drew up in battle array against the Philistines. The Philistines stood on a mountain on one side, and Israel stood on a mountain on the other side, with a valley between them.

At this time a young man named David was sent by his father Jesse to check on the other sons of Jesse who were in Saul's army. When he arrived on the scene, he witnessed a shocking sight. A Philistine soldier was taunting the Israelite army, asking that one soldier from Israel's ranks would fight him, one-on-one, with a winner take all prize. David listened to the verbal assault this giant of a man continued to hurl at the cowering soldiers. No one would take the challenge.

David listened, and his anger was aroused because no one in Israel's army would take the challenge to fight the giant. So, David began to make an inquiry into the matter.

Then David spoke to the men who stood by him saying, "What shall be done for the man who kills this Philistine and takes away the reproach from Israel? For who is this uncircumcised Philistine, that he should defy the armies of the living God."
(1 Samuel 17:26)

David then approached King Saul, saying that he would fight the Philistine giant. And surprisingly Saul agreed! What an astounding display of God's providential grace. Here is this young shepherd boy who had just been sent by his father to check on his brothers. He has no military training. He has not been through whatever form of boot camp the Israelite soldiers would have to complete before going into battle. He had no knowledge of the rules of war. He only knew that the uncircumcised Philistine champion was making a mockery of the God of Israel, and he was not willing to listen to it any longer.

King Saul granted permission for David to engage in one-on-one, hand-to-hand combat with Goliath. And it was there that this young shepherd killed the giant, winning the victory for the Israelite army over the Philistines.

This should have proven to be a time of great rejoicing for Saul and the army of Israel. And it was, at least for a short period. But when they returned home from this great victory, the accolades were divided between Saul and David. However, it was during this victory celebration that Saul became jealous of David. Why? Because as they entered the city, the crowds shouted:

> Saul has slain his thousands, and David his ten thousands.
>
> (1 Samuel 18:7)

David received the applause and the appreciation of the people for his part in the defeat of the Philistines, and rightfully so. The only problem was that he received more credit than Saul. And this resulted in Saul becoming incensed with jealousy. It was because of this that Saul turned against David. The following verse tells the tale:

> Then Saul was very angry, and the saying displeased him; and he said, "They have ascribed to David ten thousands, and to me they have

ascribed *only* thousands. Now *what* more can he have but the kingdom?" So Saul eyed David from that day forward.

(1 Samuel 18:8–9)

Saul "eyed" David. This literally means that Saul viewed David with suspicion. He became incensed with jealousy of David. He envied him. And this jealousy exploded with animosity and hatred against David. Beginning the very next day, this envy led Saul to begin trying to kill David. He allowed his insane jealousy to distort his thinking, and to cause him to begin plotting ways in which he could murder Israel's newest hero. It is astonishing what uncontrolled envy can do to a person. It distorts everything. With Saul, it became the one all-consuming desire to get rid of the person he viewed as his greatest threat.

Over the next several chapters of First Samuel we have recorded the attempts that Saul made on David's life. He was obsessed with his uncontrollable desire to destroy this man who had received more praise than he. Time after time he plotted and schemed, striving to find a way to get rid of David. Nothing else mattered. Everything else took a secondary place of importance on Saul's list of priorities. His one insatiable desire, his uncontrollable urge, was to kill the young man who had stolen the spotlight.

That is what jealousy will do if left unchecked. And we need to know that jealousy can become the downfall of anyone who allows it to become a stronghold in their life. We have seen some graphic examples of this reality in recent times. Just a few years ago, a mother, who undoubtedly loved her daughter very, very much, was overcome with jealousy and hired a hitman to kill another young girl who was in competition with her daughter for a position as cheerleader. The ironic thing about this whole ordeal was that the mothers and the daughters were best of friends before this incident. Another illustration of the insanity of jealousy was witnessed in the winter Olympic games a few years ago when a young, aspiring Olympic skater was struck down with an iron rod, probably due to jealousy and envy more than any other factor. Jealousy can take over in a person's life, and destroy that life, along with other lives as well.

There have been numerous reports on news broadcasts where a young man would kill a young woman because of his insane jealousy. There have been reports of marriages which were destroyed, ending in bitter divorces, because one of the marriage partners was uncontrollably jealous. There have been episodes of jealousy that have ruined the lives of church members, and even entire church bodies. There have been too many occasions to count of the churches which have been ruined because of the jealousy of certain staff members. There have been numerous occasions in which churches split because of the bitterness and strife which ensues when jealousy runs rampant between different ministers on church staffs.

And then, there are those times when jealousy ruins long time relationships between church members. Perhaps one individual in a local congregation is given a position that another member wanted, and he or she instantly becomes jealous of that individual. If this is left unchecked, it can cause dissension and division in the body.

It is obvious that the pothole of jealousy is one which is devastating and destructive. This is clearly evident in the story of Saul. These studies are called portraits of providence for people in potholes, and each of the previous studies has ended with God providentially working in the lives of the people involved in such a way as to deliver them from their pothole. But that isn't the case with Saul. His story doesn't end with victory over the problem, but rather his story ends with his destruction. So where, we might ask, is the providence of God in this story?

The providence of God is seen throughout the narrative. A quick review of the events which led to Saul becoming the first king of Israel would prove to helpful at this point. The people of Israel went to the prophet Samuel and told him they wanted to be like all the other nations by having a king over them. Samuel warned them that to make such a decision would be to turn their backs on God.

The nation of Israel was to be a theocracy – a nation governed and ruled by God. But the people had obviously grown tired of being a theocracy and wanted to be a monarchy. They persisted in their desire to be ruled by a king. God, in response to their persistence, instructed Samuel to anoint a king for the nation. He then providentially chose Saul to be their first king.

Saul started out well. He proved to be an invaluable asset to the people, leading them in several great military victories. God's hand was evidently upon Saul, and he had the potential of becoming a truly great leader.

However, Saul began doing things which were not the responsibility of the king. He began rejecting the clear teachings of the Mosaic law, and he eventually came to the point when he willfully disobeyed a direct order from God when the Israelites were engaged with the Amalekites in battle. God gave clear instructions in what He wanted Saul to do in that battle, but Saul compromised. He only performed part of what God commanded and left the rest undone. To see the full impact of the magnitude of his action, lets allow the text to speak for itself.

And Saul said to Samuel, "But I have obeyed the voice of the Lord, and gone on the mission on which the Lord sent me, and brought back Agag king of Amalek; I have utterly destroyed the Amalekites. But the people took of the plunder, sheep and oxen, the best of the things which should have been utterly destroyed, to sacrifice to the Lord your God in Gilgal."

So Samuel said:

"Has the Lord *as great* delight in burnt offerings
and sacrifices,
As in obeying the voice of the Lord?
Behold, to obey is better than sacrifice,
And to heed than the fat of rams.
For rebellion *is as* the sin of witchcraft,

And stubbornness *is as* iniquity and idolatry.
Because you have rejected the word of the Lord,
He also has rejected you from *being* king."
(1 Samuel 15:20–23)

Those are some strong words spoken by Samuel, and we need to make sure we grasp the full impact of the message. Just as God had providentially chosen Saul to be the king and had providentially led him in his initial victories as king, He also prophetically revealed that the kingdom would be taken from him, and then providentially led in that downfall.

Why? Because Saul disobeyed, willfully rebelling against God's will, and he allowed himself to forget who he was. He was the chosen servant of God, not the self-appointed king of Israel. And when he became jealous over a position, then God providentially led to his downfall, and his ultimate destruction. The obvious lesson from this story is simply that jealousy is a devastating sin which will ultimately lead to destruction if not kept in check.

We certainly don't want to end up as Saul did, so how can we safeguard ourselves against making the same mistake? There are a few practical pointers we can learn which will help us deal with jealousy when we feel ourselves being tempted to be jealous of another person.

First, remember that God created us in His image, and then endowed each individual with their particular personality, their particular spiritual gift, their particular talents and abilities. Remember that God designed them so that they could use their talents for His glory, and He designed you so that you could use yours for His glory. He didn't design us all to do the same things, so let's not be jealous that someone else can do something that we are not capable of doing. Rather, we should celebrate our differences and thank God that He has made us as we are so that we might serve Him as individuals, not as mere clones that look alike, act alike, etc.

Second, remember that even if you do have the same gift as another person, but the other person is given a position and you are passed over, you should praise the Lord for the other person's position, while also remembering that God has something for you to do as well. Serving in church is not a competition – it is a participation. We are all to serve the Lord through the different ministries in the church, thank Him for allowing us to serve in that capacity, and praise Him for the positions He providentially places others in. There is no room for jealousy in the Lord's work.

This spirit of jealousy is seen far too often in the lives of pastors. One is jealous of another because of his ability to craft sermons. Another is jealous because he can't deliver the sermon as he would like, and this is because he compares himself with others. Still others are jealous because another pastor has been called to minister in a church with thousands of attendees, while he is still serving a congregation of fifty. Jealousy runs deep when we begin comparing ourselves with others. Instead of doing that, let's be thankful for the ministry to which God has entrusted us, and celebrate with others as they serve where He has placed them.

This is true among others as well. In the world of sports it is easy to become jealous of another athlete who is more capable in his position than others. Some may be on the starting lineup, while others are only on the practice squad. They are on the team, but have very little hope of every getting in a real game. In the business world there is jealousy and envy among competitors. One company bursts on the scene with amazing sales, and literally shoots to the top of the Dow exchange. Another company struggles to make ends meet at the end of the quarter. They are selling basically the same line of products, but one outshines the other. Jealousy can destroy one by being envious of the other.

Jealousy is a reality in all areas of life and livelihood. Countless is the number of those who have fallen into this pothole, many of whom were never able to escape.

Third, if you have already fallen prey to the temptation to be jealous of another, then you need to agree with God that your action is sinful. Agreeing with God is what the Bible calls confession. Jealousy is a sin against God as well as a sin against the individual of whom you are jealous. Confess your sin to God and ask for His forgiveness. It might also be necessary for you to ask the individual for forgiveness. If you have wronged another by being jealous of them and have begun to talk to others about the situation, then you need to also go to each person to whom you have spoken about the matter. Jealousy cannot be left to run unbridled and uncontrolled. We must put forth the effort to take the high ground and not engage in this kind of behavior.

Finally, repent of the sin of jealousy. To repent means to change your mind which in turn leads you to change your action. When sincere repentance has taken place, we will no longer be jealous of others, but will thank God for them. One thing that will help guard us against being jealous of another is to put them on our prayer list. First of all, praise God for them and the ministry He has assigned to them, or the position they hold. Second, pray for God to bless their ministry, business, athletic ability, etc. Third, intercede on their behalf, asking God to place a hedge of protection around them to guard them from the assaults of Satan. It is extremely difficult to be jealous of someone and pray sincerely for them at the same time.

If we don't take these measures to rid ourselves of our sinful jealousy, then we are in danger of suffering the same kind of destruction that Saul suffered. It may not lead to our physical death, but it will lead to a bitter life. We will lose all joy in life, becoming embittered and angry because we are not what someone else is, or we don't have what they possess.

Praise God for making you the way you are. You are gifted to serve alongside others who are gifted to serve. By working together, serving together, ministering together, we see God work in marvelous ways. But if we bicker and fight among ourselves because someone is put in a position we desired, or if someone has been promoted in some way and we were passed over, then that spirit of jealousy will lead to a life of discontent and bitterness.

But if we praise the Lord for them, and for what He is allowing us to do in kingdom work, or in the business world, or on the football field, it will enhance our ability to rejoice with others over the abilities God has assigned them.

QUESTIONS FOR THOUGHT AND DISCUSSION

1. What caused Saul to begin a downward spiral that ultimately led to his destruction?
2. Have you ever been jealous of another person? Exactly what was it that caused your jealousy? Talent? Job? Career? Family? Possessions? Something else?
3. Did your jealousy cause a wedge to come between you and the person of whom you were jealous?
4. The author suggested some ways to safeguard ourselves against becoming jealous of others. Have you ever used any of these to help you overcome a spirit of jealousy?

   a. Praise God for the other person.
   b. Praise God for the other person's gifts and abilities.
   c. Praise God for the other person's position.
   d. Praise God for the other person's promotion.

5. In dealing with jealousy it was suggested that we do these things:

   a. Confess the sin of jealousy.
   b. Repent of the sin of jealousy.
   c. Ask forgiveness from the one you have wronged.
   d. Seek restoration with God and with others.

CHAPTER 9

DAVID

The Pothole of Integrity

David therefore sent out spies, and understood that Saul had indeed come.

So David arose and came to the place where Saul had encamped. And David saw the place where Saul lay, and Abner the son of Ner, the commander of his army. Now Saul lay within the camp, with the people encamped all around him. Then David answered, and said to Ahimelech the Hittite and to Abishai the son of Zeruiah, brother of Joab, saying, "Who will go down with me to Saul in the camp?"

And Abishai said, "I will go down with you."

So David and Abishai came to the people by night; and there Saul lay sleeping within the camp, with his spear stuck in the ground by his head. And Abner and the people lay all around him. Then Abishai said to David, "God has delivered your enemy into your hand this day. Now therefore, please, let me strike him at once with the spear, right to the earth; and I will not *have to strike* him a second time!"

But David said to Abishai, "Do not destroy him; for who can stretch out his hand against the Lord's anointed, and be guiltless?" David said furthermore, "*As* the Lord lives, the Lord shall strike him, or his day shall come to die, or he shall go out to battle and perish. The Lord forbid that I should stretch out my hand against the Lord's anointed. But please, take now the spear and the jug of water that *are* by his head, and let us go." So David took the spear and the jug of water *by* Saul's head, and they got away; and no man saw or knew *it* or awoke. For they *were* all asleep, because a deep sleep from the Lord had fallen on them.

(1 Samuel 26:4–12)

H onesty. Uprightness. Rectitude. Honor. Honorableness. Morality. Nobility. Trustworthiness. Truthfulness. Ethics. High-mindedness. Right-mindedness.

Each of the above terms are identified as synonyms for the word "integrity". It is easy to see that integrity is a multifaceted word that is difficult to define and explain. It is often equated with the word "honesty", but it goes much farther than simply telling the truth. As a matter of fact, not one of the words identified as a synonym is equal in meaning to integrity. Each of the synonyms can be used in different contexts, with the context describing one of the many aspects of integrity, but none can be used as an equal to the word. The meaning of integrity is too broad and expansive to be reduced to equality with any one of the other words.

There are many individuals throughout the pages of Scripture who could be identified as persons of integrity. But even the best of the best had lapses in which they made decisions that were not a display of integrity. Abraham, a man of great faith and commitment to God, was for the most part a man of integrity. But even this great man could be dishonest on occasion. Noah, a man who found favor in the eyes of the Lord, became intoxicated after being saved through the global flood. Moses, the great emancipator of the nation of Israel from their Egyptian bondage, displayed his ability to disobey the Lord when he struck the rock that God had told him to only speak to. That act of disobedience was the cause of God forbidding him to cross over into the promised land.

These and many others are glaring examples of Godly individuals who, for the most part were people of integrity, but who could lapse into moments in which their integrity was compromised. No one is capable of maintaining a life of integrity one hundred percent of their life.

David was one such individual whose life was characterized by integrity, but who also had moments in which his integrity was compromised terribly. He was a man committed to following the

Lord, but in several moments of spiritual weakness he was capable of some of the most heinous acts of sinful rebellion imaginable.

As we gaze into the pothole of integrity, attention will be given to two different episodes from David's life. The first will be one in which his integrity was compromised; the second will focus on one in which he maintained his integrity in the face of extreme temptation.

A COMPROMISE OF INTEGRITY

David had inherited the throne as king of Judah after the death of Saul. He reigned in Hebron for a period of seven and a half years, while Ishbosheth, a son of Saul, ruled over Israel. During those years, the house of David continued to grow stronger while the house of Saul grew weaker. Finally, the kingdom was united under David's rule, and after ruling from Hebron for seven and a half years the throne was moved to the city of Jerusalem.

David continued to be a successful leader of the nation, leading in many military campaigns. However, after being king for approximately eighteen years, he made a decision that would negatively affect the remainder of his life. It doesn't seem to be an extremely important decision at first sight, but it proved to be disastrous. The decision was that he chose to stay in Jerusalem at the time that nations usually engaged in warfare. The account speaks for itself. It was the time of year when kings go out to war. But this time, King David chose not to go with the army of Israel.

It happened in the spring of the year, at the time when kings go out *to battle,* that David sent Joab and his servants with him, and all Israel; and they destroyed the people of Ammon and besieged Rabbah. But David remained at Jerusalem.

Then it happened one evening that David arose from his bed and walked on the roof of the king's house. And from the roof he saw a woman bathing, and the woman *was* very beautiful to behold. So David sent and inquired about the woman. And *someone* said, "*Is* this not Bathsheba, the daughter of Eliam, the wife of Uriah the Hittite?" Then David sent messengers, and took her; and she came to him, and he lay with her, for she was cleansed from her impurity; and she returned to her house. And the woman conceived; so she sent and told David, and said, "I *am* with child."

(2 Samuel 11:1–5)

The text does not reveal any details as to why David decided to remain in Jerusalem. There is no need to speculate, as there is really no way to know his reasoning. But one thing we can know for sure: if he had been where kings were supposed to be, then the encounter with Bathsheba would not have taken place.

However, the text reveals that it did take place. David, seemingly restless and not able to sleep, took a stroll on the roof of the palace. While there, he saw in the distance a beautiful woman, bathing on her roof. He inquired about the identity of the woman and was told she was the wife of Uriah the Hittite. Even after discovering that she was a married woman (and David, by the way, was a married man!), David sent for her to be brought to him. David and Bathsheba then had a sexual encounter after which she returned to her place of residence.

It wasn't long after this sexual liaison that Bathsheba sent word to David that she was pregnant. This caused a dilemma for David – it put him in a horrific pothole of integrity crisis. His integrity had been compromised, and he was now faced with the problem of somehow covering up the whole sordid affair.

He comes up with a plan that he thinks will solve his dilemma. It is an awful plan, to be sure, but it shows what great lengths someone will go to when their integrity has been compromised, and they are unwilling to simply own up to their horrible mistake. David's first attempt at covering up his sin is by having Uriah brought home from the war under the guise of getting a report as to how things are going on the battle front. It certainly sounds like a reasonable plan, doesn't it? After all, who would ever think anything strange about such a request from the king?

Then David sent to Joab, *saying,* "Send me Uriah the Hittite." And Joab sent Uriah to David. When Uriah had come to him, David asked how Joab was doing, and how the people were doing, and how the war prospered. And David said to Uriah, "Go down to your house and wash your feet." So Uriah departed from the king's house, and a gift *of food* from the king followed him. But Uriah slept at the door of the king's house with all the servants of his lord, and did not go down to his house. So when they told David, saying, "Uriah did not go down to his house," David said to Uriah, "Did you not come from a journey? Why did you not go down to your house?"

> And Uriah said to David, "The ark and Israel and Judah are dwelling in tents, and my lord Joab and the servants of my lord are encamped in the open fields. Shall I then go to my house to eat and drink, and to lie with my wife? *As* you live, and *as* your soul lives, I will not do this thing."
> (2 Samuel 11:6–11)

It obviously seemed in David's mind to be a plan that would surely work. Who would ever think anything about instructing Uriah to go home and enjoy an evening with his wife before heading back to the front line of battle? But Uriah proves to be a man of genuine integrity, while David tries his best to cover up his lack of integrity. The irony of the story is powerful. David, who was believed to be a man of genuine and sincere integrity, proves to be far less. Uriah, on the other hand, whom David must have thought was a man that could be manipulated, proved to be one of true integrity. David has his well-thought-out plan completely backfire on him as Uriah refuses to enjoy the comforts of home and the company of his wife while his fellow soldiers are at war.

Again, David is left with the same dilemma. And again, he refuses to own up to his actions, confess his sin, and experience the amazing forgiveness of God. So, he is going to have to come up with another plan. This one is more horrible than the first. If only Uriah had gone home to his wife and enjoyed an evening of intimacy with her David's dilemma would be over. But since Uriah refused, David comes up with a fail-proof plan that would completely rid him of his problem. The text tells of the horror of his plan:

> In the morning it happened that David wrote a letter to Joab and sent *it* by the hand of Uriah. And he wrote in the letter, saying, "Set Uriah in the forefront of the hottest battle, and retreat from him, that he may be struck down and die." So it was, while Joab besieged the city, that he assigned Uriah to a place where he knew there *were* valiant men. Then the men of the city came out and fought with Joab. And *some* of the people of the servants of David fell; and Uriah the Hittite died also.
>
> (2 Samuel 11:14–17)

David has gone rapidly down a slippery slope of integrity compromise. It all began with being in the wrong place at the wrong time. He wasn't supposed to be in Jerusalem: He was supposed to be with the army as they squared off in battle with the enemy. He wasn't supposed to be on the roof watching a beautiful woman bathe on her roof in the distance. He wasn't supposed to make an inquiry into the woman's identify, obviously because of his attraction to her beauty. He wasn't supposed to send for her, with the obvious intent of engaging in sexual relations with her.

No, he wasn't supposed to do any of these things. He was supposed to be a man of integrity – a man after God's heart. He was supposed to be an upright man of morality and righteousness. But here he failed miserably.

And then came the crashing blow that closed the case – at least in his imagination. He has Uriah put in the most heated area of the battle and has the soldiers around him retreat, leaving Uriah hopelessly vulnerable to the enemy's attack. David: Adulterer, deceiver, murderer! Integrity? Gone. Cover-up? Just beginning.

After Uriah's death, and after a reasonable time of mourning, David has Bathsheba brought to the palace to become his wife. And they live happily ever after, right? Nothing could be further from the truth. Sin has a way of catching up and coming out. So it was with King David. God sends the prophet Nathan to confront the king about his sin and cover-up. He tells David a story that will cause David to finally confess his sin.

Then the Lord sent Nathan to David. And he came to him, and said to him: "There were two men in one city, one rich and the other poor. The rich *man* had exceedingly many flocks and herds. But the poor *man* had nothing, except one little ewe lamb which he had bought and nourished; and it grew up together with him and with his children. It ate of his own food and drank from his own cup and lay in his bosom; and it was like a daughter to him. And a traveler came to the rich man, who refused to take from his own flock and from his own herd to prepare one for the wayfaring man who had come to him; but he took the poor man's lamb and prepared it for the man who had come to him."

So David's anger was greatly aroused against the man, and he said to Nathan, *"As* the Lord lives, the man who has done this shall surely die! And he shall restore fourfold for the lamb, because he did this thing and because he had no pity."

Then Nathan said to David, "You *are* the man!"
(2 Samuel 12:1–7)

This confrontation took place a full year after David's adultery and subsequent act of murder. He has been hiding it for all those months, and undoubtedly had been successful in the cover-up. No one knew. How could they? He had covered his tracks well and thought that there was no way anyone could ever find out. He was probably rather proud of himself for coming up with such a fail-proof cover-up. No one would ever discover the truth. He was, after all, the king!

But God! God revealed it to Nathan, and Nathan confronted the king.

David could no longer conceal his sordid secret. His sin was out in the open. His actions were known by Nathan and would soon be known by all. The reputation of the king would be tainted from this time forward. It is recorded in the Bible as a permanent testimony to what can happen in the life of one whose integrity is compromised.

David's sin had been discovered and had come crashing down. He and his family would now suffer the consequences for generations to come. Compromised integrity has an extremely high price.

A COMMITMENT TO INTEGRITY

But David's life was not always without integrity. As a matter of fact, for the most part, his life is characterized by integrity. God would never have identified David as a man after God's heart if his life was nothing but a continual and consistent display of dishonesty, infidelity, murder, and conspiracy to cover it all up. There are plenty of episodes in his life that clearly show that he was a man of integrity, with the exception of a few lapses.

One of the relationships in David's life that was a clear display of integrity is David's relationship with King Saul. After Saul was anointed as king, he proved to be a great military leader, leading the nation in many successful military exploits. However, things changed abruptly for him after a certain battle with the Philistines. It was at this battle that David killed the Philistine giant, Goliath, after which the crowds gave more praise to David than to Saul. This led to Saul being incensed with jealousy, which in turn proved to be the compelling, driving force of Saul being consumed with the desire to kill David.

Saul later committed a gross error in disobeying God by offering a sacrifice, an activity which was to be done by the priest, not the king. It was after this act of disobedience that God revealed to Samuel that Saul's kingdom would be taken from him. Samuel was then instructed by God to anoint David as the one who would succeed Saul on the throne.

All these things added to the fuel on the fire of Saul's jealousy and wrath. He set out to kill David, thinking that perhaps in doing so it would secure the throne for his family line. More than a dozen times he attempted to take the life of David or have someone else do it for him.

On at least two of those occasions, David spared Saul's life when he had the opportunity to kill him or have one of his men do the job for him. The following passage records one of those occasions.

David therefore sent out spies, and understood that Saul had indeed come.

So David arose and came to the place where Saul had encamped. And David saw the place where Saul lay, and Abner the son of Ner, the commander of his army. Now Saul lay within the camp, with the people encamped all around him. Then David answered, and said to Ahimelech the Hittite and to Abishai the son of Zeruiah, brother of Joab, saying, "Who will go down with me to Saul in the camp?"

And Abishai said, "I will go down with you."

So David and Abishai came to the people by night; and there Saul lay sleeping within the camp, with his spear stuck in the ground by his head. And Abner and the people lay all around him. Then Abishai said to David, "God has delivered your enemy into your hand this day. Now therefore, please, let me strike him at once with the spear, right to the earth; and I will not *have to strike* him a second time!"

> But David said to Abishai, "Do not destroy him; for who can stretch out his hand against the Lord's anointed, and be guiltless?" David said furthermore, "*As* the Lord lives, the Lord shall strike him, or his day shall come to die, or he shall go out to battle and perish. The Lord forbid that I should stretch out my hand against the Lord's anointed. But please, take now the spear and the jug of water that *are* by his head, and let us go." So David took the spear and the jug of water *by* Saul's head, and they got away; and no man saw or knew *it* or awoke. For they *were* all asleep, because a deep sleep from the Lord had fallen on them.
>
> (1 Samuel 26:4–12)

David is in a position in which he can easily take the life of Saul. He has been hunted by this man for years, with Saul seizing every opportunity to take David's life. And on this occasion, David hears of Saul being in a certain location which could easily be infiltrated if they were very careful. So, David asks who among his men would go with him into the camp of Saul. Abishai then boldly tells the king that he would go with him, so they set out on their journey to go into Saul's encampment.

When they arrive in Saul's camp, they find that Saul, along with his men, are all sound asleep. No one is stirring. Not even those men who had the assignment of guarding the king. They were all sleeping so soundly that David and Abishai were able to walk right past those who were sleeping around the king, making their way right to the spot where Saul was sleeping.

Abishai obviously saw this as God's divine intervention on behalf of David. David now has the opportunity to assassinate King Saul and take the throne by coup. God had, after all, already chosen David to be the next king of the nation. Samuel had already anointed him to be the next king. So it would be only natural for Abishai to assume that this was the way God had ordained for David to take the throne.

It all makes perfectly good sense, doesn't it? Abishai certainly thinks it does. Listen again to his reasoning:

God has delivered your enemy into your hand this day. Now therefore, please, let me strike him at once with the spear, right to the earth; and I will not *have to strike* him a second time!

Abishai is convinced that God had now providentially orchestrated this entire series of events so that David could seize the throne by taking Saul's life. In Abishai's mind, God had graciously given David an amazing gift. How could this be anything other than the work of God to remove Saul from the throne? And now he is trying to convince David that he is right. "God has delivered." This is clearly the hand of God at work. He has seen how David has been afflicted by the attempts of Saul to kill him. He has seen how David and his men have been on the run for years and years, hiding in caves, living off the land. God has seen all the trauma they have been put through as they have had to drag their families around the country as fugitives.

Who would not see the hand of God at work in this? It seems so clear, so absolutely obvious, that God has orchestrated the events which have led up to this moment. All of David's suffering at the hands of Saul could be over in an instant. Saul had shown moments of absolute insanity in his pursuit of David. And now, he is sound asleep at David's feet. How could this not be the orchestrated work of God?

Abishai tells David to give him permission to strike Saul in his sleep. He says that he will do it right with the first strike – there will be no need to strike him a second time. He will get the job done. And again, don't miss the emphasis he places on his belief that this is God's work.

There are times when we may be in situations in which it appears crystal clear that it must be God's will to go in a certain direction. The apostle Paul had one such experience which he writes about in his correspondence with the Corinthian church.

But I will tarry in Ephesus until Pentecost. For a great and effective door has opened to me, and *there are* many adversaries.

(1 Corinthians 16:8–9)

This is such an amazing testimony to a commitment of integrity. Paul could have used the presence of many adversaries as a reason to leave and go elsewhere. He could have convinced himself that these adversaries were a warning from God that it was time for him to leave, to escape the trouble he would surely face if he decided to stay. As a direct result of his total commitment to God, and his commitment to be a man of impeccable integrity, he chooses to remain. Paul obviously felt in his heart that he was exactly where God wanted him to be at the time and refused to allow the presence of adversity to become an excuse for seeking a more peaceful place of ministry.

David could have taken Abishai's advice and decided that this must be God's handiwork. How else could he explain the fact that Saul is in a helpless situation, with no one to come to his aid. Even his trusted armor bearer had fallen into a deep sleep when he should have been standing guard over the king. Surely this had to be the work of God.

At that point – that most momentous moment in time – He could have given Abishai permission to strike Saul, taking his life and giving David the throne. But David knew that to do so would be to circumvent the plan of God. God had revealed to David that he would be the next king, but He had not told him to take the throne by force. God would handle the task in his own way and according to His own timetable.

This is seen even more clearly in another of those times when David was being chased by Saul. David had the opportunity to take Saul's life when Saul entered a cave where David and his men were hiding out. When given the opportunity to kill Saul, he said to his men:

> The LORD forbid that I should do this thing to my master, the LORD's anointed, to stretch out my hand against him, seeing he *is* the anointed of the LORD.
>
> (1 Samuel 24:6)

David realized that there was no need for him to raise his hand against Saul because God would take care of him in His own way. So, he refused to take the life of the king because he knew that God had anointed him to serve in that position, and God would handle the situation as He desired to do so. David assured Saul that he meant him no harm.

Through all this David proved himself to be a man of great integrity.

So how do we reconcile his lack of integrity in his adulterous relationship with Bathsheba and his subsequent attempts to cover it up by having her husband killed in battle, and his commitment to integrity in sparing Saul's life? We reconcile his inconsistencies by recognizing that we all have them. Every Biblical character had their moments of weakness in which their integrity was compromised. However, their lives were characterized by a commitment to integrity even though they experienced these lapses.

We are to strive for purity in our integrity, but we can be assured that when we do have momentary setbacks as we give in to the temptations of life that we have an Advocate with the Father, Jesus Christ. He is ever in intercession between God and man. And we can be restored, as was David, from our momentary setbacks through the forgiving grace of God.

QUESTIONS FOR THOUGHT AND DISCUSSION

1. How would you define "integrity"?
2. Thinking about David being described as a man after God's own heart, how would you explain his momentary lapses into sin?
3. What can we do to safeguard ourselves against falling away from a life of integrity?
4. Do you know anyone who has fallen away? What could you do to help them find their way back to God?
5. Paul used the presence of adversaries as a reason to stay and continue to minister. Why do we often take the presence of adversaries as a reason to go elsewhere?

CHAPTER 10

AHAB

The Pothole of Greed

And it came to pass after these things *that* Naboth the Jezreelite had a vineyard which *was* in Jezreel, next to the palace of Ahab king of Samaria. So Ahab spoke to Naboth, saying, "Give me your vineyard, that I may have it for a vegetable garden, because it *is* near, next to my house; and for it I will give you a vineyard better than it. *Or,* if it seems good to you, I will give you its worth in money."

But Naboth said to Ahab, "The Lord forbid that I should give the inheritance of my fathers to you!"

So Ahab went into his house sullen and displeased because of the word which Naboth the Jezreelite had spoken to him; for he had said, "I will not give you the inheritance of my fathers." And he lay down on his bed, and turned away his face, and would eat no food.

(1 Kings 21:1–4)

It was a time of prosperity and political power for the nation of Israel. Through the forming of political alliances, as well as the intermarrying of the royal line with descendants of the royal line in other nations, Israel was becoming more and more prominent on the world scene. This time of prosperity was long in coming. Things had not always looked so bright and promising for the nation.

This time of prosperity and political clout followed closely on the heels of a time of political upheaval in the nation. King Elah was assassinated, and this assassination led to civil war as different men sought to take the throne. A man named Omri was a general in the army of King Elah, and after Elah's assassination, Omri was acclaimed king by his own forces in the field. He prevailed in the ensuing civil war, and soon afterward moved the capital city from Tirzah to Samaria. He began to strengthen his political clout by making alliances with surrounding nations, one of which was the nation of Phoenicia.

After his death, Omri was succeeded on the throne by his son. Wanting to continue on in the success of his father, the new king continued to make alliances with other nations. He secured the alliance with the Phoenicians by marrying the Phoenician king's daughter. This cemented the relationship with the country of Phoenicia, but it did tremendous damage to the nation of Israel.

Omri's son's name was Ahab, and the Phoenician princess he married was named Jezebel. Ahab came to be remembered as one of the most wicked and evil kings who ever ruled the nation of Israel. His rebellion against the Lord brought the nation to new levels of spiritual anarchy as they began worshiping other gods, erecting altars to these false deities, and leading the people to follow his example. He and his wife were instigators of such wickedness and evil during his reign as king that they have nothing good recorded of them in the Bible.

Listen to the following scathing testimony given of King Ahab:

> Now Ahab the son of Omri did evil in the sight of the LORD, more than all who *were* before him. And it came to pass, as though it had been a trivial thing for him to walk in the sins of Jeroboam the son of Nebat, that he took as wife Jezebel the daughter of Ethbaal, king of the Sidonians; and he went and served Baal and worshiped him. Then he set up an altar for Baal in the temple of Baal, which he had built in Samaria. And Ahab made a wooden image. Ahab did more to provoke the LORD God of Israel to anger than all the kings of Israel who were before him.
>
> (1 Kings 16:30–33)

That is not a very pretty picture. It shows a man who had allowed himself to be consumed by the insatiable desire to fulfill his personal wants. What Ahab wanted, Ahab got, and it mattered not what means he had to utilize in order to fulfill his desires. There are many evil character traits which were obvious in Ahab's life. Each one of them would be a worthwhile study in sinful human behavior, as there are many lessons we could learn from such a wicked man. Perhaps in studying some of his wicked traits we could be warned about the consequences of making those same choices.

There is one trait which seems to stand out from the rest. It is one that will be the ruin of Ahab and will eventually lead to his destruction. Ahab's entire life was characterized by the breaking of several of the ten commandments. In the verses quoted above we learn about his breaking the commandment to have no other gods before him, and to make no graven images. He committed both evils at the very beginning of his reign as king.

But what was it that caused him to commit these abominable acts? What could have possibly convinced him that this was the correct course of action for the king of Israel to take? To answer that question, let's review for a moment the Ten Commandments.

You shall have no other gods before Me.
You shall not make for yourself a carved image.
You shall not take the name of the Lord your God
in vain.
Remember the Sabbath day, to keep it holy.
Honor your father and your mother.
You shall not murder.
You shall not commit adultery.
You shall not steal.
You shall not bear false witness.
You shall not covet.

One of those ten commandments seems to be in a class by itself. It is completely different from the other nine. It stands alone. Nine of the commandments deal exclusively with external actions. But one of the ten deals with what we are internally. Look at them again. The first nine deal with external actions. They refer to things we do. But the tenth commandment – you shall not covet – is not necessarily an external act, but rather it is what we are, internally. As a matter of fact, every time we break one of the first nine commandments, we also break the tenth.

Ahab's life was characterized by a total disregard for this tenth commandment, which in turn led him to break several of the others. We could honestly say that he not only fell into the pothole of covetousness – he took up residence in that pothole. Covetousness was his trademark. Covetousness is a devastating sin which will result in the ruin of the one who consistently commits it. This is obvious in the life of Ahab.

Let's try to keep the story in its proper setting. As already mentioned, this was a time of political and material prosperity for the nation of Israel. Ahab, being the king, would have been an extremely wealthy man. He would have lacked nothing. Everything he could ever possibly want would be his at his request.

However, for Ahab, as for so many others, to have it all is

never enough. Ahab always wanted more, and he seemed to never have enough to satisfy. There is an episode in Ahab's life that is recorded in First Kings 21 which clearly depicts this truth. It is there that we learn about a certain man named Naboth. Let's allow the text to speak for itself:

> And it came to pass after these things *that* Naboth the Jezreelite had a vineyard which *was* in Jezreel, next to the palace of Ahab king of Samaria. So Ahab spoke to Naboth, saying, "Give me your vineyard, that I may have it for a vegetable garden, because it *is* near, next to my house; and for it I will give you a vineyard better than it. *Or,* if it seems good to you, I will give you its worth in money."
>
> (1 Kings 21:1–2)

That sounds like a reasonable proposition, doesn't it? Ahab is making a simple business proposal to Naboth, who owns a piece of land that Ahab wants. So, he makes a reasonable offer to purchase the piece of property. He tells Naboth that he will give him a piece of property that is worth more than the property owned by Naboth. This could have been a profitable proposition for Naboth, as he could have taken the more expensive plot of land and sold it for more than his original property was worth. Wise investors make these kinds of deals all the time.

I know of several people who have started their own business of flipping houses. They will purchase a house that needs upgrading and renovation. Then, they will make all the necessary upgrades, making sure the house meets all the codes and requirements for putting it on the market. They will then sell the property for a large profit. Naboth could have taken the trade, then sold the new property for a profit.

But there was one small problem: Naboth wasn't interested in selling the property. This piece of land had been in Naboth's family for generations. It had been passed down from each succeeding generation to the next, and Naboth would not consider the possibility of selling it or trading it for another plot of earth. His answer to Ahab is direct and to the point:

> But Naboth said to Ahab, "The Lord forbid that I should give the inheritance of my fathers to you!"
>
> (1 Kings 21:3)

Naboth asserted his refusal to accept Ahab's offer. Even if Ahab was willing to pay an exorbitant price for the land, Naboth would not consider giving up his rightful inheritance He had every right to maintain ownership of the land and that was his final decision.

Ahab was distraught. The next verse tells the tale:

> So Ahab went into his house sullen and displeased because of the word which Naboth the Jezreelite had spoken to him; for he had said, "I will not give you the inheritance of my fathers." And he lay down on his bed, and turned away his face, and would eat no food.
>
> (1 Kings 21:4)

Ahab allowed his desire to have Naboth's property to put him into a state of mental and emotional misery. This is exactly what greed will do to anyone who allows himself to be consumed by it. Greed is insatiable. There is never enough to satisfy the sinful desires of greed. The more greed gets, the more greed wants. It becomes the controlling, driving force in the life of the one who has become ensnared by its tentacles. Ahab had allowed himself to be so consumed with his greedy desire to have Naboth's vineyard that it literally drove him into a state of despair, refusing even to eat. This action of Ahab was certainly not befitting a king as he acted so childishly. His actions were like that of a pouting child pitching a temper tantrum because he did not get what he wanted.

However, the story doesn't end there. The following verses tell us that his wife Jezebel took matters into her own hands, plotting the death of Naboth so that Ahab could take possession of his vineyard. The plan was to have men bear false witness against Naboth in order to have him executed. This act of Jezebel broke at least two more of the ten commandments. When she brought forth witnesses to bear false testimony against Naboth, and when she ordered Naboth's death so Ahab could take possession of Naboth's property. Covetousness; bearing false witness; murder. Greed has no boundaries when it sets its sights on something. Greed will drive us to lose control of our mental faculties, pushing us forward to concoct a plan through which we can obtain that which we so desperately desire.

Let's take this a step further. The New Testament condenses the ten commandments into two commandments. When Jesus was asked which was the greatest commandment, He answered:

> The first of all the commandments *is:* "*Hear, O Israel, the* LORD *our* God, the LORD *is one. And you shall love the* LORD *your God with all your heart, with all your soul, with all your mind, and with all your strength.*" This *is* the first commandment. And the second, like *it, is* this: "*You shall love your neighbor as yourself.*" There is no other commandment greater than these.
>
> (Mark 12:29–31)

The sin of covetousness clearly breaks both of these commandments. If we love the Lord with all our being, then we will make every effort to obey His teachings. Jesus told His disciples that if they loved Him they would keep His commandments. Obedience is one of the most definitive ways to identify a sincere follower of Jesus Christ. And then if we love our neighbor as we love ourself, then we would never want to defraud them in any way, as Ahab and Jezebel clearly did with Naboth. Ahab did neither. He did not love God enough to be content with what he had, and he did not love his fellow man enough to rejoice with him in his good fortune. Instead Ahab became envious of Naboth's good fortune.

In our consideration of portraits of providence for people in potholes, we have seen in some cases that God's providence proves to be positive, while in other cases it proves to be negative. In the case of Ahab, it once again proves to be negative in nature. In response to Ahab's life of total disregard for the commandments of God, God sends a prophet to Ahab to pronounce judgment, not only upon him, but upon his house, or his lineage. Listen to these somber words:

> Then the word of the LORD came to Elijah the Tishbite, saying, "Arise, go down to meet Ahab king of Israel, who *lives* in Samaria. There *he is,* in the vineyard of Naboth, where he has gone down to take possession of it. You shall speak to him, saying, "'Thus says the LORD: Have you murdered and also taken possession?'" And you shall speak to him, saying, ""'Thus says the LORD: ""'In the place where dogs licked the blood of Naboth, dogs shall lick your blood, even yours'.""
>
> (1 Kings 21:17–19)

This prophetic word was fulfilled in 1 Kings 22, when Ahab died in battle, and the dogs licked his blood according to the word of the Lord. It should be obvious to all who read this account that God does not take lightly those who commit the sin of covetousness. Those who commit such acts of sinfulness will be held accountable by God.

So, how do we safeguard ourselves against committing this atrocious act? I believe if we make application of two points mentioned earlier in this chapter we may very well build a strong defense against this sin.

First, let's love God enough to be content. Paul had learned this lesson, as he says that he had learned in whatever state he found himself to be content. There are a couple of things we need to always try to remember in relation to this matter of contentment. One, if we are not content, then it could mean that we have lost the vitality of an intimate fellowship with God. Our contentment should be an outgrowth of our relationship with Him. Contentment should be a consistent realilty as we remember that God is God and that whatever we encounter along life's way is because He has sovereignly planned it for us. Two, if we are not content, it could possibly mean that we have ceased to be submissive to God's will. We cease to be content when we feel that we deserve more than we have. So, what we must do is to nurture our love for God until we reach the point in which we are content with what He supplies.

Second, we should love our fellow man enough to not be envious of what they have. It is possible to envy any number of things. We can be envious of another person's wealth, of another person's house, automobile, job, wife, children, talents, education. In the church, we could even be envious of another believer's spiritual gifts. The only sure cure for that sort of envy is to love our fellow man to the point that we actually rejoice in their good fortune, rather than wishing them ill fortune because they have something we wish we had.

From the experiences of Ahab, we learn that covetousness is a most horrible sin which will result in the destruction of the one committing that sin. May God help us to love Him and to love our fellow man in such a way as to safeguard ourselves against living a life of covetousness.

QUESTIONS FOR THOUGHT AND DISCUSSION

1. Why is the sin of covetousness in a category by itself?
2. Do you agree with the assessment that in order to commit any of the first nine commandments, a person must commit the sin of coveting?
3. Does anyone who is given over to greed ever have enough? Why or why not?
4. To guard ourselves against the sin of greed and covetousness we are encouraged to do two things:

   a. Love the Lord enough to be content with what He supplies.
   b. Love our neighbor enough that we do not covet what he has.
   c. Has there ever been a time in your life in which one or the other of these two were not true? How did you get over the sin of covetousness?

5. Ahab was obviously given over to a desire to have what did not belong to him. What can we learn from his poor example? Write down your answer and then share it with a friend or family member.
6. Jezebel proved to be even more evil than Ahab. What can we learn from her poor example? Write down your answer and then share it with a friend or family member.

CHAPTER 11

JEREMIAH

The Pothole of Depression

Great is Thy Faithfulness
Great is Thy faithfulness, O God my Father,
There is no shadow of turning with Thee;
Thou changest not, Thy compassions they fail not;
As Thou hast been, Thou forever wilt be.

Summer and winter and springtime and harvest,
Sun, moon, and stars in their courses above,
Join with all nature in manifold witness
To Thy great faithfulness, mercy and love.

Pardon for sin and a peace that endureth,
Thine own dear presence to cheer and to guide;
Strength for today, and bright hope for tomorrow.
Blessings all mine, with ten thousand beside!

Great is Thy faithfulness! Great is Thy faithfulness!
Morning by morning new mercies I see;
All I have needed Thy hand hath provided;
Great is Thy faithfulness, Lord unto me!

Thomas O. Chisholm

What a gloriously beautiful hymn of praise! That is one of those beautiful old hymns that is great to use in our prayer time, as we contemplate God's great faithfulness to us in every area of life. When we begin to focus our attention on His wonderful faithfulness, then it facilitates even more our ability to praise Him in prayer.

The truly amazing thing about that song is the circumstances in which it was written. It sounds as if the individual writing these words was experiencing the manifold blessings of God. It sounds as if he were living a life that was carefree and filled with peace and prosperity. But, that is not the case at all. The song was penned by a man who had experienced health problems the entirety of his life. In a letter penned by the song writer, dated 1941, he wrote:

> My income has not been large at any time due to impaired health in the earlier years which has followed me on until now. Although I must not fail to record here the unfailing faithfulness of a covenant-keeping God and that He has given me many wonderful displays of His providing care, for which I am filled with astonishing gratefulness.

The testimony of the hymn becomes even more meaningful for us when we realize that this man's faith was a living faith, and his belief in the faithfulness of God was not based on a life of ease and comfort but based on the reality of God's faithfulness even in the midst of a life of trouble and pain.

So it was with the man who penned the words which inspired Thomas Chisolm to write that hymn of praise. The words are found in the Old Testament book of Lamentations. It is there that we hear the prophet Jeremiah speak of God's great faithfulness. It is there that the prophet says the compassions of God fail not, but that they are new every morning. Words which are clearly reiterated in the hymn.

And again, the amazing thing about the words of the prophet, just as the words of the hymn writer, is that they were written in a time of personal crisis. The prophet was in a pothole. A pothole of tremendous magnitude. A pothole of overwhelming proportion. A pothole that all too many of us find ourselves in far too many times. For the sake of our study, we will call it simply the pothole of depression.

> Through the Lord's mercies we are not consumed, because His compassions fail not. They are new every morning; great is Your faithfulness. "The Lord is my portion," says my soul, "'Therefore I hope in Him!
>
> (Lamentations 3:22–24)

To help better understand what is happening in Jeremiah's life when he pens these words, we need to do a brief review of the years of his prophetic ministry. Jeremiah received his calling from God to be a prophet in the thirteenth year of King Josiah's reign, which would be the year 627 BC. It was then that God informed Jeremiah that he would be a prophet of God, who would be God's spokesman to His people during these pivotal years of Israelite history.

During Josiah's reign as king, the nation experienced a wonderful time of spiritual renewal. It was under Josiah's leadership that great religious reform took place. It is interesting to note that Jeremiah doesn't record anything about this positive spiritual renewal in his prophecy. This could possibly be because he did not actually begin his prophetic ministry until after Josiah's death, and after the people began to turn back again toward the sinfulness of pre-Josiah days.

It was during the latter days of Josiah's reign that tensions began to escalate between surrounding nations. The Assyrian Empire began a time of rapid decline after the death of King Ashurbanipal. At the same time Nabopolassar began a 21-year reign as king of Babylon, with his reign culminating as his son, Nebuchadnezzar, came to the throne. With Babylonian forces now ready to attack and subdue Assyria, the Assyrians turned to Egypt for assistance in fighting the Babylonians. The Babylonian army became stronger, winning decisive battles against those who opposed them. In an attempt to thwart the expansion of the Babylonian empire, the Egyptians joined forces once again with the weakened Assyrian army. Pharaoh Necho led the army of Egypt through Palestine without informing Josiah of his plans to pass through without altercation. Making the assumption that this was an assault against Palestine, Josiah led an attack against the Egyptians in the plain of Megiddo. He suffered a fatal wound in battle and later died in Jerusalem from the injuries.

It was in the midst of this turbulence that Jeremiah begins his prophetic ministry. God's initial call upon his life, as recorded in the first chapter of his prophecy, reveals the magnitude of his task. God says to His chosen prophet:

> Behold, I have put My words in your mouth.
> See, I have this day set you over the nations and
> over the kingdoms,
> To root out and to pull down,
> To destroy and to throw down,
> To build and to plant.
> Therefore prepare yourself and arise,
> And speak to them all that I command you.
> Do not be dismayed before their faces,
> Lest I dismay you before them.
> For behold, I have made you this day
> A fortified city and an iron pillar,
> And bronze walls against the whole land—
> Against the kings of Judah,
> Against its princes,
> Against its priests,
> And against the people of the land.

> They will fight against you,
> But they shall not prevail against you.
> For I *am* with you, says the Lord, to deliver you.
> (Jeremiah 1:9b–10; 17–19)

God sets the tone for Jeremiah's ministry at the very outset of his calling, and that tone is not one which would have been very appealing to the young prophet. It would be a ministry which would for the most part be negative in its implementation. The six-fold ministry as announced by the Lord shows that it would be at least four parts negative (root out, pull down, destroy, and throw down) to two parts positive (build and plant). Jeremiah would definitely need to be a fortified city and a bronze wall. He would need to be hedged in and about by the Lord in order to survive such a ministry as this.

During the years that follow, Jeremiah involves himself to the best of his ability in fulfilling God's call upon his life. God commands him to confront the people concerning their sinfulness. Jeremiah proclaims to them in his temple sermons (recorded in chapters 7 and 23) that God is very much displeased with their sinfulness, telling them that they have misplaced faith. They are trusting in the temple, not in the presence of God in the temple. They have come to believe that nothing can ever happen to them because they are God's people, and He is their God. Jeremiah tells them otherwise. He warns them that God's displeasure will result in judgment if they are unwilling to heed his message and sincerely repent.

As a result of his faithfulness to God, Jeremiah suffers greatly at the hands of his fellow Israelites. He is taken into custody and imprisoned. He is thrown into a cistern where he is left to die. His own family members turn on him. There is no wonder that Jeremiah experienced bouts of deep depression. Some of these bouts are recorded for us in the pages of his book.

Righteous are You, O Lord, when I plead with You; yet let me talk with You about Your judgments. Why does the way of the wicked prosper? Why are those happy who deal so treacherously? You have planted them, yes, they have taken root; they grow, yes, they bear fruit.

(Jeremiah 12:1–2a)

Jeremiah is confused by what must have appeared to be unjust and unfair behavior from God. He is perplexed by the fact that the wicked were prospering, and he sees this as a direct result of God's blessing on them. He states assertively that he believes it is because of God's blessings that they are now prospering and bearing fruit. He is asking a question that has been asked by countless others throughout human history: why do the wicked prosper while the righteous suffer?

So how does the Lord respond to this complaint and question from Jeremiah?

If you have run with the footmen, and they have wearied you, then how can you contend with horses? And if in the land of peace, in which you trusted, they wearied you, then how will you do in the floodplain of the Jordan?

(Jeremiah 12:5)

This is definitely not the response Jeremiah was hoping to receive. He is seeking answers to one of life's most profound problems – the prosperity of the wicked and the suffering of the righteous – and the Lord answers with what appears to be a riddle. In essence God says, if you are weary simply because you have been contending with people, how are you going to fare when things get really tough? If you can't handle things when you have been in a peaceful, calm situation, how will you survive when you are in the turbulence of raging flood waters?

This response of the Lord should have let Jeremiah know that God was not threatened by his questions, nor by the seeming unfairness Jeremiah asks about. But, Jeremiah isn't finished with his questions and complaints. A little later in his prophetic writings he says:

> Woe is me, my mother, that you have borne me, a man of strife and a man of contention to the whole earth! I have neither lent for interest, nor have men lent to me for interest. Every one of the curses me.
>
> Why is my pain perpetual and my wound incurable, which refuses to be healed? Will You surely be to me like an unreliable stream, as waters that fail?
> (Jeremiah 15:10, 18)

The depths of Jeremiah's depression are glaringly evident. He asks the question: "Will you surely be to me like an unreliable stream?" The despair is couched in a metaphor, but the point is unmistakable. He is obviously saying that he feels God has been an unreliable partner in his ministry. Think about the seriousness of that accusative statement. Jeremiah is actually saying that God can't trusted – that He has proven to be undependable. Jeremiah is insinuating clearly that he feels as if God has not acted justly toward him.

It sounds as if Jeremiah is about to experience a mental and emotional crash. He is struggling spiritually, striving to find answers to his present state of perpetual pain. He is also struggling emotionally, bemoaning the day of his birth, citing the fact that, from his perspective, his life has been nothing but strife and contention. And note how his statement is actually a gross exaggeration: he says that he has been contending with the whole earth. As Jeremiah surveys his present state, he sees nothing but pain and problem. Everyone curses him!

This is what happens when we allow our present state of

circumstances to define us. All Jeremiah can see is what is happening to him at the moment. He can't seem to see beyond what is happening right then. He had developed tunnel-vision. What was happening to him right then became his obsession. It consumed his thoughts, his words, and his actions. He allows himself to get so wrapped up in his "woe is me" attitude that he begins making accusations against God, saying that God was like an unreliable stream to him.

We, too, can allow this to happen to us. Perhaps we find ourselves in a particularly trying situation. If we are not careful, that situation will consume us. It will enslave us, becoming that "thing" that is always uppermost in our mind. It will be the focus of our conversations with others. It could get to the point where we begin blaming God for His unfair actions toward us. As Jeremiah, we may begin looking at God as being unreliable.

Trying circumstances in life can become so powerful and overwhelming that we can't see anything but the problem. We become consumed with the problem to the point that we can't think about anything else. It is our first thought in the morning, and our last thought at night. Our minds are drawn to it countless times throughout the day. We speak of it to everyone who will listen. We lose sight of everything else.

It may even get so bad that we think there is no hope to ever get over the problem. We become convinced that no one else has ever faced anything like this before. We feel that there is no one to whom we can turn for counsel since we are the first person to ever experience such an ordeal. We may even reach the conclusion that nothing could possibly be worse than what we are experiencing right then. We are so consumed with the problem that we begin thinking there is no way we will survive. Things are as bad as they could ever be.

But things can always be worse!

Jeremiah is going to learn quickly and painfully that things are never as bad as they could be. He is going to reach the bottom emotionally, mentally, physically and spiritually before he makes a turn toward understanding and embracing his call from God. This is seen in his final complaint to God, which reveals how dark and obsessive he had become in his thinking. He is in the throes of despair, and can't seem to shake himself free from the deep, dark spiritual state he has come to be in. Read these painful words slowly, allowing the anguish of this prophet of God to speak directly to your heart:

> Cursed is the day in which I was born! Let the day not be blessed in which my mother bore me! Let the man be cursed who brought news to my father, saying, "A male child has been born to you!" making him very glad. And let that man be like the cities which the Lord overthrew and did not relent; let him hear the cry in the morning, and the shouting at noon, because he did not kill me from the womb, that my mother might have been my grave, and her womb always enlarged with me. Why did I come from the womb to see labor and sorrow, that my days should be consumed with shame?
>
> (Jeremiah 20:14–18)

What a horrible, graphic portrayal of the depths of depression. This certainly makes it clear beyond doubt that Jeremiah was overwhelmed with a depth of depression that consumed his every thought and distorted his view of reality. Deep, dark depression. His depression is so entrenched in his mind that he sees no way out. He cannot understand what God is doing, and why God is allowing him to experience such trauma and tragedy. Instead of crying out to God, his depression causes him to cry out against God, and to even curse the day of his birth.

What could have caused Jeremiah to express such grief and sorrow? What could possibly be so bad that he would even lash out at God as he did in these bouts of depression? Why would someone who has been called by God begin making accusations against God for being unreliable and less than dependable? The answer is obvious. During the years of his ministry, he had been ostracized, beaten, abandoned by both family and friend. He had experienced the anguish of spirit of being a lone voice for the Lord, even being commanded by God to preach a message denouncing the work of the spiritual leaders of his day. He felt abandoned by man and God alike. And it was more than he could take. So, in his anguished, broken spirit, he rails against God for His careless treatment of His prophet.

However, after this last complaint against God, Jeremiah continues to preach God's word to the people. But even to the very end, the people rejected him and his message. And this rejection, along with the verbal and physical abuse he suffered at the hands of his kinsmen, drove him deeper and deeper into the depths of despair.

After all of his warnings, and his pleading with his people to repent, they still refused to give heed to his admonitions. As a result of their obstinance toward Jeremiah and the message of repentance he preached, Jerusalem was besieged by the Babylonians. Jeremiah witnessed the Babylonian invasion of his beloved city. Jerusalem is encircled by the hordes of Babylonian soldiers who completely cut the city off from the outside world. For eighteen months the Babylonians lay siege to this city. Food supplies could not be brought in. Body waste could not be carried out. The stench of disease and death became commonplace. Conditions inside the city walls were so bad that those inside were forced to turn to cannibalism to survive.

Finally, in the year 586 BC, the walls were broken through, and the city was destroyed. Jeremiah's message of repentance had fallen on deaf ears, and the people were now experiencing the severe hand of judgment. God's warnings of impending judgment now had become painful reality.

Jeremiah was given the opportunity to either remain in the city, or go to Babylon with the other captives, or to move elsewhere. He decided to remain in the city. However, this is short-lived, as not long hence he is forcibly taken to Egypt. It is probably there, as he reviews in his mind the events of the past several decades of serving the Lord, that Jeremiah is brought to terms with the sincerity of God's faithfulness. Listen to him as he thinks about the events which he has personally witnessed. and as he triumphantly sounds his banner of faith.

> *Through* the Lord's mercies we are not consumed,
> Because His compassions fail not.
> *They are* new every morning;
> Great *is* Your faithfulness.
> "The Lord *is* my portion," says my soul,
> Therefore I hope in Him!
> The Lord *is* good to those who wait for Him,
> To the soul *who* seeks Him.
> *It is* good that *one* should hope and wait quietly
> For the salvation of the Lord.
> (Lamentations 3:22–26)

As Jeremiah now has time to reflect on the events of the years of his ministry, he begins to realize that the providential hand of God has been at work all along. Even in the midst of the tragedies he has witnessed, both personally and nationally, Jeremiah can see through the eyes of faith that God was with him, and them, all along. Through these reflections on the past Jeremiah is able to give testimony of his faith in God, and more importantly, of God's faithfulness to him.

Sometimes life seems so unfair. Sometimes it appears that God must have left us to fend for ourselves. It just seems that if He were there, things couldn't be quite as bad as they sometimes get.

But the reality is, He is there, and sometimes the tragedies are only an outworking of His providential plans and purposes for our lives. Jeremiah had to learn this lesson, but before he finally learned it he sank into the depths of depression. It was after he had experienced the black hole of depression that he learned, finally, that God can be trusted in every circumstance of life.

Depression is becoming more and more a common occurrence of life. Multitudes suffer from the ravages of this disorder. Cases of depression can range from mild to extreme. There are lessons we can learn from Jeremiah that would be of tremendous help to us when we are experiencing a bout with the darkness caused by depression..

The first thing we can learn from Jeremiah's experience is that when depression hits us, we should not try to develop a grin and bear it approach to life. Pretending that it doesn't exist will not make it go away. We need to confront the problem, and deal with it accordingly. Far too many have succumbed to the power of depression and despair, tragically taking their own life. Often the sentiment from those close to the one who takes his own life is that they never would have suspected the individual had any problems with depression. They had hidden it so well, wearing a mask to cover the real pain they were experiencing, that no one saw any need to offer help. It is imperative to seek counsel and assistance when we feel ourselves being overwhelmed with feelings of depression and despair. Don't take for granted that someone will notice and come to the rescue. Seek out those who are trained to assist in times of depression.

Through over forty years of pastoral ministry, I have witnessed first-hand the devastating results of depression. I have been called to the scene of a suicide, and the aftermath of such a tragedy is overwhelming. I have heard loved ones and friends say that they couldn't believe that this person, who loved life deeply and enjoyed life immensely, would do such a thing. They had hidden their deep-seated depression so well that no one knew that they were struggling with such deep, dark thoughts.

One of the worst things anyone can do when suffering bouts of depression is to wear that mask of pretense. Confide in someone you trust what you are going through. Seek professional help if necessary. Don't let the darkness of depression take control.

Second, we need to try to maintain a proper perspective in life. It was those episodes in Jeremiah's life when he took his eyes off the Lord that caused him the most grief. Remember that one of his major complaints was that the wicked prospered. In order for him to be troubled with the prosperity of the wicked would require that he focus his attention on them rather than on God. We need to keep our eyes on the Lord, and remember that His plans are being fulfilled, even in the midst of what appears to be utter chaos.

This is one of the most common causes of depression among Christians. We are so easily distracted from what should be the focus of our lives. We are admonished over and over in the pages of Scripture to focus on Jesus Christ. "Look to Jesus, the author and finisher of our faith", the writer of Hebrews says. Don't be distracted by those multitudes of things that could so easily and quickly cause us to sink into a state of depression.

There are so many things clamoring for our attention that will quickly divert our focus off the main thing if we are not extremely careful. With Jeremiah, the prosperity of the wicked so captured his attention that he lost sight of what really matters in life. The focal point of the disciple of Jesus Christ should be Jesus Himself. Paul admonished his readers to think on heavenly things, not on things of the earth. Keeping our focus where it should be will help safeguard us against depression.

Third, we need to try to maintain a level of commitment to the Lord, even when we can't understand what He is doing. Jeremiah wanted to quit, but he never did. He wanted to stop preaching the messages God gave him to preach, but he never stopped. He held true to his commitment to God, even when it would have been so much more comfortable for him to keep his mouth shut.

Our faith in God, and our faithfulness to God, are of paramount importance in maintaining a proper perspective in life. Trusting Him even when we can't comprehend what He has allowed to happen to us personally, and being faithful to Him through those episodes, will enable us to see beyond the "now".

And fourth, try to remember that God is faithful, even when He seems to have forgotten about us. When the terminal illnesses come, when loved ones die, when tragedies invade our lives, remember that God has not ceased to be faithful. He can be nothing but faithful. But sometimes His ways are hard to understand. In those times, remember that God is still God, and keep going with Him.

QUESTIONS FOR THOUGHT AND DISCUSSION

1. Depression is a very real and serious problem. Have you ever experienced bouts of depression? If so, write down a recent experience, describing it in detail.
2. If you identified a bout of depression, and you feel comfortable doing so, share the details of that experience with someone whom you trust.
3. Thinking about any experiences you have had with depression; how did you get through them? Be specific.
4. The author suggested four actions that we an take when suffering with depression. Think about these, and write down your personal ideas relative to each of these:

   a. Don't "wear a mask" of pretense.
   b. Maintain a proper perspective toward life.
   c. Maintain a life of commitment to the Lord.
   d. Focus on the faithfulness of the Lord.

5. Do you know anyone who suffers with bouts of depression? What could you learn from Jeremiah's experiences that might be of help to them.
6. If you know of someone whom you think may be trying to hide their depression, approach them in love, asking if there is anything bothering them. They probably will not seek your help, so go to them.

CHAPTER 12

DANIEL

The Pothole of Standing Alone

But Daniel purposed in his heart that he would not defile himself with the portion of the king's delicacies, nor with the wine which he drank; therefore he requested of the chief of the eunuchs that he might not defile himself. Now God had brought Daniel into the favor and goodwill of the chief of the eunuchs. And the chief of the eunuchs said to Daniel, "I fear my lord the king, who has appointed your food and drink. For why should he see your faces looking worse than the young men who *are* your age? Then you would endanger my head before the king."

(Daniel 1:8–10)

I t wasn't a good time to be an Israelite living in Jerusalem, or any other part of the Southern Kingdom of Judah. The prophets had long been warning the residents of Judah that God was about to send punishment because of their rebellion and hard-heartedness. They had been called time and again to repent, to be restored to God, and to be relieved of coming disaster.

But they refused to listen, and they refused to repent. They continued head-strong in their sinful behavior. Worshiping false deities had become the norm, as they had developed a syncretistic method of maintaining the outward appearance of commitment to God while at the same time worshipping other "gods". They had obviously convinced themselves that God would never allow His chosen people to suffer the indignation of being defeated by the godless peoples of surrounding nations. They believed that God would always protect and preserve His chosen people, regardless of anything they might ever do.

However, things began to quickly change. On the world scene, the Babylonians, under the able leadership of Nabopolassar, began their methodical dismantling of the Assyrian Empire. For a short time, the Babylonian Empire had the distinction of being the most prominent world power. Nabopolassar was succeeded on the throne by his son, Nebuchadnezzar, who ruled the empire from 604-562 BC. Under his leadership, the city of Babylon became the fabled city of luxury and splendor with which its name is commonly associated. At the same time the Babylonian empire extended its borders through military exploits.

Part of their expansion program included the nation of Judah. It was in the year 605 BC that the first deportation of exiles was taken from Jerusalem to Babylon. Among those taken by the Babylonians were four young Hebrew boys – Daniel, Hananiah, Mishael, and Azariah. It is thought that Daniel would have been about fifteen years of age at the time of this deportation, and after being taken from his home, he was never privileged to return. He remained in Babylon the remainder of his life.

During his life, Daniel became a powerful political figure in the Babylonian empire. Not long after being taken to Babylon, he began to establish a reputation for his intelligence and his fidelity to God. After a period of training in the Babylonian court, Daniel began a career which would last approximately 70 years.

It is during those many years that he spent in Babylon that Daniel was allowed by the providential grace of God to fall headlong into a most difficult pothole – the pothole of standing alone. It is obvious that Daniel had received some solid instruction and training as a young boy back over in Jerusalem that enabled him to remain true to his beliefs and religious customs. We don't know anything about his years of childhood and youth, but it seems obvious that his parents saw to it that he was instructed in the things of God. It appears to be obvious that even at the young age when he was taken from home, from family, from everything that he had grown up with, and from everything that he had grown accustomed to, he had already made a firm commitment of faithfulness to God. This is made unmistakably clear from his first days in the court of the king of Babylon.

The story is familiar to most believers. The first chapter of Daniel tells us that he and his three friends, among others, were placed under the care of Ashpenaz. The text tells us:

> Then the king instructed Ashpenaz, the master of his eunuchs, to bring some of the children of Israel and some of the king's descendants and some of the nobles, young men in whom there was no blemish, but good-looking, gifted in all wisdom, possessing knowledge and quick to understand, who had ability to serve in the king's palace, and whom they might teach the language and literature of the Chaldeans.
>
> (Daniel 1:3–4)

Daniel, Hananiah, Mishael and Azariah were among those selected to begin this rigid training program. Part of the program included feeding the trainees from the luxurious delicacies of the king's table. However, Daniel refused to partake of these foods and wines of the king. Why?

But Daniel purposed in his heart that he would not defile himself with the portion of the king's delicacies, nor with the wine which he drank: therefore he requested of the chief of the eunuchs that he might not defile himself.

(Daniel 1:8)

This decision of Daniel is a powerful testimony to his level of commitment to the Lord. The reason that Daniel refused to eat the food and drink the wine was because to do so would have been to defile himself. In other words, he remembered, from that training he had received from his parents, that there were certain foods and drinks that were unclean and forbidden according to the law of God. So, Daniel decided that he would rather be true to God than to enjoy the delicacies of the luxurious food put before him by the king's servant.

The remainder of chapter one is truly amazing. The king's servant agreed to allow them a trial period in which they only drank water and ate foods that were acceptable to the teachings of God's word. To his amazement, after that trial period he found that they were healthier than everyone else. This is only the beginning of a life lived totally to the glory of God, and in total commitment to the word of God.

But that doesn't mean that it was easy. As a matter of fact, it was anything but easy. Through a strange turn of events (strange from our perspective, but providentially planned from God's perspective), Daniel is elevated to a position of prominence in the king's court. As strange as this may sound, this all began with a dream. Nebuchadnezzar had a dream which none of his wise men could interpret. Of course, the king made it rather difficult for anyone to be able to give an interpretation. Not only did he want them to give the interpretation of the dream, but he demanded that first they reveal to him the content of the dream. None of them could do that! They even argued that no king had ever made such a request of his wise men. They asked that he first tell them the dream, and that they would then interpret it for him.

This would certainly have been an unusual thing for any king to demand of his wise men. How could they possibly be able to reveal to him the content of the dream? That was an impossible task. No one could ever do that, and it was excessively cruel of the king to demand it – at least from the wise men's perspective.

Maybe Nebuchadnezzar thought to himself that it would be a rather simple thing for someone to give an interpretation to a dream. After all, anyone with any imagination at all could come up with a reasonable and believable interpretation just by making it up. The truth of the matter would not be known until enough time had elapsed for the fulfillment of the interpretation. But Nebuchadnezzar refused their appeals for him to disclose the details of the dream.

This, perhaps, would be a good lesson for anyone who turns to mediums, diviners, and fortune tellers. The next time you approach one of these for information about your future, ask them first to tell you about your past. Not just generalities, but specifics. If they can't tell you specific details about your past, then how could you ever expect them to know your future? The Bible warns against turning to mediums and fortune tellers. Believers are simply to turn to the word of God, and to God Himself through prayer as we seek guidance for our future.

At the inability of the wise men to reveal the dream and its interpretation, Nebuchadnezzar became infuriated with the whole lot of them, and issued a command that all the wise men in the entire kingdom be executed. However, it is here that God providentially reveals the dream and its interpretation to Daniel. The result of this is that Nebuchadnezzar promoted Daniel, and his three friends, to positions of leadership and power in the kingdom. His response says it all:

> Then King Nebuchadnezzar fell on his face, prostrate before Daniel, and commanded that they should present an offering and incense to him. The king answered Daniel, and said, "Truly your God *is* the God of gods, the Lord of kings, and a revealer of secrets, since you could reveal this secret." Then the king promoted Daniel and gave him many great gifts; and he made him ruler over the whole province of Babylon, and chief administrator over all the wise *men* of Babylon. Also Daniel petitioned the king, and he set Shadrach, Meshach, and Abed-Nego over the affairs of the province of Babylon; but Daniel *sat* in the gate of the king.
>
> (Daniel 2:46–49)

What a powerful testimony to their commitment of faithfulness to God. Daniel and his three friends decide to stand alone, and as a result of their unwavering commitment to God, they are promoted to positions of prominence and power within the ranks of the most powerful nation on the face of the earth. Certainly, God is honoring their integrity and faithfulness to Him.

However, it is not all a bed of roses. Yes, there are times when standing alone will bring about positive results and great rewards. But there are other times when standing alone will do just the opposite. All four of these men experience the trauma of persecution for their willingness to stand alone. Even after being promoted by the king for his interpretation of his dream, Daniel later experiences the wrath of a different king for his willingness to stand alone, just as he had earlier experienced the blessings of King Nebuchadnezzar.

Things sometimes change in an instant. One minute we may

be experiencing the wonder of the blessings of God, and the next we might lose everything. I was asked in one of my former pastorates to visit a gentleman in the neighborhood. I arrived at his home, was welcomed cordially, offered a glass of iced tea, and began conversing with him. We talked about his job, his home, where he had been reared, how he had come to reside in this particular city – just small talk.

After a while I turned the conversation to spiritual matters. I shared with him that one of his neighbors had asked me to visit with him and invite him to visit us for one of our worship experiences at church. It was at that point of the conversation that he began to share with me his story – and what a story it was!

He shared his testimony with me – a testimony of how he had committed his life to Satan. He openly shared his "salvation" experience with me. It was at a time in his life that he had lost everything. He was contemplating suicide when someone told him about how the devil had saved his life. He thought to himself that he had nothing to lose, so he prayed to Satan, telling him that if he would get him out of the mess he had made of his life he would serve him from that time on.

He then shared with me how everything changed. His business, which had been on the verge of bankruptcy, took an amazing turn and became a successful, profitable business almost overnight. His family was reunited after he and his wife had been separated. Everything was looking bright and prosperous, so why would he ever want Jesus Christ in his life?

I shared with him my experience of God's saving grace and asked that he would simply think about it. I told him that I would come again and discuss these spiritual matters with him after he had given some thought to what I had shared.

Our visits went on for several weeks. In one of our conversations, he told me that he was thinking about buying the property directly across the street from the church where I was serving as pastor. He would then build a "church" of Satan. This never materialized. Perhaps he was trying to get some type of negative response from me, but I simply let it pass. He never brought that subject up again.

It was about three months after our initial visit that I was shocked and surprised to see this gentleman walk into our church on Sunday morning. I will never forget the words he spoke to me as he was leaving at the conclusion of the morning worship. He put his hand in mine as if he was going to give me a polite handshake, but then he held on. He then looked me straight in the eye and said, "Pastor, I believe you believe what you believe more than I believe what I believe." Needless to say, I was thrilled to hear these words. I spoke with him a little further and told him I would call the next day, which I did. We made an appointment for me to make another visit. As we sat in his living room and talked further about the Lord, he said, "Pastor, I am ready to have Christ in my life." I was thrilled and amazed beyond words!

What I said next had to come from the Lord, because I don't think I would have ever thought to say these words. I shared with him that since he had testified that he had committed his life to Satan, and that he attributed everything he had to him, that he probably needed to be prepared to lose it all. I didn't feel that God would allow him to keep what he had received from the devil. He said he didn't care if he lost everything for the sake of knowing Jesus.

He made a commitment to the Lord that night. Early the next morning I received a phone call telling me that I needed to get to the hospital as quickly as possible. When I arrived, I was informed that he had experienced some sort of health trauma and was in the intensive care unit. They were still running tests trying to determine the problem, not knowing at that time what the health issue was. They were also telling the family that his chance of survival seemed minimal under his present state.

Thanks to God's intervention, he recovered from that illness but was in rehabilitation for months. But the illness was just the beginning of his troubles. The week after his health crisis his business went bankrupt. He literally lost everything he had. But

God had given me a word of knowledge to share with him that prepared him for the tremendous loss.

The reason I share this rather long story is because this man was forced to stand alone. And he was willing to do it! It cost him dearly, but he stood firm in his new relationship with the Lord.

Back to the story of Daniel. After the Babylonian empire was replaced on the world scene by the Medo-Persian empire, Darius the Mede came to the throne. The opening verses of chapter six introduce this king:

> It pleased Darius to set over the kingdom one hundred and twenty satraps, to be over the whole kingdom; and over these, three governors, of whom Daniel *was* one, that the satraps might give account to them, so that the king would suffer no loss. Then this Daniel distinguished himself above the governors and satraps, because an excellent spirit *was* in him; and the king gave thought to setting him over the whole realm.
>
> (Daniel 6:1–3)

This is truly another amazing series of events. Daniel is still living a life of unwavering faithfulness to God, and God is still blessing him with positions of prominence in still another king's court. Only God could have orchestrated this series of promotions through which Daniel, a captive from the land of Israel, is promoted to such a high and distinguished position in the court of the king. What a powerful testimony to God's sovereign power over all the nations of the earth, and His ability to bring about His plans even through pagan kings.

However, Daniel's popularity with the king becomes a matter of contention with the other governors, so they, along with other leaders, begin devising a plan with the hopes they could cause Daniel to lose his popularity with Darius. There are those who fight against God's people for the sole reason that they are simply striving to live their lives to the glory of God. Those who opposed Daniel were obviously prejudiced against him for some reason. In their minds it may have been a perfectly legitimate reason, but it ends up backfiring on them in a totally unexpected way.

These men develop a scheme that was designed to appeal to the pride of the king. Perhaps they knew this to be a weakness in the king's character. Maybe he had shown tendencies toward acting out of pride or responding to suggestions in the past that appealed to his prideful nature.

Regardless of why they chose this approach they go to King Darius with the plan. It was truly an audacious plan, one which would be laughable in almost any situation. It was a plan that went straight to the ego of the king. Their suggestion was for the king to issue a decree that no one could pray to any man or to any god for thirty days. They would only be allowed to make their prayers and petitions to the king during this time. Anyone found praying to any god or man other than the king for those thirty days would be thrown to the lions. How absurd, right? Well, not in the mind of Darius. It appealed to his ego, and he obviously gave it serious consideration.

This is one of the most dangerous tools in the devil's arsenal: the appeal to human pride. Can you imagine how this must have made King Darius feel? It would have stroked his pride; it would have appealed to his desire to be the center of attention; it would have made his feeling of self-importance grow exponentially. This decree went straight to the heart and the head of the king.

It appears that Darius may have been somewhat blinded to the scheme behind their proposal. The text does not say that he inquired as to what prompted these leaders to suggest such a plan. Since Daniel was one of the three top leaders in his court, he was probably aware of Daniel's practice of praying to God. But it appears that when he is approached with such a wonderful plan as this, he was overtaken by the sheer delight of being the only one to whom people could pray.

An interesting observation here is that Daniel is not invited to this meeting with the king. He could have been there. Actually, he should have been there. After all, he is the one Darius had set over all the governors and satraps. A proposal of this magnitude should have involved him if for no other reason than his position. But he was not invited, and his absence was not noted by the king. This makes it all the more evident that Darius was blinded by his own ego when presented with this proposal.

Darius signs the edict, and the plan is officially endorsed and enforced. Daniel, along with everyone else in the entire kingdom, would now be expected to submit to this edict from the king. He would be expected to be a law-abiding citizen just like everyone else. As a matter of fact, the pressure on Daniel would have been greater due to his position. He would now be expected to set an example for everyone due to his prominent position in the king's court.

What does Daniel do? He has lived a lifetime of uncompromising fidelity to God. Will he now waver in his commitment? Will he now vacillate in his dedication? Daniel is faced with yet another choice to either maintain his faithfulness to God or compromise to align with the king's edict. He can either compromise his faithfulness to God and obey the edict, or he can maintain his faithfulness and continue to pray to God as had been his habitual practice, which will result in his being thrown into a den of lions.

> Now when Daniel knew that the writing was signed, he went home. And in his upper room, with his windows open toward Jerusalem, he knelt down on his knees three times that day, and prayed and gave thanks before his God, as was his custom since early days.
>
> (Daniel 6:10)

Daniel remained steadfast in his commitment to God and his devotion to God. He refused to allow the threats of these insanely jealous men to affect his unwavering faithfulness to God. Realizing the weight of the king's edict, and that it could not be renounced once it had been decreed, Daniel remained steadfast in his commitment to be a man of integrity.

In past times, God had always providentially elevated and promoted Daniel. So, what does God do for him this time? He allows Daniel to be thrown to the lions! This is one of those incidents recorded in the Bible that causes the reader to stop abruptly in disbelief. If you were reading this particular story for the first time, you would probably be shocked to see that God did not protect Daniel from being thrown to the lions.

Could God not have intervened? Could He not have caused the king to have a change of heart? Or could God not have opened the eyes of the king to realize that this was the wicked scheme of the other leaders from the very start? Surely God could have done something! And all that is true: God could have done something. He could have had the earth open underneath the other leaders who had concocted this plan as he had done before (see Numbers 16:31-33). God could have stopped this atrocious act of the king.

But, God didn't intervene. Chapter six reveals the sadness and remorse that overwhelmed Darius when he hears that Daniel has broken his law. However, there is nothing that the king can do now except abide by his own decree. He gives the command that Daniel be thrown into the lions' den with the hope that Daniel's God would deliver him from this tragedy.

We know that God did indeed deliver Daniel from the lions, but he still had to get in the den. His trust in God, and his commitment to God, did not deliver him from this terrible ordeal. It cost Daniel dearly to stand alone for God.

I remember an individual from the years of my childhood and youth, and with every remembrance of him I am brought under severe conviction. This person was a committed Christian even from a very early age. And because of that, he was the brunt of many jokes. I remember vividly and painfully how we used to make fun of him – how we used to go out of our way to make life as miserable for him as possible. And I remember how he responded. He refused to give in to the enormous pressure to turn his back on God so that he would fit in with the crowd.

As I remember it, he had very few friends. Not very many children in our neighborhood would have much to do with him. He was tempted, he was tried, he was ridiculed, he was mocked. But through it all, he remained true to his God. He refused to give in to what had to be an enormous amount of peer pressure.

But he was only doing what Daniel had done before him. And he was only doing what Jesus required of him. It was Jesus who said that we must put Him first and foremost in our lives, make Him pre-eminent in our lives, give Him prominence in our lives. He said that we must not allow any distractions to come between us and Him: whether they be friends, family, finances, positions, possessions, in short, anything. Nothing must ever take precedence in our lives over our total devotion to God. This was true in this young man's life, just as it was in Daniel's.

There is a remarkable fact about Daniel that needs to be noted, particularly in relation to this incident. This happened to Daniel quite a long while after being taken by the Babylonians in 605 BC. As a matter of fact, the incident of being cast into the den of lions probably took place when Daniel was between 80 and 90 years of age. From the time he was taken captive at the age of 15, through all those long and difficult years of his life, he never wavered in his commitment to God. He was willing to stand alone, if need be, and not turn his back on the God of Israel.

The question is, how did he manage to accomplish this? How did he maintain his commitment to God while residing all those years in a land that did not worship the God whom Daniel worshipped? There are several answers to that question.

First, it is clearly implied in this book of the Bible, even though it is not explicitly stated, that Daniel had godly parents who trained him in the ways of God. He was taken captive while just a young teen-ager, perhaps fifteen years of age. He was displaced to a heathen country, to a country that did not know the God of the

Bible. He then lived for many years in that pagan environment, where the people gave themselves to the worship of false deities. It only stands to reason that he had received sound, solid, doctrinal instruction and practical training as a child in the home of his parents. This training played a vital role in his willingness and his ability to stand alone.

Those of us who are parents need to pay close attention to this truth. Along my Christian pilgrimage, I have met a few parents who said that they allowed their children to make their own decisions pertaining to religion. They allowed their children to decide for themselves if they wanted to go to church, or to be involved in church activities. The Bible teaches us that this is irresponsibility on the part of the parent. It is our God-given responsibility to rear our children in the nurture and the admonition of the Lord. It is our responsibility to rear them to believe in God, and to know why they do. It is our responsibility to teach them about God and godliness, to instill in them principles of righteousness. Daniel certainly had that kind of parental training, and that played a pivotal role in his ability to stand alone.

A second answer to the question is that there had to come the time in Daniel's life when he made his own personal decision to live his life to the glory of God, to live a life of dedication to God. Children can't live their lives on the coattails of the parents. They must reach the point in their lives in which they begin to make decisions for themselves. Sometimes, children raised in the godliest of homes still decide that they will not adhere to the teachings of their parents. It is vitally important for parents to do everything within their power to instill in their children a love for God and godliness. This cannot be overstated or over-emphasized. A biblical reminder of parental responsibility might prove to be helpful.

> And these words which I command you today shall be in your heart. You shall teach them diligently to your children, and shall talk of them when you sit

in your house, when you walk by the way, when you lie down, and when you rise up.

(Deuteronomy 6:6–7)

And you, fathers, do not provoke your children to wrath, but bring them up in the training and admonition of the Lord.

(Ephesians 6:4)

Daniel did not fit among those who disregard their parent's biblical instruction. Rather, he had made a personal choice to live a life of total dedication to God. We are all confronted with decisions along life's way in which our actions will be the result of choices made long ago. If I am confronted with the opportunity to commit an act of adultery, then my action should be based on a decision I made long ago that I would be faithful to God and to my wife. I should not have to be put into a position to make a decision of that magnitude on the spur of the moment.

And the third thing that is evident in Daniel's life which played a major part in his fidelity to God was his committed life of devotion. When he heard the edict of the king that no one should pray to any God, Daniel goes to his house, and prays just as before. He would not allow anything to stand in his way. We must make a choice to live a life of devotion to God, and then not allow anything to interfere with that decision.

What was the result of Daniel's dedication and devotion? Did it deliver him from facing trials and difficulties? No, it didn't deliver him from them. He still had to face some really tough decisions which led to even tougher situations. But he was able to face them, and God providentially protected him, because he was a man who was true to God in every sense of the word. Let's all make the same commitment as did Daniel and live our lives to the glory of God.

QUESTIONS FOR THOUGHT AND DISCUSSION

1. Have you ever been in a situation in which you had to stand alone for your faith? If so, describe it in detail.
2. If you described a time in which you stood alone in #1, how did other people react to your decision?
3. When you read the story about the former Satan worshiper, how did you react? Do you think what the author said to the gentleman was a word from God? Why or why not?
4. It would appear that Daniel's parents played a big role in preparing him for a life of commitment to God. If you are a parent, what can you do to help your child(ren) make a commitment to follow the Lord?
5. The author suggested that two things we can learn from Daniel is to live a life of devotion, and maintain a commitment to prayer. What are you doing to make this a reality in your life?
6. If you are not already living a life of devotion and prayer, what can you do to begin?

CHAPTER 13

JOHN THE BAPTIST

The Pothole of Personal Perplexity

There was a man sent from God, whose name was John. This man came for a witness, to bear witness of the Light, that all through him might believe. He was not that Light, but was sent to bear witness of that Light.

John bore witness of Him and cried out, saying, "This is He of whom I said, "'He who comes after me is preferred before me, for He was before me'." And of His fullness we have all received, and grace for grace.

(John 1:6–8, 15–16)

H ave you ever felt as if you were out of time and out of place? Have you ever experienced the feeling that you would have gotten along better if you had been born, and lived your life, in some other historical era? Sometimes I think that I would have fit better in the Puritan era, because the more I read of the Puritans beliefs and convictions, the more I find myself more closely identified with them. Their theological convictions, doctrinal statements, and ethical practices are all more in alignment with my beliefs and practices than any others I have studied. Perhaps I would have been a better fit for that era.

Admittedly, I sometimes think about some of the strangest things. Like, for example, if my parents had not conceived me just when they did, but had rather waited another year before deciding to have another child, would the child which was born a year later have been me? Was that precise moment of conception an essential element in forming me into the person I am? If they had conceived a child later, or earlier, could they have conceived a girl rather than a boy? Was it absolutely necessary for them to conceive a child exactly when they did for that child to be me?

I guess the bottom-line question I am asking is simply this: do things, like the birth of a child, or the place of that birth, or the sex of the child, or what that child grows up to be - do all those things happen by chance? Was it by chance that I was born to Walter and Evelyn Stewart on March 5, 1952? Was that a mere coincidence? And was it by chance that Teresa Anne Harrington was born on January 26, 1955? Then, was it by chance that we met, were married, and have been blessed with three children and six grandchildren?

Is it by chance that we now reside in Fort Mill, SC? Is it by chance that we are now employed by Carowinds, an amusement park straddling the NC/SC state line? Do things happen by chance, or is there some determinative, causal force behind it all? Or, to keep things in alignment with the thesis of this book, is there a providential aspect of these events? Was God actively involved in each of the foregoing events in my life, or did they happen by chance?

We all probably have known a couple, or at least known about a couple, who were married, and a while later began trying to start a family by having their first child. Let's suppose this couple had hoped that they would have their first child within two years of their wedding. Those first two years come and go, and no child. Years three and four, and then five and six, pass, with no success in conceiving a child. They begin going to fertility specialists, who perform tests, trying to determine why they are unable to conceive.

After all the tests are run, it is determined that there is no identifiable medical reason for their inability to conceive a child. But still, they are unsuccessful in their attempts. Finally, they decide to adopt, which they do. Their adopted child is a healthy eighteen-month-old girl, whom they love dearly.

Soon after the adoption is finalized, the couple discover that they have, after all those years, been successful in conceiving a child of their own. They had given up any hope of ever having a child, but now they have two: the adopted daughter, and their soon-to-be-born baby boy.

Was all this by chance? Was it coincidence that things turned out the way they did? Or was there a guiding principle, an invisible hand of providence, that orchestrated these events, and brought them all to pass at just the right time, in just the right place, and including just the right people? Many would say that these events were just chance happenings with no other explanation needed. But maybe there are other dynamics at work in a realm that is invisible to the physical eye.

The story of John the Baptist would certainly lead us to believe that providence was at work in his birth, life and ministry. Maybe by looking at his story we can find principles that will help us better understand events such as the ones described in the hypothetical story above.

This may sound like nothing more than a lot of philosophical wranglings to some, but the fact of the matter is these are questions most of us ponder at times. The simple form of these questions may be nothing more than the age-old philosophical puzzle pertaining to life. What is life? Why am I here? Where am I going? Is there life after this life? And then out of those simple, basic questions others arise, like, not only why am I here; but why am I here *now*? And not only why am I me; but why am I not someone else?

This is another of those potholes of enormous proportion. It is a pothole that most of us probably fall into at some point in our lives. Some don't stay there very long, thinking that the questions are not important enough to ponder. Others find that they get trapped in this pothole, never finding a way of escape. It is a philosophical pothole. We will call it simply the pothole of personal perplexity. The pothole of trying to figure out all the puzzles of life. The "who am I and why am I here" pothole.

John the Baptist is one who must have been convinced that he was born in the wrong time. He was a man who must have felt as if he should have been born many years earlier than he was. He must have felt, as he began to grow toward adulthood, that his beliefs, his convictions, and even his calling from God, would have fit so much better in a day gone by. He found that he was not like other men. He discovered that his ideas were old fashioned and antiquated when compared to many of the beliefs of his day. He found that he was always butting heads with the religious elite. Those who were supposed to be the spiritual leaders of his people were actually leading them in ways contrary to the ways of God. And he found himself standing toe to toe with these religious leaders, calling them to repentance for their wickedness.

John was born at a crucial time in history. It was a time of spiritual bankruptcy, and religious callousness. He was born in a time when the voice of God had been silent for several hundreds of years. The people of his beloved nation, Israel, were languishing in spiritual darkness and political turmoil. There had not been a prophetic voice for over four hundred years. The religious leaders were enforcing legalistic demands on the people. There was ongoing tension between the Pharisees, the extremely legalistic faction of Judaism, and the Sadducees, the more liberal faction. This added to the demoralization of the people. There was a spirit of religious and political confusion among the people of Israel.

It was into this climate that John was born. His parents had prayed many years for a child to be born to them, but seemingly, their prayers had not evoked a positive response from the heart of God. His answer to their many petitions must have seemed to them to be, "No!" But, they would find out that God's answer was not, "No," but rather "Wait."

The biblical record informs us that John's parents were both advanced in years, well past the age of childbearing. We could probably safely assume from that observation that they had long ago ceased praying for a child. They had probably resigned themselves to the fact that they would die childless. This would be a natural conclusion to draw since they were far past the age that a couple would expect to conceive and have a child.

However, it was in this time of advanced age that God broke through, blessed them with a child, and promised them that this child would be great in the sight of the Lord. The parents were also informed that this child would turn many hearts toward God. These must have been exciting words to the aged couple. But it must have also brought them a sense of concern as this message would have led them to have questions about how a child born to them could ever prove to be great in God's eyes.

The parent's names were Zacharias and Elizabeth. The son was given the name John. And truly, if there was ever a man who must have felt as if he were born out of time and out of place, John must have been that man.

John fills an interesting and unique role in biblical history. When you consider his God-appointed mission and ministry, it is clear that he was an Old Testament prophet who lived in the New Testament era. He was in the lineage of the Old Testament prophets, being one who was pointing toward the coming Messiah. But unlike any of his predecessors, he was actually contemporary with the One to whom he was pointing. It was in his time that heaven invaded earth – that God became man – that eternity came into time.

It was this man's tremendous joy and privilege to be the one to announce the coming of Jesus. It was his great honor to point to Him and say, "Behold, the Lamb of God who takes away the sin of the world." But in so doing, it was also his overwhelming responsibility to call a generation to repentance. His was a most trying ministry as he was called by God to point people to Jesus, while at the same time confronting the religious leaders of his generation about their hypocrisy.

He had to stand in opposition to the liberals of his day, who were living lives which stood in stark contrast to the teachings of God's Word. They were the ones who denied the existence of angels, and the reality of an afterlife. They were also the ones who denied the resurrection of the dead, believing that this life was all that existed.

He had to also stand in the face of those legalists of his day, who were twisting the Scriptures, putting heavy burdens on the people. They were the ones who placed extreme pressure on the people to live up to the man-made law which consisted of minuscule mandates which had been developed by religious leaders, and not derived from the law of God.

John literally found himself standing between these two opposing factions of Judaism, while opposing both. It was a ministry that caused him to be hated by both of these religious factions. Everything about John made him stand out from the religious elite of his day. He didn't fit in with any group, with any segment of Jewish life. He was literally on his own.

We know very little about John's childhood and youth. Luke records an interesting bit of information about him, but leaves so much to be desires in our knowledge of him. It actually raises more questions than it supplies answers. But it does offer some insight into who John was, and a small picture into his personal development.

> So the child grew and became strong in spirit, and
> was in the deserts till the day of his manifestation
> to Israel.
>
> (Luke 1:80)

He grew strong in spirit. Is this to be understood in the sense of his spiritual well-being, or of his physical well-being? It is obvious that he grew strong in the things of the Lord, as this would be necessary to fulfill the calling of God on his life. It would take a spiritually strong man to stand in the face of the extreme opposition he would endure. It could also be a reference to his physical well-being, as he obviously showed a lot of strength in standing against those who would oppose him.

Another reference to John, and particularly a reference to his ministry, is found in Mark's Gospel.

> John came baptizing in the wilderness and
> preaching a baptism of repentance for the remission
> of sins.
>
> (Mark 1:4)

Two things of interest should be noted from this verse. First, John was involved in a ministry of baptism. This is interesting because the people of Israel saw no need for baptism. They were, after all, the children of God. Why, then, would they need to be baptized? Baptism was offered to Gentiles who chose to embrace the Jewish faith. Once they had made the decision to convert to Judaism, they would be baptized to show identification with their newly professed faith. However, a natural born Jew would see no need to be baptized.

Second, John preached a baptism of repentance. Again, they would see no need in this as they understood repentance to be something Gentiles needed, not natural born Jews. These two things would have caused his Jewish audience to become even more agitated with him and the message he preached.

Also, from all outward appearances John would be viewed as strange. His clothing was camel's hair and his diet consisted of locusts and wild honey.

> Now John was clothed with camel's hair and with a leather belt around his waist, and he ate locusts and wild honey.
>
> (Mark 1:6)

It sounds reasonably clear from these attestations that John perceived himself to be in the lineage of the OT prophets, as these are not mere coincidental similarities that he shared with them. This, also, would have been an irritant to his audience as they would be reminded of the messages calling for repentance preached by the prophets of the Old Testament era. From the testimony of the verses cited above it is reasonably clear that the people would have clearly identified John with prophets of God from preceding generations.

But who did John perceive himself to be? When asked if he were the Christ, or Elijah, or some of the other prophets, his simple answer was that he was the voice of one crying in the wilderness, calling people to prepare the way of the Lord. His message consisted of a warning of impending judgment, and a call to repentance so as to escape that judgment. Clearly, his was a message in alignment with that of the Old Testament prophets.

So again, I would submit that John was a man who probably thought of himself as being born in the right place, but at the wrong time.

And now, let's go back to the questions I posed at the outset. Why am I here? Why am I here now? Why am I me and not someone else? What is the meaning of life in general, and of my life in particular?

Let me preface my answer to these questions by first asserting that I am not a medical doctor. I do not know the intricacies of human conception and pre-natal development, and neither do I understand all that is involved in the different stages of development we all go through as we grow toward adulthood. But there are a few observations I think we can make from studying the case of John.

First, we can learn from John's conception in the womb of Elizabeth that God is intimately involved in the conception of every child. In the case of John, his parents had prayed many long years for the birth of a child. For whatever the reason, God withheld a positive response to their prayer until His own appointed time. It is interesting to note what the angel said to John's parents when he came with God's message that Zacharias and Elizabeth would have a son. The angel announced that God had heard their prayers, that they would have a son, and that they should name this son John. This teaches us that God was involved in the conception of this child in the most intimate of ways. John was who he was by the direct supervision of God.

There is an extremely interesting aside here: When did they pray? Undoubtedly many years earlier they had ceased to pray, having long since passed the age of childbearing. But the angel announces that God had heard their prayers as if they had prayed it in their quiet time that morning. Now I realize that it is possible that Zacharias and Elizabeth were still praying for a child, but I tend to believe that they were not. So, when did God hear their prayer? When they prayed it, of course! But in His own time, and according to His own will, He sovereignly appointed for this godly couple to have a child in their old age, and he saw to it that they did.

The fact that this happened with Zacharias and Elizabeth should give hope to those couples who have been trying to have a child with no success. It is possible that God has answered your prayers in the same way that he answered theirs. Perhaps His answer to you so far is not a simple no, but rather it is that you should continue to wait and trust. This is not a guarantee that things will turn out the same way for you as they did for them, but it certainly gives hope that there is a possibility that God has other plans. Therefore, continue to pray, seeking God's intervention. But also give Him praise for the outcome He chooses.

There is a second wonderful truth we can glean from this. John was not born out of time, but rather he was born at exactly the right time – the time God appointed. If there are any of us who feel that we might have fared better in another historical era, then remember the case of John – an Old Testament prophet in the New Testament era. He was who he was, and he lived when he did, by the sovereign plan of God.

And then a third observation we can make is that he was where he was by God's divine appointment. John wasn't born in Africa, or Egypt, or Arabia, or anywhere other than the place God appointed him to be born. Have you ever wondered why you were born where you were born? I assume that most who will read this book were born in the United States. For those who were, have you ever wondered why God gave you the opportunity to be reared in a country in which you have religious freedom, where you can worship God without fear of extreme forms of persecution? You are where you are according to His plans and purposes.

So, what is the point? The point is simply that you are who you are, you are where you are, and you are what you are, by the divine appointment of God. He has been intimately involved in your life at every level: conception, pre-natal development, birth, infancy, adolescence, youth, young adulthood, median adulthood, senior adulthood. Your life is not a meaningless span of disjoined events, but your life is a beautiful tapestry of God. He is weaving it as He sees fit.

And He would have us accept our lot in life as part of His plans for us. He brings things into our personal experience which He will then use for His glory. And in it all, He always works for the good of those who love Him.

Since we can learn from the life of John the Baptist that we were not born out of time and out of place, we should pray diligently that God would make us more aware of why we were born when we were and where we were. He has things for us to do here and now. And there is so much that needs to be done. It takes each of us doing our part in the kingdom's work. Let's be faithful in serving Him where we are and with the gifts, talents and abilities He has given us.

QUESTIONS FOR THOUGHT AND DISCUSSION

1. Did you find the author's "philosophical wranglings" amusing, or thought-provoking? Explain your answer.
2. Have you ever given serious thought to the philosophical questions, "who am I", and "why am I here"?
3. The prayer of Zacharias and Elizabeth was answered, and John was born. What can we learn about prayer from their experience?
4. Have you ever had an answer to a specific prayer "delayed" as it was with Zacharias and Elizabeth? Write down the specifics of that experience, then share the story with a friend or family member.
5. God has certain things for each individual Christian to do in His kingdom's work. We are who we are and where we are for reasons He has providentially planned. How would you explain your understanding of this concept?

CHAPTER 14

NICODEMUS

The Pothole of Religion

There was a man of the Pharisees named Nicodemus, a ruler of the Jews. This man came to Jesus by night and said to Him, "Rabbi, we know that You are a teacher come from God; for no one can do these signs that You do unless God is with him."

(John 3:1–2)

S ome potholes are so pronounced and obvious that you can't miss them. They are so big, and black, and ugly, and ominous, that you would have to be blind to let it sneak up on you. It is relatively easy to steer clear of those potholes: all we must do is to keep our eyes on the road ahead, and we can maneuver around those glaring potholes with ease.

However, there are other potholes which are not so easy to detect. There are those which are concealed in a blind spot in the road, and before you know it, you are on top of it - and in it - before you know what hit you, or more accurately, what you hit. Others are sometimes filled with water, and as you drive along, the pothole is completely out of sight because the water in the hole doesn't allow you to see the danger ahead. And then others are sometimes concealed by that hallucinatory heat rising off the road, and before you know it, you are in a pothole that was not visible just a split second before you hit it.

That's life: some of the potholes along life's highways and byways are out there in open view, and for the observant passerby who watches carefully, these potholes can be missed with ease. However, it is oftentimes those which are hidden from sight that catch us. And it is oftentimes those which are conspicuously concealed that do the most harm.

So it is with the pothole considered in this chapter. It is not difficult to find someone in this particular pothole. As a matter of fact, I would venture a guess that six or seven out of every ten people you see are caught in this pothole. Myriad is the number of those who are trapped in the tenacious grip of this deceiving pothole, and the sad reality is that most of them never even realize it.

The Bible is filled with persons who are in this pothole. It is difficult to turn to any book in all the Bible and not find a person trapped, and many of them destroyed, by this pothole. So was a certain individual with whom Jesus came into contact during His three-year ministry. He was a good man - some would even say that he was a godly man. He was the kind of neighbor everyone would want. He had gone to all the right schools, had rubbed shoulders with all the right people, had made contacts with all the right individuals who could help him attain his goals in life. He was respected in the community; looked up to by everyone; envied by most. He was respected as a civic leader; and revered as a spiritual leader. He had risen through the ranks, eventually becoming one of an elite group of seventy men, called the Sanhedrin, the rulers of Israel. When parents would see him on the streets, they would probably bend and whisper in the ears of their children, "Look, there goes a good and godly man. I hope that you will be like him when you are grown." Respected. Revered. Envied. All these are apt words of description for this man.

We find his story in John's Gospel. His name was Nicodemus. His pothole was religion. His dilemma was that he was trapped in a religious system which taught rules of righteousness, and which advocated a system of redemption through ritual. To use our contemporary terminology, he was lost. However, the tragedy of his condition was that he didn't know that he was lost. He thought everything was fine between him and the Lord. He thought that surely, if anyone was a member of the kingdom of God, he was certainly one.

As John weaves this important story for his readers, he reveals a few details about Nicodemus which should be carefully considered. He reveals that Nicodemus was a Pharisee. This was an extremely elitist group to which only a limited few could belong. There were never more than 6000 Pharisees at any one time. Pharisees were rigorously religious. Their 'religion' was based primarily on the law of God. However, the written law was not enough for them. They also advocated an unwritten, oral, law, which had been passed down by their forefathers. They were strict observers of the letter of the law, actually going so far as to divide the law up into over 600 precepts. In some ways this was a tedious task for them, and an even more tedious task for those who tried to live up to these hundreds of laws. However, in another way, it was liberating, at least to some degree. If you could live up to their manmade laws, then you were religious, even righteous. But it was an external form of righteousness that Jesus consistently unveiled and denounced.

We can know that Nicodemus was an extremely religious man, and also an outwardly righteous man, simply by knowing that he was a Pharisee. But John weaves more into his story. He tells us also that Nicodemus was a member of the Sanhedrin. As already mentioned, this was the ruling body of Israel. In Jesus' day, their influence was not as great as it had been at other times in Israel's history, but they were still an impressively powerful group of men who gave leadership in matters pertaining to the law, both religious and civil.

So, we know that this was no ordinary Nick off the streets of Jerusalem who is paying Jesus a visit. He is a man who has earned the respect of his peers.

John then informs his readers of the details of Nicodemus' visit with Jesus, and again it is obvious that he is a religious man simply by listening to his words. He approaches Jesus with an obvious respect as he addresses Jesus as Rabbi. This was a term of respect, describing one who is a teacher of others. Then. Nicodemus makes the rather astounding observation that he knows Jesus has come from God. This assertion was extremely strange coming from the mouth of one who is a member of an elitist group that has consistently denounced Jesus as being a fraud. However, attention should be given to the fact that this assertion is based on the things Jesus has done. Surely, there can be no question about the fact that Nicodemus was an extremely religious man who was sincerely searching for truth.

The sad reality is, however, that religion was his downfall. He was chained in the shackles of religion. His ideas about God, and his conception of God's kingdom, were tainted by his misconceptions concerning what real religion was all about. He had come to embrace a philosophy of life which was based on works righteousness. He had a visible list of rules and regulations which in itself was the entirety of his religious system of belief. He felt that if he did the right things, prayed the right prayers, said the right words, involved himself in the right activities, then by doing that he was most certainly a member of the kingdom of God. He found his self-worth in what he did rather than in who he was. But more importantly, he based his eternal destiny on what he did rather than on who he was. Somehow this good man had fallen prey to the age-old tendency of man which leads us to think that we are capable of making restitution between self and God on the basis of what we can do.

Jesus is about to teach Nicodemus a lesson that he will never forget. Jesus is about to blow away Nicodemus' nice, comfortable, philosophical/theological system of thought, belief, and practice. Jesus is about to confront Nicodemus with the truth. Truth that will not necessarily be pleasing to the ears of one of his stature. But truth, none the less.

Jesus just seems to skirt around all the pleasantries of the moment. He doesn't even acknowledge the compliments which Nicodemus lavishes on Him. Jesus just simply goes straight to the heart of the matter - and, more importantly, right to the heart of Nicodemus - with the assertion that unless a man is born again he cannot see the kingdom of God.

> Jesus answered and said to him, "Most assuredly, I say to you, unless one is born again, he cannot see the kingdom of God." Nicodemus said to Him, "How can a man be born when he is old? Can he enter a second time into this mother's womb and be born?"
>
> (John 3:4)

What a crushing blow this must have been to the ego of this religious giant. He had dedicated his life to teaching the law of God. He had studied for years under the tutelage of the great teachers of his day, and now he was one of those teachers to whom others turned for instruction. He had now attained the position of Pharisee, and to the rank of that elite group called the Sanhedrin. He knew the law of God, and he knew the God of the law. At least, he thought he did.

You can almost hear the shock and consternation in his voice as you read his astonished reply: "How can a man be born when he is old? Can he enter a second time into his mother's womb and be born?"

We have to realize that this reply is far more than an outcry of shock and amazement. We must understand that with this statement, Jesus has just blown away everything Nicodemus has ever believed. He has given his life, and staked his eternal destination, to a legalistic observance of the letter of the law. Everything he has been taught and has now taught others is based on what man can do for God. And now, Jesus informs him that you don't see the kingdom of God by what you do for Him, but by what He has done for us.

Indeed, Nicodemus is in a pothole of perplexity. He is confused, puzzled, over this strange thing Jesus has spoken. And the reality is that there are countless people, just like Nicodemus, alive today. Multitudes have bought into the same belief system. Countless throngs have sold themselves out to this religious mentality. So many have been deceived by religious systems that teach the heresy of works righteousness. And so many are now placing their faith in what they have done for God, rather than embracing the amazing work of salvation Jesus has provided.

Might I name just a few? Jehovah's Witnesses have certainly bought into this system. Do you know any Jehovah's Witnesses? If you do, then you know some of the most rigorously religious people you will ever meet. They adhere dogmatically to their doctrine. They live by the principles they are taught by their teachers in the kingdom hall. They are religious through and through. If religious fervor and activity could save anyone, then members of this religious sect would most certainly be saved. If works could save, then by all means those who embrace the teachings of the kingdom hall could rest assured in their standing with God.

Members of the Church of Jesus Christ of Latter-Day Saints (Mormons) are also extremely religious people. Morally upright. Ethically sound. Men and women of integrity. Men and women who have committed themselves wholeheartedly to their religion. But again, it is a religion of works. It has a place in its teachings for Jesus, but not the Jesus of the Bible. Jesus, according to the Bible, is the Second Person of the Trinity, very God of very God, the Savior of the World. He is the only means of salvation for lost man. He gave His life as the sacrificial Lamb of God, who made it possible for sinful man to be reconciled to God. But, according to Mormon teaching, Jesus is not the only name under heaven whereby men might be saved, as the Bible teaches. Rather, Jesus is an example, showing us that we might become sons of God just as Jesus is. And please understand, according to Mormonism, Jesus is not the eternal Son of God who takes away the sin of the world. Therefore, the Mormon church teaches heresy, a religious system that places emphasis on what man can do for God, and not on what God has done for man.

There are so many false religions in the world, most of which teach a legalistic system of works. By performing these works, an individual can earn a relationship with God. But again, the Bible teaches that no one can be saved by works. It is only through the completed work of Christ that we have hope of an eternal home in heaven.

We could go on and on listing these cultic groups which are known by their works righteousness philosophy of life. But there are others who have bought into this same system who are a little closer to home. If you think really hard, you may realize that you know some Baptists, or Methodists, or Presbyterians, or Episcopalians, or Catholics, who would fit into this same category. When we superimpose a list of rules and regulations upon ourselves and begin to think that we will be right with God when we do all these things, and when we don't do certain other things, then we have become just like Nicodemus. One doesn't have to be a member of a religious sect whose religion is based upon the works of the individual to be like Nicodemus. All one has to do is believe that they can attain a right relationship with God by what they can do for Him, not by what He has done for them.

It is so much more comfortable to think that we can do something in and of ourselves to attain entrance into the kingdom of God. It gives us a feeling of self-importance, of self-exaltation, of self-righteousness, to think that we play a part in our salvation experience.

Now, let's bring it as close to home as possible. Some of us reading this chapter have probably bought into this philosophy of life. Some of us are probably guilty of finding our self-worth in what we do for God. It gives us a feeling of self-satisfaction to think about what we have done for God, and how pleased He must be with us.

Nicodemus could have probably stood there for hours recounting to Jesus all the things he had done for God. He could have given testimony to a life of righteousness, to a life committed to God and the things of God. But that would have been to no avail. Jesus said on another occasion that unless our righteousness exceeds that of the Scribes and the Pharisees, we would not enter the kingdom of God. Nicodemus was a Pharisee, so this would have definitely been a spiritual slap in the face to him. How could anyone's righteousness exceed a Pharisee's righteousness? They were, after all, the most righteous of all Jews! But were they really righteous? Living up to a man-made list of rules and regulations does not make one righteous. But Nicodemus, along with countless others throughout human history, have been taught to think otherwise.

Obeying a self-imposed, or even a church-imposed, list of rules and regulations, is to no avail. Being religious is to no avail. Doing, doing, doing, is to no avail. No amount of work, no number of righteous deeds, no amount of charitable contributions, no amount of fervent prayers, no amount of pious singing, no amount of anything, will gain us entrance into God's wonderful presence.

Nicodemus, along with anyone else who thinks their righteousness will gain them entrance into heaven should be reminded of a few sobering truths presented in scripture. The following verses are only a sampling of many which state clearly that man cannot be good enough, or do enough good things, to measure up to God's standard of righteousness. Read these verses slowly and carefully, letting the words sink deeply into your mind and heart:

> But we are all like an unclean thing, and all our righteousnesses are like filthy rags; we all fade as a leaf, and our iniquities, like the wind, have taken us away.
>
> (Isaiah 64:6)

> The Lord looks down from heaven upon the children of men, to see if there are any who understand, who seek God. They have all turned aside, they have together become corrupt; there is none who does good, no, not one.
>
> (Psalm 14:2–3)

> There is none righteous, no, not one; there is none who understands; there is none who seeks after God. They have all turned aside; they have together become unprofitable; there is none who does good, no, not one.
>
> (Romans 3:10–12)

Nicodemus, being an expert in the law, would have been familiar with the verses from Psalms and Isaiah. He should have known that these verses applied to every person who has ever lived, with the one exception of Jesus. He should have known that he, personally, was one of whom it could be said that his righteousness was as filthy rags before God. But sadly, it is obvious that he did not recognize himself in these verses. He thought that he was a member of the family of God with a home reserved in heaven for him because of who he was and what he had done.

Jesus was saying to Nicodemus, and to us, that religion is a real killer. You think you are doing good, doing right, working righteousness, earning a place in His eternal kingdom, when in reality you are only digging your own eternal grave. Pay careful attention to these sobering words spoken by Jesus:

> Many will say to Me in that day, "Lord, Lord, have we not prophesied in Your name, cast out demons in Your name, and done many wonders in Your name?" And then I will declare to them, "I never knew you; depart from Me, you who practice lawlessness!"
>
> (Matthew 7:22–23)

Note carefully what Jesus describes as lawlessness: prophesying, casting out demons, and performing wonders. In other words, doing things for God will not gain entrance to God. And even more profoundly Jesus says He never knew them. There are multitudes who claim to know Him, but that is not the point. People of all backgrounds, of all ethnicities, of all religious beliefs and practices, know about Jesus. But does Jesus know them?

Of course, in a general sense Jesus knows everyone. He is, after all, the second Person of the Holy Trinity. Being very God of very God means that He has all the attributes and characteristics of God. This includes the attribute of omniscience. He knows all things, which would include knowing everybody. It is not this general sense of knowing that Jesus is referring to here.

Rather it is that special, familial knowledge. He doesn't know them as part of the family of God. They have never been born again into the family through faith in the saving work of Jesus. Thus, even though they claim to know Jesus, it is only knowing about Him, and not knowing Him through the experience of salvation.

If you are caught in this terrible pothole, then please hear the admonition of Jesus to be born again. Cast yourself wholly on His grace. Acknowledge that you need Him for your salvation. And place your trust in Him as your Savior. Religion is not the answer. A relationship with God through Jesus Christ is our only hope.

QUESTIONS FOR THOUGHT AND DISCUSSION

1. How would you explain the pothole of religion to someone?
2. Do you know of anyone who is trapped in this pothole?
3. If you answered yes to #2, what might you do to help them get out of this pothole?
4. Do you think Jesus really meant it when He said that He was "the way, the truth, and the life", and that no one could come to the Father except through Him?
5. If you answered yes to #4, how can you share this information with others, especially with those who are caught in the pothole of religion?
6. Why do you think it is so appealing to believe that the things we can do for God will attain for us entrance into heaven?

CHAPTER 15

JEWISH BRIDE AND GROOM

The Pothole of Procrastination

Then the kingdom of heaven shall be likened to ten virgins who took their lamps and went out to meet the bridegroom. Now five of them were wise, and five *were* foolish. Those who *were* foolish took their lamps and took no oil with them, but the wise took oil in their vessels with their lamps. But while the bridegroom was delayed, they all slumbered and slept.

(Matthew 25:1–5)

There is nothing more beautiful and touching than the pomp and ceremony of a Jewish wedding. In Jesus' day, it was an elaborate affair which consisted of many different phases. The following is the story of a first century Jewish wedding, and if you listen closely, you might be able to detect another story within the story.

> (This story is adapted from a live presentation by Zola Levitt. Zola referred to himself as a "completed Jew". Before passing away several years ago, his ministry was designed to reach people, Jew and Gentile, with the saving message of Jesus Christ. He told the story of a Jewish wedding while leading in a Passover demonstration.)

In order to appreciate these details of a first century Jewish wedding, we need to first of all strive to mentally separate ourselves from the modern-day concept of dating and marriage. There was no such thing as dating in first century Jerusalem. There was nothing remotely close to what we think of as a young man courting a young woman. The wedding between a Jewish man and woman was based upon a contract, or a covenant, rather than on the trial and error our young people go through in the dating game deciding whom they will marry. A young Jewish male would decide which Jewish girl he wanted to marry (or his father would decide for him!), and he would then approach the young woman with a contract of marriage. This contract was a binding legal document which stipulated the terms of the marriage agreement. Included in this covenant was the 'bride price', which was the price the groom was willing to pay to marry this particular bride.

After the young man had made his offer, the woman and her father would then consider the contract. If the terms were suitable, the bride and groom would then drink a cup of wine together which was a sign that the contract had now been accepted and sealed. This seal did two important things. First, it signified that the bridegroom was willing to pay the price for his bride; and second, it signified that the bride was willing to enter the marriage relationship.

Once the contract had been settled, the groom would then depart. As he departed, he would say something to the effect that he was now going to prepare a place for the two of them. Having said that, he would leave, going to his father's house where he would begin the process of building their honeymoon suite. Sometimes this building project would take several months, as the young man would do his best to build a suitable honeymoon suite for his bride.

An interesting thing about this building project is that it would be under the supervision and final judgment of the father of the groom. This really makes sense when you think about it. If the young man was left to build it alone with no supervision, he would probably throw together a grass shack and rush back for his bride. But that wasn't the case. Instead, the young man could not return for his bride until his father told him to. In other words, the day of the consummation of the marital relationship was left to the discretion of the father. It was only when he gave final approval to the building of the wedding chamber that he allowed his son to return for his bride.

So what was the bride doing all this time? In a word: waiting! Oh, she would be busy getting prepared for the day her groom returned to take her to the honeymoon suite, but for the most part she waited. According to Jewish custom and tradition, the bride and her maids were to have oil lamps ready just in case the groom was to come in the middle of the night. First century Jerusalem did not have the luxury of streetlights to guide the way in the darkness. The roads were often filled with potholes and ruts made by the flow of rainwater, and anyone who tried to walk those roads in darkness was in danger of being severely injured. The bride and her maids were to have their lamps trimmed and filled with oil, ready to be off at a moment's notice.

All during this period of waiting, the bride was considered consecrated, or set apart, or bought with a price. She was a lady in waiting, having been paid for by her bridegroom. The price he had paid guaranteed that he would return for his bride. She didn't know exactly when, but she had no doubt that he would come for her. After all, he had paid a rather high price to have her for his bride.

So, the bride would busy herself making sure that she was ready for the return of her groom. And the groom all the while was keeping himself busy preparing that bridal chamber. If by chance one of his friends would pass by the bridal chamber and ask, "When's the big day?", the groom would reply, "Only my father knows the day."

Finally, after all these weeks, or perhaps even months of building and preparing, the father would inspect the bridal chamber one last time. If it met his approval he would finally say to the son, "It's time to get your bride!" All the anticipation which had been building up over those long months was about to be relieved. The groom and his friends would set out for the bride's father's home. More often than not this would be done in the middle of the night, as the groom would make every effort to surprise the bride at a time she didn't expect him. This just added to the romance and excitement of the entire event. The bride would literally be stolen from her father's house. As the young men would make their approach to the house, one of them would be assigned the duty to give a loud shout announcing the arrival of the bridegroom.

All the young maids in the bridal party would be prepared as well, with their lamps trimmed and ready for the shout of the groom's party. Or at least they should be prepared. However, Jesus told a story about a Jewish wedding, and all the participants were not prepared.

> Then the kingdom of heaven shall be likened to ten
> virgins who took their lamps and went out to meet

the bridegroom. Now five of them were wise, and five *were* foolish. Those who *were* foolish took their lamps and took no oil with them, but the wise took oil in their vessels with their lamps. But while the bridegroom was delayed, they all slumbered and slept.

And at midnight a cry was *heard:* "Behold, the bridegroom is coming; go out to meet him!" Then all those virgins arose and trimmed their lamps. And the foolish said to the wise, "Give us *some* of your oil, for our lamps are going out." But the wise answered, saying, *"No,* lest there should not be enough for us and you; but go rather to those who sell, and buy for yourselves." And while they went to buy, the bridegroom came, and those who were ready went in with him to the wedding; and the door was shut.

Afterward the other virgins came also, saying, "Lord, Lord, open to us!" But he answered and said, "Assuredly, I say to you, I do not know you."

Watch therefore, for you know neither the day nor the hour in which the Son of Man is coming.
(Matthew 25:1–13)

There we have it: the pothole of procrastination. The pothole of putting off till tomorrow what we could have done today. The pothole of waiting, waiting, waiting, when we know the deadline is fast approaching.

We see it in all areas of life, don't we? We see it in the lives of our children. Those of us who have been blessed to have children know this all too well. Children are experts at procrastination. Give them a task, and more often than not it will not get done by the expected time. They get sidetracked with so many important things, like finishing the chapter in the book they are reading, or watching the TV program until it goes off, or finishing the game they are playing, or the phone call they are on, or, or, or... So many things take precedence, and before long they have forgotten all about the assignment.

We see it in the lives of our spouses. Like the husband who is reminded of a task his wife has asked him to complete, and he responds by saying, "I know, I know! You don't have to keep reminding every week or two!" We all have deadlines to complete the assignment, to finish the project, and yet we often put it off until tomorrow.

And yes, if we look closely enough, we will probably detect at least a degree of procrastination in that person we see staring back at us in the reflection of a mirror. The grass hasn't been cut, the car hasn't been washed, the garage hasn't been cleaned out.

In Jesus' story, He says that those who procrastinate are foolish. Eventually, the deadline will arrive, and it will catch us off guard and unprepared if we continue to procrastinate. It happens to all of us on occasion.

We all remember school deadlines, don't we? We remember that on the very first day of the semester, the professor gives an assignment, and we look at the due date and immediately say to ourselves, 'Boy, that paper isn't due until July 15! This is only June 1. I don't have to worry about that for a while!' And then, the next time you think about it is, you guessed it, July 14. The deadline has caught up with us. Time has flown. The project is due. And we are unprepared.

Every year, millions of Americans procrastinate at different times. Over ten million persons buy Valentine's Day cards on, you guessed it, Valentine's Day. We see them every year on April 15, as the hands of the clock approach midnight. There they are, scurrying to the post office, so their tax returns will be dated no later than midnight on April 15. Assignments are left undone.

Jobs are put off for a more convenient time. Procrastination has become an American pastime.

What do you think causes procrastination? Why do so many of us find ourselves so often in this frustrating pothole? The excuses offered are a dime a dozen! There are far too many to even try to begin making an exhaustive list. Let me suggest a just few possible causes of procrastination.

First, and probably most obvious, is laziness. We have an assignment to fulfill, a task to complete, and we know that it is not due for a few more days, and we are just plain lazy. We don't want to do it until we absolutely must do it. This doesn't mean that the person who does this is habitually lazy. He may be extremely energetic – a real go-getter. In most cases he is on top of the task. But on occasion, when he has an activity that needs to be done – one which he is not crazy about doing – he can sometimes get lazy. He just doesn't want to do the job.

Another possible cause of procrastination is inconvenience. We may have a job to do, and we might convince ourselves that it just isn't a convenient time to do it. So, we put it off until a more convenient time, like a minute till midnight on April 15, or the night before the big paper is due, or scurrying around looking for an appropriate Valentine's Day card on Valentine's Day. Yes, it is much more convenient to do it as the deadline approaches, with all the frustration and aggravation that causes, than to do it at a more appropriate and opportune time.

A third possible cause of procrastination is rebellion. Rebellion is a form of disobedience, and when we have an assigned duty which we fail to keep, then we have been disobedient to those in authority over us. A parent tells a child to wash the dishes, but the child was angry at the parent for not giving them permission to visit a friend's house. So, the child "punishes" the parent by not doing the dishes. Or the parent tells the child to take out the trash, but instead he piles it on the back porch. Why? Because he was upset at his parents for not allowing him to stay up late to watch the football game. Adults sometimes procrastinate in rebellion against their employer for a multitude of possible reasons.

Sometimes, procrastination is merely a cause of personal frustration or aggravation. Like when we don't cut the grass for a long period of time. Then, when we finally decide to cut it we find that it is much more difficult to accomplish than it would have been had we done it earlier. Or, when we have that assignment to finish for our professors, it is a matter of aggravation when we must stay up all night the night before it is due just to get it done.

Other times, however, procrastination is much more serious than that. Take, for instance, the story Jesus tells of the wedding feast. He says that those who were foolish, and who had procrastinated in preparing themselves for the coming of the groom, were shut out of the wedding feast. This procrastination proved to be eternally destructive, as these were not prepared for the coming of the Lord.

We find a story of this type of procrastination in the Bible. In the Book of Acts there is the story of a certain king named Felix. When the apostle Paul confronted him with the claims off the Gospel, Felix told him to go away and come back at a more convenient time. His procrastination was eternally foolish.

There are those who play this game with eternity. They say things like, "I will accept Christ one day, but not today." But they know not the day or the hour when they will be called to give account of themselves before the Lord.

So how do we overcome procrastination? We need to understand that it is a continual, lifelong battle, but we can be overcomers. Let me suggest a few possible remedies which can be implemented in our lives to help us overcome this pothole.

First, I would suggest that we be people of commitment. When we have acquired a position, or have been assigned a duty, or have accepted a responsibility, which makes demands on us to accomplish certain things by certain deadlines, then we need to make a commitment to fulfill the challenge. This may be an assignment at school, or at the office, or at home. The place is irrelevant. The commitment is essential. As Christians, we should take our responsibilities very seriously, as everything we do is a direct reflection on Jesus Christ. We should strive to do all that we do for God's glory. This would include how we handle our responsibilities without procrastination.

Second, I would suggest that we develop accountability partners, with whom we would share our commitments. Make them aware of any deadlines we have to meet, or any responsibilities we have to fulfill. Then, ask them to lovingly check up on us on occasion to make sure that we are holding true to our commitments.

And third, I would suggest that we all work hard toward organization. For some of us this comes naturally; for others, it is something we have to work diligently toward. But it is definitely worth the effort. I have always encouraged my college students to take seriously their assignments given at the first of a semester. If they were taking four courses, I would suggest that they get a calendar, and begin putting assignments on the calendar by due date. The course did not matter. Whichever was due first took priority. Start on it immediately. Then, once that one is completed go to the next. Then the next. And so on. By doing this nothing should have to be done in a mad rush the night before it is due.

And fourth, and absolutely most essential of all, is that we don't procrastinate in developing a relationship, and then maintaining fellowship, with our Lord. This takes first priority in our lives. We make appointments for other things, so why not have a standing appointment with the Lord every day for prayer and Bible reading/study? It is simply a matter of putting things in their proper order of importance.

QUESTIONS FOR THOUGHT AND DISCUSSION

1. What is the most common reason for your times of procrastination?

    a. Laziness.
    b. Inconvenience.
    c. Rebellion.

2. Have you ever experienced a problem due to procrastination?
3. The author gave several suggestions on how to guard against procrastinating. How could you use each of these to fight the tendency to procrastinate?

    a. Commitment to complete the task.
    b. Accountability partners to hold us accountable for the task.
    c. Organizing tasks according to date/time deadlines.
    d. Make personal appointments with God for daily prayer/Bible reading.

4. Keep a journal of episodes of procrastination over the next month. At the end of the month review the episodes to strive to identify the root cause of your procrastination. Come up with a plan based on the observations of this chapter to assist you in overcoming this tendency.

CHAPTER 16

MARY AND JOSEPH

The Pothole of Shame

Now the birth of Jesus Christ was as follows: After His mother Mary was betrothed to Joseph, before they came together, she was found with child of the Holy Spirit. Then Joseph her husband, being a just *man,* and not wanting to make her a public example, was minded to put her away secretly. But while he thought about these things, behold, an angel of the Lord appeared to him in a dream, saying, "Joseph, son of David, do not be afraid to take to you Mary your wife, for that which is conceived in her is of the Holy Spirit. And she will bring forth a Son, and you shall call His name JESUS, for He will save His people from their sins."

(Matthew 1:18–21)

I t is so easy to read passages of Scripture relating the facts of the birth of Jesus Christ and be so enraptured with the miraculous element of the story, or of the wonder of the birth, or of the magnitude of God's love, or of the majesty of His grace, that we just read over the human-interest story which is so clearly presented there. Of course, the focus of the story is the birth of our Savior, and we should always keep that thought central any time we read the account. However, there are other thoughts which are presented there which should be given some attention, as we can glean some wonderful truths from the text which will help us better live the Christian life.

The two accounts present us with information pertaining to the angel relaying the news to both Mary and Joseph that she will give birth to God's Son. This is remarkable news, seeing that Mary was a virgin, having never had intimate relations with a man. Jesus would be both the Son of man and the Son of God. This could only be accomplished through the miraculous virgin conception of our Lord. Actually, if we want to be absolutely correct in speaking of this matter, we should refer to it as the virgin conception. The birth took place just as any other birth. It was the conception of Jesus in the womb of Mary which was miraculous. As a matter of fact, the Roman Catholic doctrine of perpetual virginity was an outgrowth of the belief in the virgin birth. And of course, the Bible itself refutes the belief in perpetual virginity, as it speaks of Jesus' brothers and sisters who were born after His birth.

As we read these accounts, we see the reaction of both Mary and Joseph after they are made aware of this miracle which will radically change their lives. Mary responds in simple, child-like faith, as she submits herself to the will of God. It is a remarkable testimony of an individual who is willing to live a life of faith and trust in God as she contemplates the cost of accepting His will. This would be no easy path to follow for her, but she is willing to accept anything that comes her way in order to fulfill God's will for her life. The Bible records her simple yet profound acceptance of the message of God's messenger. Read these words slowly, allowing the impact of her commitment, with all of its possible ramifications, to speak directly to your heart.

> Now in the sixth month the angel Gabriel was sent by God to a city of Galilee named Nazareth, to a virgin betrothed to a man whose name was Joseph, of the house of David. The virgin's name *was* Mary. And having come in, the angel said to her, "Rejoice, highly favored *one,* the Lord *is* with you; blessed *are* you among women!"

> But when she saw *him,* she was troubled at his saying, and considered what manner of greeting this was. Then the angel said to her, "Do not be afraid, Mary, for you have found favor with God. And behold, you will conceive in your womb and bring forth a Son, and shall call His name Jesus."

> Then Mary said, "Behold the maidservant of the Lord! Let it be to me according to your word.' And the angel departed from her."
>
> (Luke 1:26–31; 38)

Mary makes a commitment that will affect her for the duration of her life. Can you imagine her having to explain being pregnant before she and Joseph had officially been married? She would carry a stigma the rest of her life of being unfaithful to Joseph. She would be ridiculed and mocked as a woman who had been unfaithful to her betrothed husband before they came together as husband and wife. This would be a horrible ordeal for this young girl to bear: a tremendous burden to carry.

And what about Joseph? How did he handle the news that his betrothed wife was pregnant? He has a right, by law, to make one of several choices. He could have Mary stoned to death, which was one of the sentences that could be carried out against a woman who had been unfaithful to her husband. Or, Joseph could have had her put to an open humiliation. But he did not choose either of these. Again, the Bible records the story of the angel appearing to Joseph with the news of Mary's pregnancy – news that will turn his world upside down.

> Then Joseph her husband, being a just *man,* and not wanting to make her a public example, was minded to put her away secretly. But while he thought about these things, behold, an angel of the Lord appeared to him in a dream, saying, "Joseph, son of David, do not be afraid to take to you Mary your wife, for that which is conceived in her is of the Holy Spirit. And she will bring forth a Son, and you shall call His name JESUS, for He will save His people from their sins."
>
> Then Joseph, being aroused from sleep, did as the angel of the Lord commanded him and took to him his wife, and did not know her till she had brought forth her firstborn Son. And he called His name JESUS.
>
> (Matthew 1:19–21; 24–25)

Joseph discovered in some undisclosed way that Mary was pregnant. Having received this news, he decides to "put her away secretly". He did not want to shame Mary any more than she was already going to be, so he took the path of least harm to her. These facts show the obvious love and affection he had for Mary. It also shows his deep concern for her, as the law would allow having her stoned to death for adultery. Joseph loved her far too deeply to allow that to happen. So, after he is informed by the angel that Mary's child was not one which had been conceived in an illicit relationship with another man, but one which had been conceived through the miraculous work of God, he makes the same choice Mary had already made. They both willingly submit themselves to this wonderful plan of God to bring His Son into the world.

The text then quietly passes over any reaction which might have resulted from this pregnancy. However, there are two words which probably could be used to describe the reaction of others toward Mary and Joseph when news spread that Mary was expecting a child before she and Joseph had been married. Those two words are shame and reproach.

Webster's Dictionary defines reproach as "to charge with a fault; to rebuke; to censure; to upbraid; to bring disgrace to; blame for something considered reprehensible; source of discredit; disgrace; object of contempt, scorn or derision."

Shame is defined as "the painful feeling arising from the consciousness of something dishonorable, improper, ridiculous, or the like done by oneself or another, or of being in a situation offensive to decency, self-respect, or pride; a fact or circumstance bringing disgrace or discredit."

Surely, this had to be a most horrible pothole for Mary and Joseph. Can you imagine the hushed whispers behind their backs? Can you imagine the sneers, the jokes, the ridicule, the mockery, they must have been subjected to? Can you imagine how their families must have felt when they heard the news? They must have been the brunt of many jokes, the focus of many cutting remarks, the center of much negative attention. They probably suffered the brunt of countless episodes of hurtful, distasteful, shame and reproach.

Even though sexual promiscuity was a common thing among the pagans of the world at the time of Jesus' birth, it was viewed as a horrible sin among the people of Israel. And, as has already been mentioned, adultery was punishable by death if the innocent party so desired. Joseph, even before he realized that the child was the Son of God, decided that he would put Mary away privately, or quietly, but he was not going to stand by and allow himself to be put to shame because of the supposed sin of his betrothed wife. He was not going to allow his name to be defamed along with hers. Her reputation was ruined. His need not be. She had brought the shame and reproach upon herself. He was going to protect his name from being smeared along with hers.

But things change quickly for Joseph. Just as Mary had been visited by the heavenly messenger, Joseph then has his own encounter with this same messenger. He is assured by the angel that Mary had not been unfaithful, but that she had been chosen by God to give birth to His Son. As unbelievable as all this must have seemed to Joseph, he accepted the message and obeyed the instruction. Joseph and Mary, in total commitment to the fulfillment of God's will for their lives, make the choice to face all the ridicule, harassment, sneers, reproach and shame of their families and friends. These would follow them for the remainder of their lives.

Why? Because people will be people. Mary and Joseph's commitment to God would still not stop the people from hurling their cutting, condemning, critical remarks at this couple. People are going to believe what they want to believe. And even if Mary and Joseph attempted to tell them the truth, that the child was the Son of God, how many do you feel would have believed such an outlandish story? I mean, we have it recorded in the inerrant Word of God, and multitudes today still think of it as an absurdity, a biological impossibility! Do you feel it would have been any different in their day? Certainly not.

So, the miracle would have been met with murmuring and disbelief. Their commitment would have been the cause of much criticism and condemnation. Their submission to God would have been the brunt of excessive cries sarcasm. Even though they knew full well what they were doing and why they were doing it, they also had to be fully cognizant of the fact that they would be the cause of their families being maligned, and they had to know that they would be the topic for every gossip's wagging tongue for a long time to come.

But this is the way it so often happens. Those who strive to faithfully follow the Lord are many times the recipients of much unwarranted shame and reproach. The Bible is full of such people who suffered shame for following the Lord.

Can you imagine the ridicule and reproach Noah must have suffered at the hands of wicked and evil men? Think about what he must have faced as he obeyed the command of the Lord to build that huge ark. His actions would probably been the focus of many jokes and much ridicule. Many probably would have been convinced that Noah had to be completely insane. After all, who in their right mind would spend over one hundred years building a gigantic boat on dry ground! A hundred and twenty years he labored building that boat. Surely he and his sons would have been viewed as the neighborhood fools! Until. Until the rains fell, the flood waters rose, the ark was shut, and they all perished.

Can you imagine the shame Jeremiah experienced? He faithfully preached God's word to the people of his day for close to half a century. He was denounced by the priests, the prophets, and the people at large. He was the laughingstock of his own hometown of Anathoth. He suffered unbelievable shame and reproach from those who thought God would never bring judgment against His own chosen people. Until. Until the Babylonian army surrounded the beloved city of Jerusalem and besieged it for eighteen months. The residents of the city had to resort to cannibalism to survive before the siege ended and they were taken into bondage in Babylon.

And what about Ezekiel? God led him to do some of the most unorthodox and bizarre things you can possibly imagine getting his message across to his people. He must have been viewed by his contemporaries as eccentric at best, and completely mad at worst.

And what about those men who gave up their livelihoods to follow Jesus? These men had forsaken everything to be His disciples. But then, their Leader had been crucified, and they are left cowering behind closed doors. Until. Until after the resurrection and they had experienced the power of the Holy Spirit. But even then, unbelievers would still think of them as insane for carrying on the work of a dead man. Their lives must have been inundated with continual shame and reproach.

Think about Paul, who had been an aspiring young student and an up-and-coming leader of Israel, who gave it all up to follow Jesus. Those political and religious leaders of Israel with whom he had worked would now view him as a traitor. They would hold him in derision, causing all manner of shame and reproach to follow him the remainder of his life. It would ultimately cost his life, as he died for his faith in Jesus Christ.

And John, was a faithful follower of the Lord for several decades. He wrote five of the books of the New Testament, and loved the Lord with all this heart. And yet, he spent some of the latter years of his life in exile on the Island of Patmos, because of his commitment to the Lord.

Then think of those throughout history who have followed in the footsteps of these in the Biblical record. Think of Martin Luther, who literally put his reputation, and even his physical life, on the line to stand for what he knew God wanted him to do. Think of John Bunyan, who wrote his "Pilgrim's Progress" while incarcerated because of his faith. Think of the multitudes who have been executed for their commitment to God and His calling upon their lives.

It is a matter of record: shame and reproach have been the constant companion of those who would live their lives totally to the Lord.

Some reading these pages may be in this pothole of reproach. Not reproach because of a sinful lifestyle, but reproach because to the best of your ability you are striving to follow God. We live in a society which is rapidly becoming more and more anti-Christian with each passing day. Those old Judeo-Christian values of morality are being ridiculed by those who are living shameful lives. We live in a society in which, for the most part, right has become wrong and wrong has become right. And those who are still striving to live right are being accused of being wrong. Those who still hold staunchly to the moral values taught in the Bible are the laughingstock of our sin-laden society. When we decide to do right, then we are opening ourselves up for all manner of ridicule and reproach.

You can rest assured that when Mary surrendered herself to obey God, and when Joseph surrendered himself to be part of God's wonderful plan, they became overnight the center of every wicked, unkind, cutting remark conceivable. And today, when we commit ourselves to the plans of God, we too, will bear the brunt of this same kind of reproach.

So how did Mary and Joseph handle it? What was it that enabled them to face the ridicule, to handle the reproach, to conquer the shame? There are a few things that can be noted in particular that will help us understand what enabled them to carry on in the midst of all that was thrown at them.

One thing that strengthened them for the task was their commitment to God. It is obvious that Mary was an extremely righteous person. I think we could safely assume that God would not have chosen an unrighteous woman to bring His Son into the world. She was undoubtedly already committed to God and striving to serve Him faithfully before God announced to her that she would give birth to Jesus.

And Joseph, too, was undoubtedly a man who sought to serve God. It is obvious that he was a man with strong moral convictions. These convictions were probably due to his unwavering commitment to God. This character trait of commitment to God was obviously one the outstanding traits of this couple. And if we are to succeed in facing the onslaught of ridicule and contempt thrown at us for living Godly lives it will take this same kind of commitment to God.

There is something we must do if we are to be successful in following God and being able to bear the brunt of unwarranted shame and reproach. We must have already made a decision to live a life of commitment to God. This type of commitment is seen over and over in the pages of Scripture. Daniel, Shadrach, Meshach, and Abednego obviously had made a total commitment to God before being taken to Babylon, and it was that commitment that guided and strengthened them to face the temptations to which they were subjected. Joseph is another example as he remained faithful to God even in a foreign land with all of its enticements to sin.

And we, today, are still called to live lives of commitment which lead to holiness and righteousness. It is becoming more and more difficult in our post-Christian culture to maintain this kind of commitment to God. Professing believers are faced with the same temptations as non-believers are faced with. We are faced with the temptation to lie, to steal, to give our employers less than what they pay us for, to steal, to commit adultery, to engage in pre-marital sex, to choose an alternative lifestyle that is clearly forbidden in Scripture, or any of countless others. What will keep us from falling prey to these worldly temptations? Our commitment to God.

And when we are faced with the shame and reproach of our fellow employees, our friends, and even our own family members because we choose to live a life of moral integrity rather than going along with the sinful dictates of our society, the only thing that will keep us going is our commitment to God.

Perhaps another thing that kept Mary and Joseph going in the face of the shame and reproach they must have suffered was their obedience to God. Their obedience to God was a direct outgrowth of their commitment to God. Jesus told His disciples that if they really loved Him, it would be evidenced in their obedience to Him. One thing that will oftentimes keep us going when we are faced with ridicule and reproach is our obedience to God.

Obedience is certainly not the easiest route to take. Sometimes circumstances make it extremely difficult to do the right thing. Peer pressure is sometimes so overwhelming that, if we haven't already made up our minds as to what we will do when faced with the decision, we may give in to the desire to be part of the crowd. Peer pressure can be so powerful if we aren't prepared for it.

At other times it may be pressure we feel on the job. We may have submitted our name for consideration for the promotion that has just been announced. Only one person will be promoted, and there are several others who would like to get it besides you. It might be tempting to try to make some of the others look bad, thinking it would make you look good, which would in turn give you a better chance at getting the promotion. However, to be obedient to the Lord would mean that we would let our record speak for itself, and hope that we are the one chosen. But even if not, we would celebrate with the one who did get the promotion. Obedience to the Lord will guard us against giving in to the pressure to be deceitful in our ethical behavior in the workplace.

One final thing that probably helped Mary and Joseph during this difficult time was their understanding of the fact that God was in control - that it was His plans which were being fulfilled through them. They realized that no matter how severe the shame and reproach might become, it will only be for a season.

We are here for such a short period of time. And the glory set out before us is of such great magnitude, such wonder and splendor, that we should be motivated to face the troubles and trials of this life with the assurance that we have something far better to look forward to. Perhaps focusing their attention on a bright future helped Mary and Joseph face the harsh realities of a painful present.

Maybe you are suffering from the scrapes, scratches, and bruises of falling headlong into the pothole of reproach. If it is because of your faithfulness to God, then take heart. Continue to be true, committed to the plan God has laid out for your life. Obey Him completely, fully, and look to the future, because no matter what happens here and now, God will turn the painful present into a glorious future for those who follow Him.

QUESTIONS FOR THOUGHT AND DISCUSSION

1. Have you ever faced shame and/or reproach for being a follower of Jesus Christ?
2. If you answered 'yes' to #1, describe the experience in detail.
3. What was the cause of the shame/reproach? Were others involved?
4. What were the results of this experience? Did you grow spiritually as you faced the potential hurt?
5. The author suggested four things that possibly aided Mary and Joseph in facing the shame and reproach. Explain these in your own words.

   a. Commitment to God.
   b. Obedience to God.
   c. Striving for holiness and righteousness.
   d. Remembering that God is in control, and what is happening to you is happening because He is allowing it for reasons sometimes unknown to us.

CHAPTER 17

EPHESIANS 5:22-33

The Pothole of Family Crisis

Wives, submit to your own husbands, as to the Lord. For the husband is head of the wife, as also Christ is head of the church; and He is the Savior of the body. Therefore, just as the church is subject to Christ, so *let* the wives *be* to their own husbands in everything.

Husbands, love your wives, just as Christ also loved the church and gave Himself for her, that He might sanctify and cleanse her with the washing of water by the word, that He might present her to Himself a glorious church, not having spot or wrinkle or any such thing, but that she should be holy and without blemish. So husbands ought to love their own wives as their own bodies; he who loves his wife loves himself. For no one ever hated his own flesh, but nourishes and cherishes it, just as the Lord *does* the church. For we are members of His body, of His flesh and of His bones. " *For this reason a man shall leave his father and mother and be joined to his wife, and the two shall become one flesh.*" This is a great mystery, but I speak concerning Christ and

235

the church. Nevertheless let each one of you in particular so love his own wife as himself, and let the wife *see* that she respects *her* husband.

(Ephesians 5:22–33)

We see it everywhere we look: Families in crisis. Husbands and wives who can no longer get along. At one time they were head over heels in love with each other, and now one can't seem to stand the sight of the other. They used to love spending every spare moment together, enjoying the things that years before had attracted them to one another. Now, they would much rather spend their spare time with their friends, without having the other tagging along. They have grown miles and miles apart, with almost no common interests anymore.

Parents and children have the tendency to do the same thing. Parents, who at one time loved spending time with the children – playing in the yard, throwing the football, going to sporting events and watching movies together, planning vacations with the kids in mind - begin enjoying those rare times away from the kids. Instead of going to the movies with them, the parents drop them off at the entrance to the movies. Instead of attending the sporting event together, they let the kids go alone or with their friends.

And the reverse of that is just as true: Children begin enjoying doing things without the parents being there. This is natural as they grow into their teenage years, but it is happening with more and more frequency at earlier ages as well. Children will stay in their bedrooms with the door securely shut, playing their video games, watching their TVs, talking to their friends on the phone, and a thousand other things. These activities are not bad in and of themselves, but when they cause a wedge to be driven between parents and children then irreparable harm can be done. Oftentimes these types of things will cause crisis in the family.

Added to these examples of problems within the traditional family, there are now alternate lifestyles, and alternate sexual preferences, and alternate "marriages", all of which are adding to the crisis in family relationships. Couples living together outside of the marriage is a common occurrence in our contemporary culture. These, as common as they may be, are contrary to the clear teachings of scripture. The Bible speaks of only one

God-ordained marriage – that of one man being married to one woman, until death parts them.

The divorce rate continues to soar among American families. Children are being reared in single-parent homes. This is often the result of pre-marital sexual activity which leads to an unwanted pregnancy. Many times, when the male figure (I'll not refer to him as a father, he is only an active participant in an illicit sexual liaison) in the relationship finds out his sexual partner is expecting, he will quickly vanish from sight, wanting nothing to do with rearing a child. At other times the child is conceived in a traditional marriage relationship, but the couple divorces leaving one or the other, usually the mother, to rear the child alone.

Then there are those families in which strife and division, arguing and fighting, are common experiences. The couple cannot seem to get along anymore, so there is constant tension between them.

I was serving as pastor of a church about mid-way through my forty-year pastoral ministry. Soon after arriving, and as I was striving to get established in my new field of ministry, one of the couples in the church, who were leaders in the music ministry of the church, came to me with a bit of surprising information. They sat in my office and began to relate to me the present state of their relationship. Rather matter-of-factly, the husband told me that they had been married twenty years, and during that time they had three children. The oldest child at the time of this conversation was sixteen years of age.

Then, she began to speak, informing me that there were no longer any feelings of love toward one another. He nodded his head in agreement. They wanted to let me know that they were only staying together until all three children had graduated from high school, and at that time they were going to divorce.

This was just the tip of the iceberg. It was not long after this couple shared with me their story that I heard of several other couples in the church family who were having serious difficulties in their marriages. Learning about all these couples who were experiencing crises in their families motivated me and my wife to be trained to do marriage retreats with the prayer that it would enable us to assist these struggling couples. Through the years, by the amazing grace of God, we have witnessed several couples whose marriages were saved through the retreats we have led.

Perhaps your marriage is in a state of crisis, and you feel as if you are just about ready to throw in the towel and walk away. Or perhaps you and your spouse are committed to each other in the marriage relationship, but you have a wayward son or daughter that is beginning to drive a wedge between the two of you because of a difference of opinion as to how to handle the situation.

Is there any hope? Is there a way to get out of the pothole of family crisis? I am thrilled to tell you that there is a way out. The Bible presents us with several passages of scripture that provide wonderful instruction and insight into this matter. One is found in Paul's letter to the Ephesians (quoted at the beginning of this chapter) to which we will turn to glean information that could radically improve relations in a family in crisis. We will do this by looking at the four persons mentioned in Paul's text: Jesus Christ, husband, wife, and child.

THE EXAMPLE OF JESUS

Since Jesus is the solid foundation of a successful marriage, we will begin with Him. Paul makes several statements about Jesus in this passage from which we can gain much-needed assistance in times of family crisis.

> Wives, submit to your own husbands, as to the Lord. For the husband is head of the wife, as also Christ is head of the church; and He is the Savior of the body.

> Husbands, love your wives, just as Christ also
> loved the church and gave Himself for her.
>
> For no one ever hated his own flesh, but nourishes
> and cherishes it, just as the Lord *does* the church.
> (Ephesians 5:22–23; 25; 29)

First, Paul speaks of Jesus' love for the church. An important fact to remember is that the church is referred to as the bride of Christ in the Bible. A few verses will suffice to show this relational concept between the church and Jesus Christ.

> Let us be glad and rejoice and give Him glory, for
> the marriage of the Lamb has come, and His wife
> has made herself ready.
> (Revelation 19:7)

> For I am jealous for you with godly jealousy. For
> I have betrothed you to one husband, that I may
> present *you as* a chaste virgin to Christ.
> (2 Corinthians 11:2)

> Then I, John, saw the holy city, New Jerusalem,
> coming down out of heaven from God, prepared
> as a bride adorned for her husband.
> (Revelation 21:2)

These verses give ample evidence that the relationship between Christ and the church is likened to that of a husband and wife. What principles can we glean from this understanding that will assist us in our marriage relationships?

First, Paul makes a statement that has caused much debate, especially in our modern, post-Christian, pro-feminism, liberal-leaning culture. He says that Christ is the head of the church.

This is not the only time this truth is found in scripture. Paul also refers to Christ being the head of the church in Colossians:

And He is before all things, and in Him all things consist. And He is the head of the body, the church, who is the beginning, the firstborn from the dead, that in all things He may have the preeminence.
(Colossians 1:17–18)

Jesus is head of the church which means that the church, His bride, should submit to His headship. This is an extremely important factor in the relationship between Christ and the church as well as between husband and wife. The husband is head of his wife as Christ is head over the church.

It is extremely easy to read a passage such as this and completely miss the emphasis of what is being taught. Jesus shows His headship over the church by caring deeply for the churches well-being. He lavishes love on the church, nourishing and cherishing her. He showers her with care and compassion, ministering to her every need.

Second, Paul draws attention to the love Jesus has for His bride. He says that He loved the church and gave Himself for her. His love for His bride compelled Him to lay His life down for her. He gave His life so that she, His bride, might be sanctified and cleansed.

Husbands, if we love our wives as Christ loved the church and gave His life for her, it will be so attractive to our wife that she will naturally submit to your godly headship. We will address this more fully in the section concerning the role of the wife and mother.

Third, Paul says that Jesus washed His bride with the water of the word, so that He might present her as a glorious church, and that she should be holy and without blemish.

Each of these truths pertaining to the relationship between

Jesus and His bride have direct application to the relationship between a husband and wife.

THE ROLE AND RESPONSIBILITIES OF THE HUSBAND/FATHER

Before discussing the application of the above-mentioned relationships between Christ and the church, please note carefully that I am not against equity between male and female. According to the Bible both were created in the image of God. However, this does not mean that God created male and female as equals. He ordained that man would be head of his wife, and head of his household. What does this look like in the marriage relationship?

As Paul says, husbands are to be the head of the wife as Christ is head of the church. What exactly does this look like? How are we to understand this role of the husband in the marriage relationship?

We must understand one all-important truth: Christ is not a dictatorial leader of the church. The Bible does give directives as to how the church is to be submitted to the headship of the Lord. The church is to turn to the written word of God, the Bible, to get directions from the living word of God, Jesus Christ. And there is one foundational, underlying truth that must be understood from the Bible's teachings. Jesus is head of the church in a loving way. He loved the church and gave Himself for her.

The husband is to love his wife in the same way. I have often said in marriage retreats and seminars that if a husband truly loved his wife as Christ loved the church, then his wife would never have any problem submitting to his headship over her. But too many Christian men use this passage as a battering ram of sorts to try to force their wives into submission. This will never turn out well but will always be viewed by the wife as a source of antagonistic domineering.

Therefore, husbands, love your wife sacrificially just as Christ love the church and gave Himself for His bride. But there is more. Paul also says that Christ sanctified His bride. He set her apart for Himself. This is a crucial aspect of the marriage relationship that is oftentimes overlooked.

Exactly how are husbands to do this? By being the spiritual leader in the home. Husbands, when was the last time you prayed with your wife? When was the last time you led your wife in a time of devotion? Do you have a regular schedule of spending time together in spiritual growth and development? Do you regularly talk about spiritual matters? Husbands are to take the lead in these activities that will facilitate spiritual growth. This is one of the many ways we can be the head of our wives.

But what of the relationship of the father and the child? Paul speaks to this issue as well.

And you, fathers, do not provoke your children to wrath, but bring them up in the training and admonition of the Lord.

(Ephesians 6:4)

It's interesting to note that Paul addresses this statement specifically to fathers. He could have just as easily used the word "parents" as he had in the previous verse (which we will consider in a moment), but he used the word "fathers" instead. Is Paul insinuating from this that mothers are never guilty of provoking their children to wrath? Of course not, but in my personal and pastoral experience I have noticed that fathers are far more prone to be guilty of this type of behavior than are mothers.

Parents, particularly fathers, are sometimes guilty of breaking the spirit of their child(ren). Harsh, overly hard disciplinary fathers can be so tough on their child that the child eventually grows to detest the father. They develop a rebellious spirit and begin to disobey what the father is striving to teach. The father may be well-meaning in his actions, but his hardness begins to wear the child down, eventually breaking the spirit of the child.

My own father was a strict disciplinarian. Let me preface my remarks here by saying that he was a very good man, a wonderful provider for our family, and a loving husband to our mother. But he was, in my estimation, too hard and strict. He was more apt to say no than yes when my siblings or I would ask permission to do something with our friends.

One of my most painful memories was when my father told me that I should be more like my brother. There was nothing really wrong about that. I am two years younger than my brother, and he was one that could have been followed as a good example. But what hurt me so deeply and is still like a fresh wound even after many, many years, is the fact that my father never complimented me on being a good example. Granted, in my teenage years I wasn't much of an example for anyone to follow, but to hear your father say something like that can scar a child for life.

One more example from my childhood. I remember vividly an occasion when it was pouring rain – really pouring. It was more than raining cats and dogs; it was more like it was raining hippos and elephants. It was really raining! Now please understand that it was not storming. There were no high winds, and no thunder and lightning. It was just raining – hard.

So, wanting to get a close-up view of the rainfall, I took an umbrella, went out into the front yard, and sat down on a lawn chair. I just wanted to watch it rain. My father came to the door and called for me to come in out of the rain. Once I had gotten back in the house, I was punished for doing something so insane as that. As I recall, I was never asked for an explanation. I was just punished.

Now those two examples may not sound like much, but I want to make a very important point. Please note carefully what I am about to write. Both of those incidents took place when I was very young. I am now 70 years of age, and those memories are still etched in my mind. Parents, especially fathers, we need to guard ourselves carefully so that we are not guilty of provoking our children to wrath. I am not suggesting that either of these incidents, or a combination of the two, had anything to do with my rebellion against my parents, but it may very well have. When you are punished with no explanation as to why, it tends to build a spirit of resentment.

So, parents, let's strive to help our children grow up loving the Lord and serving Him faithfully. How? Again, Paul gives the answer: by bringing them up in the training and admonition of the Lord. Teach them from the Bible. They are not going to get all the instruction they need from attending church once or twice a week. It is incumbent upon the parents to make sure the children are getting the instruction they need. Study the Bible with them. Have daily devotions with them. Pray with them.

And second, admonish them in the Lord. Correct their wrong behavior, citing Bible verses to validate your admonition. Rebuke them when they get out of alignment with the instruction from the word of God. Be their teacher, their mentor, in assisting them in their spiritual growth.

Husband, love and cherish your wife. Father, train and admonish your child. Follow the guidelines of scripture and you will safeguard your family against undue and unnecessary crises.

THE ROLE AND RESPONSIBILITIES OF THE WIFE/MOTHER

What of the role of the wife and mother? Once again Paul gives us timely instruction in how to be the kind of wife and mother that will prove to be a buffer against the crises many families face.

Paul tells the wife to submit to her own husband. Before we get into the marital significance of this statement, we need to make an extremely important observation. Note carefully that Paul emphasizes wives submitting to their own husbands. There are many men, especially in the workplace, who expect every woman to be subject to every man. That is not what Paul is saying here. He is speaking specifically about the marital relationship, not the business relationship. It is far too common for a man to try to lord himself over a woman in the office, or on the assembly line, or in some other place where the man is in a position of supervision over the woman. It is the woman's responsibility to understand his role and her role, but it is not her responsibility to submit to any demands he might place on her that has nothing to do with her performing her job. Wives are to submit to their own husbands, not to every male who would exert some unwarranted pressure on her simply because he is male, and she is female.

Now, enough for that soapbox! Let's look at the Biblical role of the wife and mother. Paul says that wives are to be submissive to their own husbands. This again has nothing to do with being less important or significant as far as personhood goes. As stated earlier, both man and woman were created in the image of God. That means we should have equity, but not equality. Let me explain what I mean.

Equality means that two things are exactly the same. It is a state of being, where everyone is at the same level. Equity, on the other hand, is a virtue of being just and impartial. It provides everyone with opportunities to grow and develop, without being stereotyped because of their ethnicity, the color of their skin, or any other litmus test to which one might be subjected. Equity provides equal pay for equal work. If a man and a woman both perform the same job, then their pay should be in alignment. That is equity.

God created male and female in His own image. But then He assigned certain roles and responsibilities to each. It is by His design that man was assigned the role of head of the household. It was also by His design that woman was assigned the role of being submissive to the husband's headship.

So how does this look in a marital relationship? The husband loves, nurtures and cherishes his wife. He is attentive to her needs and strives to meet those needs in a loving manner. He cherishes his wife by treating her as the treasure she is. She is his companion, one who was designed by God to walk alongside her husband, giving support and encouragement to his endeavors while not neglecting her own. She is to respect him for who he is and the role he has been assigned by God. She is to respect him for being the leader of the house and the household.

She is also to play a role in the rearing of the children. They are to be trained and admonished, mainly by the father, but when it becomes a joint effort between the two it tends to solidify the relations between every member of the family.

THE ROLE AND RESPONSIBILITIES OF THE CHILD

And finally, we will turn our attention to the role and responsibilities of the child(ren). Paul shares the following advice for them:

> Children, obey your parents in the Lord, for this is right. "Honor your father and mother," which is the first commandment with promise: "that it may be well with you and you may live long on the earth."
>
> (Ephesians 6:1–3)

Children are to obey their parents. This is followed by the instruction to honor father and mother. When these two ideas are thought of as complementing one another it helps us grasp the meaning. If a child honors his parents, then he shows them the respect that is theirs by virtue of the role they play in the family. They would respect the fact that God has placed them under the authority of their parents. To honor one is to recognize their rightful place and give them due recognition. Out of that recognition comes respect for the parents and the desire to obey them.

In another letter penned by Paul, he warns of the spiritual climate that will be prevalent during the latter days. This is a crucial passage for our understanding of why things have deteriorated in family relations in the recent past.

> But know this, that in the last days perilous times will come: For men will be lovers of themselves, lovers of money, boasters, proud, blasphemers, disobedient to parents, unthankful, unholy, unloving, unforgiving, slanderers, without self-control, brutal, despisers of good, traitors, headstrong, haughty, lovers of pleasure rather than lovers of God, having a form of godliness but denying its power. And from such people turn away!
>
> (2 Timothy 3:1–5)

Note particularly the words, "disobedient to parents." This will be one of the visible character traits of many children as the latter days progress. We have all probably witnessed the disobedient, disrespectful actions of children. In the marketplace, in the amusement park, at the zoo, just about anywhere and everywhere you go there are those children who have no respect for their parents, nor do they show any desire to obey. Children will throw temper tantrums in the store because they want a certain toy. The parent continues to say no, but the child's insistence continues to grow. Finally, in an attempt of desperation to convince the child to quieten down, the parent gives in. What does this ultimately teach the child? If I scream loud enough and long enough, I'll get my way. It is teaching them to disregard, disrespect and disobey. It is the parent's responsibility to teach them otherwise.

Family crises are often caused because the husband/father, the wife/mother, or the child is not accepting their role and fulfilling their responsibilities as prescribed in Scripture. And usually, the pothole of family crisis not only affects one member of the family, but more often than not the entire family crashes down into the pothole, sometimes doing irreparable harm.

THE NECESSITY OF MUTUAL RESPECT AND MUTUAL SUBMISSION

In the passage quoted at the beginning of this chapter, I purposely started the quote a few verses beyond one of the key factors in striving to guard ourselves and our families against falling into the pothole of family crisis. Let's go back now and allow those verses to bring this chapter to a fitting conclusion.

> ...speaking to one another in psalms and hymns and spiritual songs, singing and making melody in your heart to the Lord, giving thanks always for all things to God the Father in the name of our Lord Jesus Christ, submitting to one another in the fear of God.
>
> (Ephesians 5:19-21)

How would it affect your family if you spoke to one another with the joy of the Lord directing your thoughts? How would your family benefit from sharing the words of psalms, hymns and spiritual songs together?

And most importantly, how would it affect your family relations if every member of the family showed mutual respect to one another. Husbands submitting to his wives. Wives submitting to their husbands. Children submitting to their parents. Parents respecting their children. This could possibly radically revolutionize many homes, families and relations.

Let's not allow this pothole to entrap us, but let's put forth every effort as parents to guide and guard our families against the peril of this devastating pothole.

QUESTIONS FOR THOUGHT AND DISCUSSION

1. Describe in your own words the role of the husband in the marital relationship.
2. Describe in your own words the role of the wife in the marital relationship.
3. Describe in your own words what it means for a wife to be submissive to her husband.
4. Describe in your own words what it means for a husband to love his wife as Christ loves the church.
5. What does Paul mean by his words to fathers, "Do not provoke your children to wrath"?
6. How could the application of Ephesians 5:19-21 to family relations assist in growing strong families?

————— CHAPTER 18 —————

THE APOSTLE PAUL

The Pothole of Persecution

Are they ministers of Christ?—I speak as a fool—I *am* more: in labors more abundant, in stripes above measure, in prisons more frequently, in deaths often. From the Jews five times I received forty *stripes* minus one. Three times I was beaten with rods; once I was stoned; three times I was shipwrecked; a night and a day I have been in the deep; in journeys often, *in* perils of waters, *in* perils of robbers, *in* perils of *my own* countrymen, *in* perils of the Gentiles, *in* perils in the city, *in* perils in the wilderness, *in* perils in the sea, *in* perils among false brethren; in weariness and toil, in sleeplessness often, in hunger and thirst, in fastings often, in cold and nakedness—besides the other things, what comes upon me daily: my deep concern for all the churches.

(2 Corinthians 11:23–28)

The church of Jesus Christ is no stranger to persecution. From its inception, persecution has been a constant in the church. Ever since the death, burial and resurrection of Jesus, the church has undergone seasons of intense persecution from an unbelieving world.

It was soon after the crucifixion of the Lord that persecution became a reality for those early believers. Luke's record of events in the Book of Acts tells us of the explosive growth of the church, and along with its numerical growth came the intense animosity of the world. That animosity came from a multitude of sources: the religious leaders, the political rulers, the legalists Jews, the liberal Jews, pagans, worshippers of a plethora of false deities, and so many more. It seemed as if the entire world was against this small band of disciples of the now deceased Jesus Christ. Luke records a few of the acts of violence toward those early believers that will show just how intense that early persecution was.

> Now as they spoke to the people, the priests, the captain of the temple, and the Sadducees came upon them, being greatly disturbed that they taught the people and preached in Jesus the resurrection from the dead. And they laid hands on them, and put *them* in custody until the next day, for it was already evening.

> So they called them and commanded them not to speak at all nor teach in the name of Jesus.

> Then the high priest rose up, and all those who *were* with him (which is the sect of the Sadducees), and they were filled with indignation, and laid

their hands on the apostles and put them in the
common prison.

At that time a great persecution arose against the
church which was at Jerusalem; and they were
all scattered throughout the regions of Judea and
Samaria, except the apostles.

(Acts 4:1–3; 4:18; 5:17–18; 8:1)

These are only a few of the passages in Acts relating details
of the persecution leveled against the early church. Nothing has
changed much since. The church of Jesus Christ has always faced
the reality of intense persecution.

In this chapter attention will be focused on the apostle Paul
as our example. It is obvious in the passage on the title page of
this chapter that Paul suffered through many different kinds of
persecution, and many different occasions of that persecution.

It is quite ironic to note that Paul had at one time been a
persecutor of the early church. As a staunch adherer to the
teachings of the Jewish faith, and a member of the Pharisees, the
legalist branch of Judaism, he was opposed to the radical new
movement being led by the followers of Jesus Christ. It was his
desire to completely rid the world of this insidious sect that had
now invaded the world of Judaism and was causing so much
chaos and confusion among orthodox Jews.

As for Saul, he made havoc of the church, entering
every house, and dragging off men and women,
committing them to prison.

(Acts 8:3)

To guard against any confusion, the Saul mentioned in
this verse is the apostle Paul. This was his Jewish name which
God later changed to Paul. The verse reveals to us the disdain,
animosity, and anger he had against the church. In his desire to

protect what he must have deemed as the purity of his Jewish faith, he set out to destroy every vestige of this new religious sect that he viewed as a serious threat to his religion.

But then, in a turn of events that is nothing short of miraculous, Saul is personally confronted by the Lord Jesus Christ – the very One he has denied and now is attempting to bring into disrepute.

> Then Saul, still breathing threats and murder against the disciples of the Lord, went to the high priest and asked letters from him to the synagogues of Damascus, so that if he found any who were of the Way, whether men or women, he might bring them bound to Jerusalem.

> As he journeyed he came near Damascus, and suddenly a light shone around him from heaven. Then he fell to the ground, and heard a voice saying to him, "Saul, Saul, why are you persecuting Me?"
> (Acts 9:1–4)

It was at this momentous event that Saul became a believer and a follower of Jesus Christ, the very One he had set out to defame. He was "breathing threats and murder against the disciples of the Lord." You can feel the intensity of his hatred in those words. He will stop at nothing to protect his religious faith, while destroying those that he viewed as a threat to what he held so dear.

It was there that his life was radically changed. His conversion story is a tremendous account of how far God will go in His providence to seek and save those for whom Jesus died. While Saul was still an extremist in his hatred of Jesus, Jesus showered His love on Saul. Perhaps this is the very reason Paul, in his letter to the Romans, makes this amazing assertion:

But God demonstrates His own love toward us, in
that while we were still sinners, Christ died for us.
(Romans 5:8)

Paul was a changed man. His attitude toward believers took a complete turn-around. His intense hatred for believers became a burning fire of love and concern for them. His all-consuming desire from that moment on was to see Jews and Gentiles alike come to faith in Jesus Christ. No matter what it cost him personally he was going to spread the news of the Gospel with even more intensity than that which drove him earlier to try to destroy it.

But it did come at great cost to Paul. Take a moment to reread the passage on the title page of this chapter. The only thing that came close to the intensity with which he shared the Gospel was the intensity of those who fought against him. They made every effort to stop Paul from sharing the Gospel. He suffered physically as seen in his beatings, stonings, and imprisonments. He also suffered emotionally in those times of being forsaken and left alone with his own thoughts. Of course, I'm sure his thoughts would have been focused on the Lord most of the time. But it would have been very easy for the devil to try to plant seeds of doubt and even despair in his mind during those times when he was abandoned and alone.

Persecution was a constant in Paul's life. And persecution has been a constant in the church ever since it was birthed into existence on the Day of Pentecost. However, persecution should never catch a sincere believer in Jesus Christ off guard. The Bible contains plenty of warnings that should let us know that it will continue to be a reality until the Lord returns. Jesus Himself spoke of the suffering believers would experience.

If you were of the world, the world would love its
own. Yet because you are not of the world, but I
chose you out of the world, therefore the world

hates you. Remember the word that I said to you,
"A servant is not greater than his master. If they
persecuted Me, they will also persecute you."

(John 15:19–20a)

By God's grace we have been called out of the world's ways.
We no longer think as the world thinks. We no longer have the
desires of the flesh that we had before being born into the family
of God. We are different. And because of that difference the world
will hate us just as it did Jesus. And once we begin living our lives
as citizens of the kingdom of God, displaying characteristics that
go along with that new citizenship, the worldly crowd will not
like or appreciate our new Christian disposition.

Before I became a follower of the Lord Jesus, my life was
characterized by a worldly mentality, worldly desires, and worldly
attitudes. I lived for me – self-centered and self-absorbed. As a
young teenager I developed a desire to learn to play the drums
and become a world-renowned drummer. It was an extravagant
dream, to be sure, but it was one that drove me to practice,
practice, practice so I might pursue my dream.

I started playing in my first band at the age of fifteen. At the
age of 18 I, along with four others, formed a band that stayed
together for the next eight years. Playing music literally took over
my life. I married at the age of 21, and for a very short period of
time I backed off the total commitment to the band, but that was
short-lived. It wasn't long before my wife took a back-seat to my
music. The band was practicing three nights a week, and usually
playing somewhere three nights a week, so it didn't leave much
time for anything else, including family.

I continued playing in that band until a wonderful night in
September of 1977. It was on that night, September 13, 1977,
that my wife and I were both gloriously saved. My life changed
instantly. My desires changed, including the desire to play the
kind of music I had been playing. I no longer had the desire to

be seen in the bars and dance venues we had been playing in for years.

When I shared with the other members of the band that I had been saved by the amazing grace of God and would no longer be playing in the band, I was met with a most unexpected reaction. I guess I had it in my mind that they would be thrilled to hear of my wonderful news, but just the opposite happened. They were totally put off by my news.

First, they tried to convince me that my salvation experience was nothing to worry about. It didn't have to change anything. They told me that I could still play in the band and continue to play in the same venues we had been playing. They went so far as to say that I no longer had to involve myself in the drinking and drugs that are so prevalent in those venues. But I shared with them that I could no longer be part of those types of activities, and no longer go to those places, as it would damage the testimony I was now trying to show by a changed life.

The second thing they tried was to convince me that it would just be a passing fad. They were convinced that it was not genuine, but that it would not be long before I was knocking on their door, asking to be accepted back into the band. When I assured them it was not a passing fad, but that my life had been radically changed, their attitude toward me began to change. I was no longer welcome or wanted at our practice studio.

The final thing that occurred was very painful to me. They actually turned on me. Not in a physical sense – they did not attack me physically. But their attack was just as painful, perhaps even more so, than a physical attack. They simply turned their backs on me. They would have nothing to do with me. They cut me off from any communication. We had been together as a band for eight years. And now, they treated me as if I didn't exist.

I realize that this is nothing in comparison with Paul's litany of suffering he had experienced, but it was real, and painful, and deeply scarring to me. The world, as Jesus said, will hate us because of our stance for Him, and our identification with Him.

Persecution is real for the believer in Jesus Christ. It takes so many different forms and comes at us in a variety of ways. And when it comes it should not take any of us by surprise. The Bible gives us so many warnings about the reality of persecution that will come to the life of followers of the Lord. It also gives us some words of instruction in how to handle persecution properly so that we might bear testimony to the goodness of God, as well as bring glory to God as we face the persecution. A few more passages of Scripture will make this clear:

> These things I have spoken to you, that in Me you may have peace. In the world you will have tribulation; but be of good cheer, I have overcome the world.
>
> (John 16:33)

> But you have carefully followed my doctrine, manner of life, purpose, faith, longsuffering, love, perseverance, persecutions, afflictions, which happened to me at Antioch, at Iconium, at Lystra— what persecutions I endured. And out of *them* all the Lord delivered me. Yes, and all who desire to live godly in Christ Jesus will suffer persecution.
>
> (1 Timothy 3:10–12)

> Behold, I send you out as sheep in the midst of wolves. Therefore be wise as serpents and harmless as doves. But beware of men, for they will deliver you up to councils and scourge you in their synagogues. You will be brought before governors and kings for My sake, as a testimony to them and to the Gentiles.
>
> (Matthew 10:16–18)

So many other verses could be added here, but these should be sufficient to show the reality of persecution in the life of a follower of Jesus Christ. As Jesus says, "In the world you will have tribulation." Tribulation in the life of a believer is real. It will come in so many different ways, and often it will come from the least expected sources.

Now the question remains as to how we handle persecution when it becomes a personal reality. What are we to do when it invades our personal arena of life? The remainder of this chapter will consider how the Bible instructs us to deal with it when it is our personal experience.

The following passages of Scripture should prove to be helpful and encouraging to us when we find ourselves deeply entrenched in the pothole of persecution.

> Blessed are those who are persecuted for righteousness' sake, for theirs is the kingdom of heaven. Blessed are you when they revile and persecute you, and say all kinds of evil against falsely for My sake. Rejoice and be exceedingly glad, for great is your reward in heaven, for so they persecuted the prophets who were before you.
>
> (Matthew 5:10–12)

> Do not fear any of those things which you are about to suffer. Indeed, the devil is about to throw *some* of you into prison, that you may be tested, and you will have tribulation ten days. Be faithful until death, and I will give you the crown of life.
>
> (Revelation 2:10)

> Beloved, do not think it strange concerning the fiery trial which is to try you, as though some strange thing happened to you; [13] but rejoice to the extent that you partake of Christ's sufferings, that

259

when His glory is revealed, you may also be glad
with exceeding joy.

(1 Peter 4:12–13)

To these could be added many more, but these should be
sufficient in providing us with insight and instruction that will
aid us in facing times of persecution as we live in an antagonistic,
anti-Christian, world.

First, in the passage from Matthew's Gospel, we hear Jesus
giving us a strong admonition to rejoice and be exceedingly
glad when facing episodes of persecution. This sounds almost
impossible to achieve. Who could ever rejoice in the face of
personal persecution? How could anyone ever be exceedingly
glad when experiencing of an episode of persecution? This
sounds impossible. Usually when anyone is under the pressure
of personal persecution the last thing they think of is being glad.
Persecution is not something we look forward to, or desire, or
enjoy. Why would Jesus make such a statement as this?

We need to make sure we understand fully and clearly
the kind of persecution Jesus is referring to in this powerful
statement. He says that we are to rejoice and be glad when we
suffer persecution for righteousness' sake. Then, a little further in
that same passage, He refers to people saying all manner of evil
against us for His sake. Jesus is not saying that we are to rejoice
and be glad when we are in the midst of persecution for any and
every reason. There are times when we might find ourselves
suffering some form of persecution because we have brought it
on ourselves.

But here, Jesus is speaking of being persecuted because we
are striving to live a Godly life – a life of righteousness. And
further, He refers to being persecuted for His sake – for being a
verbal, visible witness for Him and to His glory. When we suffer
some form of persecution because of this, then we are to rejoice
and be glad.

But still, this is a pretty daunting thing to consider. Persecution is persecution. Even if it is persecution that comes my way because of godly living, it is still an overwhelming thing to consider being joyful and glad about. How are we to pull that off? The answer is attitude. What is my attitude toward the reality of persecution in my life? And how do I go about developing the right kind of attitude that will enable me to rejoice in times of persecution?

One thing we can do that will aid us in times of persecution because of godly living is to prepare ourselves beforehand. If we store the word of God in our mind and heart, specifically passages such as those printed above, then the Holy Spirit will bring them to mind at just the right moment to encourage us as we face persecution. Our attitude will be positively affected as these verses come to mind, and as we realize that we are suffering for His sake.

Another way we can prepare beforehand is to grow in our understanding of the teachings of the Bible on the subject of persecution. When we understand the fact that Jesus revealed to us the reality of persecution in this world, then it should never catch us off guard. Granted, it may come our way at the hands of someone we would never expect it from, but after the initial shock we should realize that this is coming as a result of my attempt to glorify Christ.

In our present cultural climate, believers may be persecuted to some degree because of our biblical stance against abortion, homosexuality, same-sex marriages, drinking, demeaning language, among other things. We may even face persecution because we believe that morality is not determined by the shifting sands of culture, but rather on the eternal, unchanging word of God. The persecution may not be life-threatening, as it was for the Christians in the New Testament era. We may not experience the horror of being hunted down and executed for our witness for the Lord. But we may very well face persecution of other kinds. And when it comes our way, we should be glad that we have been counted worthy to suffer for His name's sake.

When faced with opposition and persecution for standing

firmly on the teachings of the authoritative word of God, then our attitude should be one of joy and gladness. Why? Because it is ultimately bringing glory to our Lord Jesus Christ.

A second thing we can learn from the passages printed above is the admonition to be courageous in the face of persecution. John quotes Jesus in the Book of Revelation. He says that we should not be afraid when faced with the trials of persecution, regardless of the personal cost of that persecution. Jesus tells us that we are to be faithful even unto death. This could be thought of in two ways. First, Jesus could be telling us that we should be faithful in the face of persecution for the duration of our lives. We are to be faithful until we leave this world through the valley of the shadow of death.

However, in the context of this statement, it could be that Jesus is admonishing us to be faithful, even if our faithfulness costs us our lives. We are seeing this happen more and more in other countries around the world where believers are being executed for no reason other than the fact that they are believers. We should not think that we in America are immune to such horrific actions against us by an unbelieving, anti-Christian culture.

Courage is a necessity to face persecution in a way that honors and glorifies our Savior. Suffering and persecution are but for a season, and the glories of heaven await the believer in Jesus Christ. Paul said that the sufferings of this present life are not worthy to be compared to the glory set before us. So, be glad and rejoice in our sufferings and persecutions, being courageous even to the point of death.

Then, another thing we can learn from the passages printed above is that we should never think it strange when we are faced with fiery trials that will sometimes confront us. We are to rejoice in the fact that we are suffering for Christ's sake. It is not a strange occurrence to face persecution and suffering in this present life. It is the common lot of believers. So, let us rejoice and be glad, living righteous, God-honoring lives even to the point of death.

These warnings about persecution against believers were

given to us so that we would not be caught off guard and surprised when we see them happening. Believers in different parts of the world have experienced horrific forms of persecution, and in many instances execution. In just the recent past we have witnessed the horror of believers being beheaded simply for being a believer in Jesus Christ. Anti-Christian sentiment is growing more intense globally as the spirit of anti-Christ is at work in the world.

It is vital for Christians to hear and heed the warnings that were sounded long ago by Jesus and the writers of Scripture. These warnings will prove to be of great benefit as we face the possibility of persecution. They will also encourage us by knowing that persecution is not to be viewed as a strange thing, but something that God can use to reveal His glory through us as we face these uncertain times.

QUESTIONS FOR THOUGHT AND DISCUSSION

1. Have you ever experienced persecution for being a Christian? Describe in detail your experience.
2. Do you think it is really possible to rejoice and be glad when we experience persecution?
3. If you answered yes to #2, explain your answer in detail.
4. The Bible admonishes believers to be courageous when facing persecution. Is this referring to natural courage or supernatural courage? Explain your answer.
5. Several passages of Scripture were quoted in this chapter with insightful information that will help us face persecution. If you have a study Bible with marginal notes, run references to discover more verses related to this topic. Make a commitment to memorize a few of these for strength and guidance.

CHAPTER 19

THE SAMARITAN WOMAN

The Pothole of Prejudice

Then God said, "Let Us make man in Our image, according to Our likeness; let them have dominion over the fish of the sea, over the birds of the air, and over the cattle, over all the earth and over every creeping thing that creeps on the earth." So God created man in His *own* image; in the image of God He created him; male and female He created them. Then God blessed them, and God said to them, "Be fruitful and multiply; fill the earth and subdue it; have dominion over the fish of the sea, over the birds of the air, and over every living thing that moves on the earth."

(Genesis 1:26–28)

I f we take the passage quoted above at face value, then we will quickly, clearly, and easily understand a major biblical truth: there is only one race – the human race. All human life, every human life, each individual human life, has been born in the lineage of the first human couple: Adam and Eve. God, according to scripture, created Adam, and then, taking a rib from Adam, formed Eve. God then blessed them and told them to multiply, fill the earth, and subdue it.

Therefore, there is only one race. So, how then are we to understand the differences that are obvious as we consider different people groups? There are, after all, reds, yellows, blacks, and whites. And even within each of these "color" groups there are many different shades of color distinction. There are light colored whites, and darker colored whites. There are light browns, dark browns, and some so dark they appear almost black. There are differing shades of red and yellow.

But what we need to remember is that each of these people groups is part of the humankind. Humankind is then divided into different ethnic groups. Yes, there are clearly different "color" groups, but each group is a part of the larger whole. All ethnic groups are part of the humankind.

And now to the question we must address: Is one ethnic group superior to the others? The answer is quite simple when we turn to the Bible: No. There is no room for a sense of superiority of one ethnic group over another. Reds, yellows, blacks, and whites are equal in the eyes of God, and so they should be in the eyes of man.

What if, hypothetically speaking, God created humans with no ability to see? What if, in this hypothetical world, the only distinction that could be made between people groups is the sound of the voice? For the sake of discussion, let's assume that in this world everyone spoke the same language, but the distinguishing mark between the groups would be the accent with which they spoke. In our country, there are clear distinctions between a Texas accent, a Southern accent, a Bostonian accent, a Mid-western accent, etc. And then, on an international level there are Russian, European, African, Asian accents, etc. If all of humanity had no ability to see, would we divide ourselves up by accent? Would people groups be determined by the way one speaks? And if so, would one accent be viewed as superior to all others?

Doesn't that sound absurd? But, if we could not see the different colors of skin, would we find some other artificial way to assess one people group as superior over all others? Or would we simply accept each other as equals? I know that this hypothetical scenario cannot answer that question, but perhaps it will give the reader a little food for thought.

There was an occasion in which Jesus had the opportunity to teach this much needed lesson to the disciples, including His followers today.

But He needed to go through Samaria.

So He came to a city of Samaria which is called Sychar, near the plot of ground that Jacob gave to his son Joseph. Now Jacob's well was there. Jesus therefore, being wearied from *His* journey, sat thus by the well. It was about the sixth hour.

A woman of Samaria came to draw water. Jesus said to her, "Give Me a drink." For His disciples had gone away into the city to buy food.

> Then the woman of Samaria said to Him, "How
> is it that You, being a Jew, ask a drink from me,
> a Samaritan woman?" For Jews have no dealings
> with Samaritans.
>
> (John 4:4–9)

As the passage reveals, the disciples had left Jesus alone to rest while they went into the village to purchase food. Jesus was "wearied" from the day's activities. However, it is imperative that we note that His weariness was not the only reason He was there.

Nor was it the main reason. The invisible hand of providence was guiding His every step.

How do we know this? There are a few informative insights revealed in the text. Jesus and His disciples were making their way from Judea to Galilee. If one was to go directly north from Judea, he would have to travel through Samaria to make the journey. However, Jews despised Samaritans so strongly that they would not travel through Samaria. Instead, they would cross the Jordan River, and travel north on the eastern side of the river until they had gone far enough to refrain from having their feet touch Samaritan soil. Such were the extreme lengths Jews would go to in order to keep themselves from being tainted by walking through Samaria.

Why bother? Why add the extra mileage just to keep from going through Samaria? Simple: Prejudice! The Jews were prejudiced against the Samaritans. The word "hate" would not be too strong to use to describe their feelings toward all Samaritans. This hatred and animosity stemmed from the fact that Samaritans were viewed by Jews as half-breeds.

After the Babylonian captivity, which took place in 587–86 BC, the Jews were taken to Babylon and assimilated into Babylonian life. The longer they stayed, the more comfortable many of them got with the culture and traditions of the Babylonian people. They grew so comfortable, in fact, that many of the Jews lowered their standards of holiness that were taught in their scriptures and began living according to Babylonian practices. One of those practices was that of intermarrying with foreigners.

God had forbidden His people to intermarry with pagan peoples. They were to maintain a pure bloodline. Many of them compromised their lifestyles which were to be based on the teachings of God's word and married men and women from Babylon. This resulted in the children of these intermarried couples being viewed as half-breeds. A spirit of contention developed between the Jews who maintained the pure bloodline and those who had now engaged in unholy and impure marriage relationships.

The disciples must have been shocked with astonishment when Jesus informed them that He needed to go through the land of the hated Samaritans. They probably would have thought to themselves, "We don't need to go through Samaria. We can simply do what all good Jews do – cross the river and travel north on the other side."

But note carefully that Jesus said He needed to go through Samaria. He needed to travel that particular route because of a divine appointment that was awaiting His arrival. That hand of providence led Him to be in just the right place at just the right time to meet just the right person. He had to be there precisely when the Samaritan woman came to draw water. Just a little amount of time either way would have hindered Him from having this meeting and subsequent conversation with her.

And it's interesting to note that she was not at the well at the usual time to draw water. The usual time to draw from the well would have been early morning before the heat of the day. However, this woman was at the well later in the day, the sixth hour, when everyone else would have come and gone. So, Jesus being there at this time reveals that He was guided by that invisible hand of providence that orchestrates events so that we are where we need to be when we need to be there.

When Jesus asks the woman to draw water for Him, she is shocked that He would make such a request. He, a Jew, is asking her, a Samaritan, to draw water for Him. There are several observations that need to be made concerning the significance of this event. In this action of Jesus, several barriers of prejudice were broken down.

First, Jesus, a man, spoke to the Samaritan, a woman. This practice was forbidden in Jewish life. Men were not to speak to any woman in public, except their own wives. This was a long-held tradition that was shattered by Jesus when He struck up a conversation with her. Some traditions are good, helpful, and healthy. Families pass down traditions from generation to generation. Some of these are simple and have meaning only to the family that practices them. Some, however, are of great significance. They pass down information and practices which ensure each succeeding generation will hold on to matters of importance relative to the family lineage.

Second, Jesus, a Jew, spoke to the woman, a Samaritan. This, again, was unheard of in this historical era. Because of the mutual hatred between the Jews and Samaritans they would never engage in any kind of social activity, which would include the simple act of conversing with one another.

This type of prejudice has always been a reality throughout the history of humankind. There have always been those who think of themselves as better than others. In the New Testament era, women were viewed as nothing more than possessions. Men were thought of as being so much more important than women. Jesus destroyed this tradition of prejudice by speaking with the Samaritan woman. Men had rights that women did not have. Men could make decisions that affected women, but women had no rights that enabled them to make such decisions. It was a man-centered era of history.

A third barrier that Jesus broke down on this occasion was that strangers would very seldom, if ever, engage in conversation with each other. There were always exceptions to his prejudicial barrier, but it was observed for the most part as this cultural tradition was passed down generation to generation. All these barriers that were commonly practiced were destroyed when Jesus engaged this Samaritan woman in conversation.

But the conversation is only part of the barrier destroying work of the Lord. He actually asked that she draw some water from the well that He might have a drink. There is nothing in the text that would lead us to believe that Jesus had any kind of drinking vessel with Him, so He was asking that she draw water in her vessel and allow Him to drink from it. No Jew would ever consider letting his lips touch the drinking vessel that belonged to a half-breed Samaritan! To do so, according to Jewish tradition, would render the one who drank from the vessel ceremonially unclean.

This is such an amazing incident in the life and ministry of Jesus. This encounter, which was divinely orchestrated by God's providence, shatters so many of the prejudices that are commonly embraced by man. Jesus broke down social barriers, ethnic barriers, and religious barriers. He refused to allow any of these differences to keep Him from reaching out to this woman who was in desperate need of His love and grace.

Prejudices run deep. There are prejudices of all kinds that cause people to hate one another. I grew up in the days of racial integration. Tensions ran deep between blacks and whites (and sadly, they still do!). I was entering the eleventh grade when the two high schools in my hometown were combined. One was the all-black school, and the other was the all-white school. As a result of this action, the ninth and tenth grades were to go to one campus while the eleventh and twelfth went to the other. The tension between blacks and whites was extreme in those opening days of the school year. Fights broke out between individuals. School security was heightened. Local law enforcement was always on high alert for any trouble that might break out on either of the campuses.

Where do prejudices of this sort originate? Why does one ethnic group think of themselves as being superior to another? Why are whites against blacks and blacks against whites; Asians against Hispanics and Hispanics against Asians; blacks against Hispanics and Hispanics against blacks? What gives one a sense of superiority over the other?

In the opinion of this writer, based on my very limited knowledge and my extremely simplistic mind, I feel that these distinctions and ideas of superiority are based on a faulty way of thinking. This kind of thinking is pervasive in our society and is a cultural stronghold that desperately needs to be destroyed.

I, personally, feel that if parents could do so much to effect change in the world by beginning the change process in their respective homes. If parents would go out of their way to instill in the minds of their young children the fact that all are created equal and have equal standing before God, then maybe they would grow to see everyone as equal, with no sense of superiority. And, by the way, children have to be taught to view one people group as superior to another. Left to themselves children just simply get along with other children, regardless of skin color. Unless, of course, they have been indoctrinated to do otherwise.

We are the human race. We are different, to be sure, in so many ways. There are cultural differences, societal differences, traditional differences, religious differences, historical differences, national differences, etc. But these types of differences should not be categorized on a scale of the most superior to the most inferior. They should simply be viewed for what they are: differences between people groups.

As a matter of fact, this writer would surmise that not only should the differences not be viewed as a way of determining superiority of one over the other, but rather they should be recognized and celebrated, as one sees the significance of each people group for what it is: a group of individuals who are all created in the image of God, and are of equal value in the eyes of the One Who created them.

This is especially true for followers of Jesus Christ. Jesus was no respecter of persons, nor should His disciples be. Those who have been born again into the family of God should take seriously the family relationship: We are brothers and sisters in Christ. We are family. We have the same Father, and we are all the brothers and sisters of the Lord Jesus Christ. Paul states this clearly and assertively, and what He says should be taken to heart.

> For whom He foreknew, He also predestined *to be* conformed to the image of His Son, that He might be the firstborn among many brethren.
>
> (Romans 8:29)

We are the brethren of the Lord Jesus. This is such an astounding thing to consider. We are the brothers and sisters of Jesus Christ. Of course, we must understand and remember that He is the preeminent Son of God, and we will never attain His status as the Eternal second Person in the Holy Trinity. But by the power of His sacrificial, propitiatory death we are given the privilege of becoming sons and daughters of God.

But as brothers and sisters in the family of faith, we should never look down on anyone because of the color of their skin. We are all members of the same family. Paul says it this way in his discourse on the mysteries of God:

> For He Himself is our peace, who has made both one, and has broken down the middle wall of separation, having abolished in His flesh the enmity, *that is,* the law of commandments *contained* in ordinances, so as to create in Himself one new man *from* the two, *thus* making peace, and that He might reconcile them both to God in one body through the cross, thereby putting to death the enmity.
>
> (Ephesians 2:14-16)

In this passage Paul is talking about the division between Jew and Gentile. He states clearly that in Christ the wall of separation that once divided them has been destroyed through the power of the saving work of Jesus Christ. Therefore, there should be no more division among us, but we should be at peace with one another just as in Christ we are now at peace with God.

Perhaps the song we learned as young children could be a good starting point for each of us to begin celebrating the human race:

Jesus loves the little children
All the children of the world
Red and yellow, black and white
They are precious in His sight
Jesus loves the little children of the world.

QUESTIONS FOR THOUGHT AND DISCUSSION

1. Do you agree with the author's assessment that there is only one race? Why or why not?
2. If there is only one race, what should that teach us about how we view people of other ethnic groups?
3. Jesus broke down barriers in His conversation with the Samaritan woman. Are these barriers still observable today?

   a. Social barriers.
   b. Cultural barriers.
   c. Ethnic barriers.
   d. Traditional barriers.
   e. Superiority barriers.

4. Why did you answer the way you did on each of the barriers mentioned in #3?
5. Have you been guilty of any of these barriers? If so, what can you do to change your attitudes and actions?

CHAPTER 20

THE NATION ISRAEL

The Pothole of Compromise

However, Manasseh did not drive out *the inhabitants of* Beth Shean and its villages, or Taanach and its villages, or the inhabitants of Dor and its villages, or the inhabitants of Ibleam and its villages, or the inhabitants of Megiddo and its villages; for the Canaanites were determined to dwell in that land. And it came to pass, when Israel was strong, that they put the Canaanites under tribute, but did not completely drive them out.

Nor did Ephraim...

Nor did Zebulun...

Nor did Asher...

Nor did Naphtali...

And the Amorites forced the children of Dan into the mountains, for they would not allow them to come down to the valley; and the Amorites were determined to dwell in Mount Heres, in Aijalon, and in Shaalbim; yet when the strength of the house of Joseph became greater, they were put under tribute.

(Judges 1:27-35)

Potholes! As we have observed in the preceding chapters, they come in all different shapes and sizes. Sometimes they seem to be almost insignificant, while at other times they seem to be insurmountable. Each of the previous chapters has dealt with individuals who had to deal with different types of problems and situations on an individual basis. Their potholes may have affected others, and others may have been involved in some way or another, as we observed in Esther's pothole of prominence and Saul's pothole of jealousy, but the pothole itself was directly related to the individual's choices.

As we come to the end of this work, there is one final pothole that should be addressed. It differs from those in the preceding chapters because it is not focused on an individual. It also differs from the others in the sense that the ramifications of this pothole are much more far-reaching than the previous studies. The pothole in this closing chapter deals with an entire nation. The nation of Israel, the nation that God created for His purposes, the nation that was designed by God to be a theocracy, a nation of people ruled by God, failed to live up to God's design. They refused to live by His teachings, and they failed to follow His guidance. They were guilty of compromise in so many ways. A brief review of biblical history will clearly reveal this truth.

The nation had come into existence by the sovereign action of God in calling one man, Abram (Abraham), and making of him a great nation that would impact the entire world. Every nation of the world would be affected in some way through their interaction with, and their relationship to, the nation of Israel. God made Abraham some truly incredible promises that would prove to be true in all succeeding generations, and in relation to all nations in the world. These promises are still at work in the world today and will continue to be active until God sees fit to bring this era of human history to a close. It would be wise to remind ourselves of these promises God made to Abraham long ago.

Now the Lord had said to Abram:
"'Get out of your country,
From your family
And from your father's house,
To a land that I will show you.
I will make you a great nation;
I will bless you
And make your name great;
And you shall be a blessing.
I will bless those who bless you,
And I will curse him who curses you;
And in you all the families of the earth shall be
blessed.
(Genesis 12:1–3)

What phenomenal promises these were! God is taking a man of His choosing – a man out of a pagan background, and a worshipper of false gods. He is going to make of that man a nation which will be either a blessing or a curse to all nations of the world. Nations that blessed Israel would be blessed while nations that cursed Israel would be cursed. It is clear from these promises that God intended this new nation to be a missionary nation that would influence the world by sharing God's message with the world.

This was a daunting task, especially when God first revealed it to Abraham. After all, he was just one man, taken out of obscurity, and given these amazing promises from God. He had to be wondering to himself how in the world this could ever come to pass. But one thing we can rest assured of from the very beginning of God's relationship with Abraham: for this promise of God to have any chance of being successful, he would have to follow the instructions entrusted to them by God.

From the meager beginning of just one man, along with his wife Sarai, God was going to accomplish an amazing feat: a nation would be born, and through the passing of time would grow to number in the millions. God held true to His promises made in that initial calling of Abraham. His wife bore a son whom they named Isaac. Isaac and his wife, Rebekah, then had twins, Jacob and Esau. The promises of God to Abraham would then pass through the line of Jacob, to whom his wives and concubines bore twelve sons who would become the tribal leaders of the twelve tribes of Israel. Through all these years and all these experiences God kept His hand of grace on this family, and ultimately on the nation.

After hundreds of years of God's provision and protection, the nation had grown to number in the millions. As a nation they had gone through many trials and national crises. During a time of severe famine, they came, through the providence of God, to be in Egypt. They would remain there for over four hundred years. God would then raise up Moses to be the deliverer who would lead the people out of Egyptian bondage toward the land long ago promised to Abraham. Moses was the nation's leader for forty years, after which he was succeeded by Joshua, who would be the one to finally lead the nation into the promised land. It was also Joshua who led in victorious military expeditions as they took possession of the land. They finally had a place they could call home!

This, however, is when they find themselves in an enormous pothole. Sadly, it is a pothole of their own making. After Joshua's death, the nation began to go through a cycle of rebellion, repentance, and restoration. This is a period referred to as the days of the judges, and the events are recorded in the book that bears that name: Judges.

God had commanded that when they took possession of the promised land that they were to completely destroy or drive out the inhabitants of the land. They were warned solemnly that if they refused to do so their failure would result in suffering and hardship. They failed to comply with the commands of God, which resulted in the inhabitants of the land becoming thorns and snares to the people of Israel.

This is just the beginning of the troubles they were going to face. Things were going to go from bad to worse. All through the record of events in the Book of Judges we witness that pattern mentioned above. Through the compromises of the people of Israel with the inhabitants of the land of promise, the people of Israel began to engage in worship of the gods of the land.

Now, instead of the nation of Israel being set apart unto God, totally committed to God, and devoted to His teachings, they are now trying to continue to worship Him while at the same time worshipping the gods of the inhabitants of the land whom they had failed to drive out or destroy. The result was that God would allow them to be defeated by the people of the land who were left there. This would then lead to a season of suffering for the nation, which would last until they came to their spiritual senses. They would then cry out to God in a spirit of contrition, confession, and repentance.

When they sought God for deliverance, He would then raise up a deliverer – a judge – who would bring about deliverance from their oppressors. The nation would then once again enjoy God's peace and prosperity for a period of time. Then, sadly, they would do it all over again. Rebellion – repentance – restoration.

This cycle continued for hundreds of years until the days of the last judge of Israel. God had raised up a man named Samuel to give guidance to the nation. However, it was during Samuel's tenure as judge that the people would make a climactic decision. They go to Samuel and demand of him that they have a king to rule over them. Their reasoning for this demand? They wanted to be like all other nations.

Samuel was distraught. He understood the gravity of their demand. He fully understood the consequences that the implementation of such a decision would bring about. He understood that this nation that God had personally created and assigned the task of showing the world what it looked like to be a nation ruled by God would be destroyed. God's desire was that the nation would be a theocracy – a nation ruled by God.

The people were demanding to be a monarchy – a nation ruled by man.

God instructed Samuel to give in to the demands of the people. This led to the beginning of a downward spiral of the nation. The nation only enjoyed a very few years of unity under the rule of the first three kings. Saul, the first king, ruled the nation forty years. Saul thought that the rule of the nation would pass to his sons, resulting in a lasting dynasty. However, the kingdom was taken from him by a providential act of God. His rejection was the direct result of his personal disobedience against a command of God, and his compromise with the directives of God.

Saul was then followed on the throne of Israel by David, whom God had personally chosen to be Saul's successor. David was a most unlikely candidate for the position of king, but God has His own reasons for His choice of those who would rule. David was a man whom God described as being a man after God's heart.

David's reign as king lasted forty years, after which he was succeeded by his son Solomon. Solomon was an extremely wise man. His wisdom was a direct result of his prayer to God that God would grant him the wisdom necessary to rule the nation. God granted that prayer, which resulted in Solomon's wisdom being known to the far reaches of the world. However, toward the end of Solomon's life he began to compromise the direct teachings of the Word of God. He began marrying women from other nations, resulting in his having hundreds of wives and concubines. This led to his allowing his many wives to lead him to worship the gods of the nations from which they came.

These actions of Solomon led to a most pivotal moment in time in which the downward spiral of the nation becomes prominent. After Solomon's death, the nation is divided into the Northern Kingdom of Israel and the Southern Kingdom of Judah. This, then, would eventually and ultimately result in the destruction of the Northern Kingdom in 722 BC at the hands of the Assyrians, which would be followed by the captivity of the Southern Kingdom at the hands of the Babylonians in 587–86 BC.

The downfall of the nation began with compromise. It began when the people decided they did not want to be different from all the other nations of the world. This is what happens to any nation that was once committed to the God of the Bible and then decides to compromise their commitment to Him with a commitment to the gods of the world.

Please allow me to make a personal word of testimony before continuing. I love the United States of America. My patriotism runs deep. I am proud to call this nation my home and cannot think of any other place in the world I would rather live. I have been privileged to visit seven other nations and have never found one that caused me to think that I would like to make it my home.

One of the things that I love most about our nation is our rich Judeo-Christian heritage. I am so proud when I read the documents of our founding fathers, who envisioned this nation being one that honored God (the God of the Bible!). As I think back over the history of our nation, it is obvious that the hand of God has blessed this nation immensely.

Yes, I love this nation, but I must admit, I loathe what this nation has become. It has only been in the very recent past that we have witnessed a massive shift in the direction of this great nation. This nation, since its inception, has been one which was guided by the principles clearly delineated in scripture. Our educational system was built on the teachings of the Bible. The Bible was the major textbook used in the classroom. Our higher education system was established to train men and women in all fields – science, mathematics, history, etc. – and still the Bible was an essential part of their educational process.

It has been in just the recent past that this rich heritage began to erode and crumble. Revisionist historians are now rewriting history so that our rich Christian heritage has been relegated to a byline in our history books. The many contributions of Christianity – education systems, health care systems, social concern systems, emergency response systems (both national and international) – are now conspicuously missing from our history textbooks. The rich Christian legacy that has been passed down generation to generation has now seemingly passed on. We, a nation that is "under God," and one in which we say, "In God we trust," are a nation that has now pretty much forgotten God – at least the God of the Bible. All gods and deities are welcome and wanted – except the God of the Bible.

The results of this shift in direction have been devastating. Our social climate has been altered dramatically. The hot-button issues of our day – abortion, same-sex marriage, couples cohabiting outside of marriage, racial tensions, violence in the classroom and the community, and so many others – are now being treated from a non-Biblical worldview, which opens the door for "every man doing what is right in his own eyes." We have lost our moral moorings. We are a nation wandering in a spiritual wilderness with no sense of direction.

A past president of our nation made the statement, "We are no longer a Christian nation." If that is true then we are open to any philosophy of life and any theological or non-theological understanding of God, or no belief in God at all. We are a nation with no moral, spiritual, or theological compass, floating aimlessly with no rudder to stay the course.

I long for the day that America turns back to God. Is it too late for this nation to turn back? Some say we are so far removed from the spiritual heritage of our founders that we could never be restored. Yet, there is a longing for a spiritual renewal among many. There have been times in our past when we experienced such powerful spiritual revivals that the nation was affected. Could it happen again?

We need to remember that God is an all-powerful Being who can accomplish His desired will regardless of any man or nation. Yet the Bible clearly teaches that God's usual mode of operation is to bring about circumstances that will cause His people to turn back to Him. Sometimes, as is clearly shown in the Old

Testament, it took God's people suffering tragically at the hands of other nations. Oftentimes God would use a heathen, godless nation to bring judgment to the nation of Israel.

When a nation, such as Israel, or the United States, decides to turn away from God, then God will graciously and lovingly send messengers to warn the people of their deplorable spiritual state. If they respond in repentance, then the hand of God's judgment is stayed. However, if the nation refuses to heed the warnings, then God will take much more drastic measures.

A pattern has been established in the United States over the past half-century that has progressively turned this nation more and more away from our rich Christian heritage. Prayer was removed from school, murder of innocent, unborn children was made legal, a valueless curriculum was embraced by the public school system (facts, just give them the facts), and God's definition of marriage is redefined by nine Supreme Court justices. Is the pattern now too entrenched to be changed?

Let's be reminded of a powerful declaration from God's Word:

> If My people, who are called by My name, will humble themselves, and pray and seek My face, and turn from their wicked ways, then I will hear from heaven, and will forgive their sin and heal their land.
>
> (2 Chronicles 7:14)

> I realize that this verse was written specifically to and for the nation of Israel, but the application is still true for any nation that had at one time been committed to the God of the Bible. However, what we sometimes fail to do is read the preceding verse.

When I (God) shut up heaven and there is no rain,
or command the locusts to devour the land, or send
pestilence among My people, if My people...

(2 Chronicles 7:13–14a)

Please don't miss the emphasis on God's activity in bringing about judgment on His people when they turn their back on God. This is His providential work designed to call His people back to Himself. It seems to me that, in this day of post-Christianity in our nation, that it is far beyond time for believers to once again humble ourselves, pray, repent, and allow God to bring about a time of spiritual renewal.

To bring this chapter to a conclusion, let me address a question that has been posed to me on many different occasions. What happens to committed, dedicated, faithful followers of the Lord when God brings judgment against a nation that has turned its back on Him? Does God supernaturally protect them from the ravages of judgment? Are they somehow kept safe amid the far-reaching ramifications of the wrath of God?

In the Old Testament, when the people refused to heed the warnings of the prophets about impending judgment, then the entire nation suffered the consequences. This certainly doesn't mean that when God sent judgement against Israel that every individual Israelite had rebelled against Him. There was always a faithful segment, often referred to as a remnant, who had not rebelled. But when judgment came, they suffered along with everyone else in the nation.

In our present day, we have witnessed a massive turning away from the teachings of God's Word. In the past half-century, we have witnessed the spiritual climate change dramatically. We have seen a nation which at one time could claim to be a Christian nation become a religious nation – a nation in which every religion is given equal value. We, as the people of Israel in the days of the judges, have compromised our Judeo-Christian moorings and have embraced every religion of the world. Some would even say that we have gone farther than that. It seems that other religions of the world have now been embraced, and Christianity has been relegated to a religion of antiquity.

The old-fashioned, outdated ideas propagated in the Bible are now given very little, if any, value in the decision-making processes of our nation. We are a people governed by those who seem to have no spiritual moorings at all, and even if they do, their moorings are not anchored by the teachings of the Bible.

So, can we be revived? Can revival once again sweep across this great land? Yes, it can. It can, because revival is an act of God, and God's arm has not become weakened by the acts of man. The mandate we should hear loudly and clearly from this review of God's judgment on His people is the mandate to pray – to seek God's intervention before it is too late. And to trust that He will graciously respond, once again, to the cries of His people.

QUESTIONS FOR THOUGHT AND DISCUSSION

1. Do you see any parallels between the downward spiritual spiral of the nation of Israel and that of the United States?
2. If you answered yes to #1, how would you describe this nation's movement away from God?
3. God revived and renewed the nation of Israel many times in the Old Testament. Do you think He would do it again for the United States?
4. If you answered yes to #3, what would it take for this to happen?
5. Do you think the United States was envisioned by the founding fathers of this nation to be a Christian nation?
6. Do you agree with a recent past president of the United States when he said that America is no longer a Christian nation? Why or why not?

EPILOGUE

It is clear that potholes are a reality of life. It is also clear that potholes come in all different shapes and sizes as well as in all different degrees of severity. Many of them, as we have seen, are so large and devastating that they do irreparable harm, while others may more easily be handled and repaired. However, regardless of the shape, size or severity, they all present us with challenges and obstacles. In light of that, let's try to glean some much-needed insight from the examples we have considered and the potholes we have observed.

First, and of most importance, is the lesson concerning God's providence. In each of the case studies we have considered, one thing stands out with absolute clarity: God is always at work! We may sometimes have difficulty ascertaining exactly where He is and what He is doing. We may even, on some occasions, wonder if He is doing anything at all. But, according to the portraits of providence considered in this work, it is obvious that He is, with absolute certainty, always busily involved in our lives. Even though there are times in which His work is more out of sight that it is obvious, we can still rest assured that He is working – always. And, according to His promise penned by the apostle Paul, He is working in such a way as to bring about good for those who love Him (Romans 8:28).

Second, and also of great importance, is the fact that God has purposes and plans for each of us. What an amazing thing to consider! Each of us is of particular importance and significance in the economy of God. His desire is that we be aware of the fact that we are here for a purpose, and for just such a time as this. Remember that this is what Mordecai said to Esther when they were faced with the decree of the king that all Jews would be executed on a certain day. Esther was in a position – Queen of Persia – in which she could go to the king and intervene on behalf of her people. Mordecai told her that she was there for just such a time as that.

You and I are here right now, for just such a time as this. We are not here by chance or coincidence, but by divine directive. And we are here to fulfill God's design for us as individuals. So, each of us needs to strive to discover what our purpose is, and work to fulfill it. Of course the purpose of every believer is to bring glory to God and bear witness to His Son.

Our role may not prove to be as crucial as that of Esther, but we do have a purpose. We may not be one whom God uses to save a nation, but we may be the one whom He can use to share His love and grace with our next-door neighbor so that His grace of salvation might be offered to them. We should strive to join God in His work, here and now.

A third truth that we can glean from our study is so refreshing and liberating when we come to understand it and live in the continual reality of it. We have seen time and time again through the studies of these individuals that God is sovereign. His is in control of all that happens. This doesn't mean that we can place the responsibility for the depravity of man on God. He is not the author of evil. But we must understand that somehow, in a way that is far beyond our ability to understand and explain, that the existence of evil plays a role in God's created order.

We must always guard ourselves against any tendency to blame God for man's sinful deeds. We should be grateful that He can take the worse that man can do and make it work for the good of those who love Him. He can use them to bring God's purposes and plans to their appointed end. Always remember:

When man is at his absolute worst, God is still working to bring about His very best.

Still another truth we need to give attention to is the wonderful ability of God to orchestrate certain events in such a way as to manifest His glory, even in the midst of horrible circumstances. Contemporary Christianity seems to have bought into the idea that God's ultimate concern is for His children is their happiness. However, happiness is such an arbitrary thing. Happiness is based on whatever is happening in our lives at any given time.

So, when things are pleasant, there is plenty of money in the bank, we have the job of our dreams, there is plenty of food in the pantry, we have a beautiful home in a nice community, and two fancy cars in our multi-car garage, and our children are enrolled in the best schools, and they are the envy of all other parents because they are so well-behaved, then we are happy.

But let something happen that takes it all away: we lose our job, or our home, or our health, or our kids are not the best behaved, or, or, or – then all of a sudden we are no longer happy. Happiness is based on happenings.

But God's main concern is not about happiness. Now I don't think He minds us being happy. I think that He enjoys it when we are happy. I believe that He actually likes seeing His children happy, IF. If we understand happiness from His perspective. As a matter of fact, it would probably serve us better if we changed the word "happy" to "joyful". God does indeed want us to be joyful. But joy does not come from what is happening around us or to us.

Happiness can be shattered in a moment. It's that moment we get the bad news: cancer, layoff, accident, divorce, financial setback, or so many other unforeseen things that can come our way in a split second. These can instantly rob us of the euphoria of happiness.

But joy is an entirely different matter. Joy is not defined by what is happening, but rather joy is a direct byproduct of our relationship with God. This is the reason the Apostle Paul, while being chained to a guard while in prison, could write of joy and even admonish his readers to rejoice in all things.

When we give serious consideration to the providence of God and understand that everything that happens in life is part of His grand plan, then we can maintain a sincere spirit of joy, even when life throws its very worst in our direction.

Finally, let's learn that our greatest ambition in life should be to bring glory to God in all we do. He brings circumstances into our personal experiences of day-to-day life through which we can bring glory to Him. Our ultimate purpose is to bring glory to Him, to do all that we do to the glory of God. If we could live in the realization that God providentially gives us opportunities in which we can glorify Him, it would perhaps transform our way of thinking and acting. He is constantly working, giving consideration to every minute detail in our lives in such a way as to bring out good, and ultimately, to exalt His Son, our Savior, Jesus Christ.

Let's commit ourselves to live our lives in the reality of His presence, with the desire to fulfill His purpose, and to strive to bring Him glory until that wonderful day when we will join in that grand reunion in our eternal home.

Printed in the United States
by Baker & Taylor Publisher Services